Music in the Horror Film

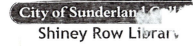
Music in the Horror Film: Listening to Fear is a collection of essays that examine the effects of music and its ability to provoke or intensify fear in this particular genre of film. Frightening images and ideas can be made even more intense when accompanied with frightening musical sounds, and music in horror film frequently makes its audience feel threatened and uncomfortable through its sudden stinger chords and other shock effects. Scholars in film studies have tended to downplay the audible over the visual, to overlook if not the presence of music in horror films then its potency within them. The essays in this collection—some of which take a thematic approach, some of which focus on a particular film— strive to address that lacuna with respect to the particular genre of film known for its ability to terrify us, the horror film. With contributions from scholars across the disciplines of music and film studies, these essays delve into blockbusters like *The Exorcist*, *The Shining*, and *The Sixth Sense*, together with lesser known but still important films like *Carnival of Souls* and *The Last House on the Left*. By leading us with the ear to hear these films in new ways, these essays allow us to see horror films with fresh eyes.

Contributors: Julie Brown; James Buhler; David J. Code; James Deaville; K. J. Donnelly; Ross J. Fenimore; Janet K. Halfyard; Claire Sisco King; Neil Lerner; Stan Link; Joe Tompkins; Lloyd Whitesell.

The *Routledge Music and Screen Media Series* offers edited collections of original essays on music in particular genres of cinema, television, video games and new media. These edited essay collections are written for an interdisciplinary audience of students and scholars of music and film and media studies.

Neil Lerner is Associate Professor of Music at Davidson College where he teaches courses in music as well as film and media studies. His work on film music has been published in numerous journals, essay collections, and encyclopedias. He is co-editor of *Sounding Off: Theorizing Disability in Music* (Routledge, 2006).

Routledge Music and Screen Media Series

Series Editor: Neil Lerner

Music in the Horror Film: Listening to Fear

Edited by Neil Lerner

Music in the Horror Film

Listening to Fear

Edited by Neil Lerner

 Routledge
Taylor & Francis Group

NEW YORK AND LONDON

First published 2010
by Routledge
270 Madison Ave, New York, NY 10016

Simultaneously published in the UK
by Routledge
2 Park Square, Milton Park, Abingdon, Oxon OX14 4RN

Routledge is an imprint of the Taylor & Francis Group, an informa business

© 2010 Taylor & Francis

Typeset in Goudy and Gill Sans by
Florence Production Ltd, Stoodleigh, Devon
Printed and bound in the United States of America
on acid-free paper by Sheridan Books, Inc.

Library of Congress Cataloging in Publication Data
Music in the horror film: listening to fear; edited by Neil Lerner.
    p. cm.—(Routledge music and screen media series)
    1. Motion pictures and music. 2. Horror films—History and
criticism. I. Lerner, Neil William, 1966–.
ML2075.M879 2008
781.5'42—dc22   2009029811

ISBN 10: 0–415–99202–8 (hbk)
ISBN 10: 0–415–99203–6 (pbk)
ISBN 10: 0–203–86031–4 (ebk)

ISBN 13: 978–0–415–99202–2 (hbk)
ISBN 13: 978–0–415–99203–9 (pbk)
ISBN 13: 978–0–203–86031–1 (ebk)

Contents

Foreword
Music and Screen Media Series

While the scholarly conversations about music in film and visual media have been expanding prodigiously since the last quarter of the twentieth century, a need remains for focused, specialized studies of particular films as they relate more broadly to genres. This series includes scholars from across the disciplines of music and film and media studies, of specialists in both the audible as well as the visual, who share the goal of broadening and deepening these scholarly dialogues about music in particular genres of cinema, television, videogames, and new media. Claiming a chronological arc from the birth of cinema in the 1890s to the most recent releases, the *Music and Screen Media* series offers collections of original essays written for an interdisciplinary audience of students and scholars of music, film and media studies in general, and interdisciplinary humanists who give strong attention to music. Driving the study of music here are the underlying assumptions that music together with screen media (understood broadly to accommodate rapidly developing new technologies) participates in important ways in the creation of meaning and that including music in an analysis opens up the possibility for interpretations that remain invisible when only using the eye.

The series was designed with the goal of providing a thematically unified group of supplemental essays in a single volume that can be assigned in a variety of undergraduate and graduate courses (including courses in film studies, in film music, and other interdisciplinary topics). We look forward to adding future volumes addressing emerging technologies and reflecting the growth of the academic study of screen media. Rather than attempting an exhaustive history or unified theory, these studies—persuasive explications supported by textual and contextual evidence—will pose questions of musical style, strategies of rhetoric, and critical cultural analysis as they help us to see, to hear, and ultimately to understand these texts in new ways.

Neil Lerner
Series Editor

Preface
Listening to Fear/Listening with Fear

Neil Lerner

One of the most familiar responses to the gruesome moments of a horror film is to cover or close one's eyes in fear. Yet, as Robynn Stilwell has pointed out about film sound in general, we can't cover our ears with the same certainty of muting the unwanted sounds as we can avert our gaze to stop seeing something.[1] Human anatomy lacks the equipment necessary for actually closing our ears—there is no earlid as there is an eyelid, and a finger only dampens, not obliterates, sound waves—and perhaps that says something about the fundamental utility of hearing in our development as a species. Thinking more specifically about the role of music in human evolution, Charles Darwin related all music back to its usefulness in sexual selection, noting the function of song in bird courtship. Songs could be used to attract mates as well as to define territory, yet Darwin thought only certain types of emotions could be affected by music; in *The Descent of Man*, Darwin wrote that "Music arouses in us various emotions, but not the more terrible ones of horror, fear, rage, etc. It awakens the gentler feelings of tenderness and love, which readily pass into devotion."[2] Such an assertion confirms for us that Darwin never saw a horror film, because of all the cinematic genres, horror gives music a heightened responsibility for triggering feelings of horror, fear, and rage, and so Darwin's statement rings particularly hollow in this context.

Scholars in film studies have tended to downplay the audible over the visual, to overlook if not the presence of music in horror films—music's presence in horror has long been noted—then its potency within them. For instance, Carol J. Clover's important work on the horror film draws attention to what she calls "the eye of horror."[3] Accurately situating the work of horror around "eyes watching horror"[4] and its self-reflexive voyeurism, Clover does mention the role of the sound track in a paragraph-length parenthetical aside:

> (We also take it in the ear, of course. Although my interest here and throughout is with the ocular, it would be remiss not to mention sound in connection with horror's directly assaultive effects. The

shower sequence of *Psycho* shocks at the auditory as well as the visual level; preceded by an ominous silence [the unadorned natural sounds of Marion's preparations], the attack triggers the sound of "shrieking violins" whose hammering thrusts duplicate both the stabbing action of the diegesis and the editorial shattering of the image. Some viewers claim that they are more disturbed by the "music" of horror movies than the images, and that they cover not their eyes but their ears in the "scary parts." Sound in cinema in general has been undertheorized, and horror sound scarcely theorized at all.)[5]

Music in the Horror Film: Listening to Fear includes twelve essays that strive to address that lacuna, although they are hardly the first to do so. K. J. Donnelly's essay "Demonic Possession: Horror Film Music" provides an important theoretical framework for music in horror films, offering a historical survey of significant horror film scores and techniques together with the broader theme of music's role in making film (horror films in particular) a visceral experience for the audience, of film music being "able to *embody* horror, providing a demonic presence in itself."[6] Horror film's repetitive drones, clashing dissonances, and stingers (those assaultive blasts that coincide with shock or revelation) affect us at a primal level, perhaps instinctually taking us back to a much earlier time when the ability to perceive a variety of sounds alerted us (as a species) to approaching predators or other threats.

Music's Presence in Horror

Stylistically, music in horror films tended to allow greater freedom for composers to experiment with harmony and instrumentation. It may be regarded as a commonplace of twentieth-century music history that film music absorbed some of the practices of aesthetic modernism from the concert hall, and that in particular the genre of the horror film turned to unresolved dissonance, atonality, and timbral experimentation as part of its characteristic stylistic qualities. Frightening images and ideas can be made even more intense when accompanied with frightening musical sounds, and music in horror film frequently makes us feel threatened and uncomfortable through its sudden stinger chords and other shock effects. Yet the modernist experiments of the twentieth-century concert hall are not the only models for music in horror film. In the important collection of essays about horror film that he co-edited, film scholar Robin Wood includes an essay on Schubert's famous *Lied*, "Der Erlkönig" (1815).[7] Examining Goethe's poem as well as Schubert's musical setting of it through a psychoanalytic lens, Wood draws attention to the ways music and words work together to deal with repressed desires regarded as sacrosanct by civilization. Woods's basic formulation of the horror film—

"normality is threatened by the Monster"—focuses attention on the important ways the genre allows for the contemplation of taboo topics through various levels of subterfuge and subtext.[8]

As Woods's essay on Schubert makes clear, composers long before the twentieth century, and without recourse to unresolved dissonances or timbral experimentation, found multiple ways to create a sense of unease or dread. The unexpected recontextualization of a consonant and familiar-sounding musical work can also create dread. For instance, the return of the happy-sounding waltz (Arditi's *Il Bacio*) in *Dr. Jekyll and Mr. Hyde* (1931), a work that first appears during a romantic kiss and that essentially serves as a love theme in the film, nonetheless twists the knife in our heart as we hear it at the end of the film, while Jekyll breaks up with his beloved Muriel. The most trivial tonal music can also become terrifying when it calmly and euphoniously accompanies scenes of brutal violence, as Stan Link so eloquently discusses in "Sympathy with the Devil? Music of the Psycho Post-*Psycho*."[9]

Organization: Joining the Eye of Horror with Horror's Ear

While all of the essays in this collection examine closely the ways that music works in horror films, the first three chapters take a more thematic approach (e.g. the presence of organs, tritones, and children's music) while the remaining nine delve into a particular film or group of films with an eye—and ear!—towards finding new understandings of these filmic texts through a careful reflection upon the music. Although the essays here do not offer an exhaustive survey of every horror film or every technique, they nonetheless bring with them fresh insights (note visual metaphor) of well-known films such as *The Exorcist*, *The Shining*, and *The Sixth Sense* just as they also expand our knowledge of lesser known but still important films like *Carnival of Souls* and *The Last House on the Left*. Ultimately, the essays in this collection interrogate a number of different ways that music functions in horror films, with an underlying assumption that music in a horror film, just as in any other cinematic genre, participates crucially in the creation of the film's meaning, and so close attention to the score with both the eye *and* the ear will generate readings of the film that do not emerge when considering only the visual and cinematographic elements. By leading us with the ear to hear these films in new ways, these essays also allow us to see these horror films with fresh eyes.

Notes

1   Robynn Stilwell, "Sound and Empathy: Subjectivity, Gender and the Cinematic Soundscape," in *Film Music: Critical Approaches*, edited by K. J. Donnelly (Edinburgh: Edinburgh University Press, 2001), 171.
2   *The Works of Charles Darwin*, edited by Paul H. Barrett and R. B. Freeman, volume 22 (New York: New York University Press, 1989), 594.
3   "The Eye of Horror" is the title of the fourth chapter in Carol J. Clover's book *Men, Woman, and Chain Saws: Gender in the Modern Horror Film* (Princeton, NJ: Princeton University Press, 1992).
4   Ibid., 167.
5   Ibid., 204.
6   K. J. Donnelly, *The Spectre of Sound: Music in Film and Television* (London: British Film Institute, 2005), 106.
7   Robin Wood, "Der Erlkönig: The Ambiguities of Horror," in *American Nightmare: Essays on the Horror Film*, edited by Andrew Britton, Richard Lippe, Tony Williams, and Robin Wood (Toronto: Festival of Festivals, 1979), 29–31.
8   Wood, "An Introduction to the American Horror Film," in Britton et al. (eds) *American Nightmare: Essays on the Horror Film*, 14.
9   Stan Link, "Sympathy with the Devil? Music of the Psycho Post-*Psycho*," *Screen* 45/1 (Spring 2004), 1–20.

Acknowledgments

This volume could never have happened without the considerable assistance of several individuals. The initial ideas for this book and the series it inaugurates benefitted from the vision of Larry Todd, Bryan Gilliam, and Constance Ditzel, Music Acquisitions Editor at Routledge. Clark Ross, Dean of the Faculty at Davidson College, and the Davidson College Faculty Committee on Study and Research supported this project through grants that allowed for travel to several archives, visits that were made especially fruitful with expertise from archivists: Barbara Hall, Jenny Romero, and Warren Sherk at the Margaret Herrick Library; Nicolette Dobrowolski at the Syracuse University Library Special Collections Research Center; and Alice Birney and Laura Kells at the Library of Congress. Tim Carter and Annegret Fauser helped me track down some vital archival sources. A number of colleagues at Davidson College provided crucial feedback, conversation, and encouragement: Mauro Botelho, Jessica Cooley, Scott Denham, Ann Fox, Van Hillard, Burkhard Henke, Randy Ingram, Ray Sprague, Jennifer Stasack, and the students in the Fall 2008 seminar CIS 421, The Horror Film. The Davidson College Library staff, and especially Interlibrary Loan coordinator Joe Gutekanst, regularly led me to necessary materials. My special thanks go to Stan Link for coming up with the book's subtitle and most especially to all of the contributors for their horrifically interesting work.

Neil Lerner

Chapter 1

Carnival of Souls and the Organs of Horror

Julie Brown

Watch a horror movie and there is a good chance you will hear an organ, probably a pipe organ. Screenwriters and directors even add organs to stories whose literary sources have none. Robert Louis Stevenson's 1886 novella *The Strange Case of Dr. Jekyll and Mr. Hyde* contains no mention of a pipe organ and yet the 1931 film of the story by Rouben Mamoulian opens with Dr. Jekyll playing one in his grand home; the Edgar Allan Poe story to which Edgar G. Ulmer's 1934 *The Black Cat* alludes (admittedly only vaguely) likewise has no organ even though the film does. Herk Harvey's one-off, low-budget cult film *Carnival of Souls* of 1962 is perhaps the *ne plus ultra* of horror movies with an organ. Its central character is an organist, its soundtrack consists exclusively of organ music, and the film moves to and from two locations of organ imagining: a church and an abandoned fairground-cum-entertainment pavilion. The minute we hear the organ underscoring we know something is up. Much as K. J. Donnelly argues we can consider films to be generally haunted by the "ghosts" and half-remembered sounds of film music, that "repository of reminders, half-memories and outbursts of emotion," we might consider this film to be thoroughly haunted by organ music, certainly to the same extent as its central character seems haunted by demons and ghosts.[1]

Horror movies as a genre are often read as safe explorations of the audience's worst fears. Steven Schneider, for instance, argues that horror "serves a variety of psychological functions in society."[2] In addition to catharsis and escape, it provides audiences with "a relatively safe (because relatively disguised/distorted) forum for the expression of socio-cultural fears." *Carnival of Souls* is a little more like the films of Hitchcock or Cocteau in that it presents its fantastical events as if they might be a psychological effect on its central character. *Carnival of Souls'* Mary Henry (Candace Hilligoss) even sees a psychoanalyst. The plot, which can be interpreted in various ways, was neutrally summarized in *The Daily Cinema* in 1967:

The survivor of a car crash, organist Mary is given up for lost, but emerges apparently unscathed from the river into which the car plunged. She takes a job as a church organist; but her solitary life is haunted by a strange, elusive man (whom no one else can see). At times she can make no contact with the people around her and she is drawn to a deserted pavilion. A stray relationship with a flirtatious neighbour merely accentuates her sense of isolation. Sacked by the vicar for playing profane music over which she has no control, Mary attempts to leave town, but instead is drawn to the pavilion where she encounters other doomed souls. In the morning, Mary has disappeared, but when the car in which she crashed is fished out of the river, her dead body is also recovered.[3]

The final scene thus tells us that normal-looking Mary's ghostly and horrifying experiences arise from the fact that *she* is the zombie—this six years before that cornerstone of zombie films, *The Night of the Living Dead*.

Judging by his screenplay to *Carnival of Souls*, John Clifford well understands a point made by Terry Castle: namely, that "the most influential of modern theories of the mind—psychoanalysis—has internalized the ghost-seeing metaphor: the Freudian account of psychic events . . . is . . . suffused with crypto-supernaturalism."[4] Like so many horror films, *Carnival of Souls* is not only helpfully explicated by psychoanalysis, but the relationship is mutually supportive. "Without a soul," sexually "cold," and "off her rocker," as variously described, Mary Henry is understood by Dr. Samuels (Stan Levitt) (the type of doctor is left open) to be acting the way she does because of her traumatic experience:

Look, look. You've had a fright. Hysteria won't solve anything . . . You've had a shock . . . It's been less than a week since you were in a car that crashed into the river. How you got out of that, no-one seems to know. But that experience must have been a serious emotional shock . . . The point is this: our imaginations play tricks on us. They often misinterpret what we see and hear. Do you agree? . . . If that can happen in ordinary times, go a step further. Look what can happen in a high fever, or following a serious emotional shock.

Or perhaps the whole thing is a nightmare; as such, the obvious nightmare sequence that starts when she is at a garage on a car hoist is a nightmare within a nightmare. What is certain is that the film reflects the post-Freudian view that mental apparitions have a demonic hold over us. The (ghostly) man who haunts her throughout may, for instance, be the embodiment of Mary's general fears about men. By the very end, however, the logic of genre kicks in, and, for horror, the film provides a more straightforwardly supernatural explanation: Mary herself belonged to the world of the dead.

The way in which the organ music is deployed in the film strongly supports this fantastical world. But why the organ? The organ is one of the spectral presences in *Carnival of Souls*, summoning up, or being summoned up by, the various allusions in the film to cinema's past. The screenwriter explains its inclusion as the result of a series of location choices.[5] As this was a very low budget independent film, and the first feature film by a director and screenwriter who had previously shot only industrial films, it made sense for affordable locations to drive the plot. Director Herk Harvey chose Salt Air, the enormous and highly atmospheric abandoned amusement pavilion sitting in the middle of a lake just outside Salt Lake City, and said that he wanted the film to include creatures emerging from the water and dancing on the dance floor of the abandoned pavilion (Figure 1.1).[6] He gave screenwriter John Clifford carte blanche to write the rest of the story. Before doing so, Clifford identified a good second location: the Reuter Organ Company in Salt Lake City, which had a big room where they tested their organs (Figure 1.2). From this came the idea of making Mary an organist, according to Clifford. There is no reason to doubt this account of the story's genesis, but making these

Figure 1.1 Zombies dancing on dance floor of the deserted entertainment pavilion, in *Carnival of Souls*

Figure 1.2 Mary Henry in the Reuter Organ Company testing room, in *Carnival of Souls*

conceptual connections presupposes a knowledge of the horror genre and the significance of the pipe organ to it.

Herk Harvey admits that he feels the sequences shot in the organ factory add to the "Gothic look" of the film. Yet *Carnival of Souls* is not Gothic in the sense in which we typically understand the term. The term has a rather loose definition, but broadly refers to a sense of an earlier time, usually the Middle Ages, and one of necromancers and superstition. The eighteenth- and nineteenth-century gothic novel, which partly gave rise to genre horror film, asserted itself from the beginning "as the literature of collapsing structures, evil enclosures, forbidden feelings, and supernatural chaos. Its primary crisis would be entrapment or fear of entrapment for the innocent and evil characters alike . . ."[7] Yet it was a universe of "*pleasing* horror." In this sense, its "ruined magnificence, beautiful disorder, attractive decay, dreadful spectacle, and supernatural extravagance" provided a kind of aesthetic relief from the emotional starvation of the neoclassic value system. For Frederick S. Frank, the Gothic was a response to the political and religious insecurity of the time in which it emerged. The crumbling pavilion, the images of immense pipe organs, and the church scenes, render *Carnival of Souls* a contemporary spin on the Gothic.

The broader attraction of horror films to the pipe organ must be partly a function of the instrument's suitability to the genre's recurring, often Gothic themes. The instrument's clear religious associations enable it to serve as a musical sign of religious ponderings (in *Bride of Frankenstein* [James Whale, 1935]), when a blind man takes the monster into his isolated hut and thanks God for sending him a friend, non-diegetic organ music is heard), esoteric knowledge (in *The Black Cat* we see Boris Karloff's character sitting at the organ and later presiding over a bizarre futurist rite while another man plays the organ), and possible death followed by funerals (in Hammer horror *The Gorgon* [Terence Fisher, 1964], when a character reaches a coffin lid). The organ's usual locations—inside churches and cathedrals, near crypts—alludes to the spaces of the Gothic novel, joining with tolling cathedral bells and choral voices in horror films in this respect.[8] The immensity of the sound of a pipe organ seems well suited to a horror film's sense of monumentality, and its desire both to scare and to create larger-than-life characters. Its effect might be likened to Edmund Burke's notion of the sublime. While for Burke beautiful objects are associated with smallness and delicacy, huge objects evoke awe and terror—a sense of the sublime.[9] The huge sound of the organ might be thought of in this way. With their baroque and various other fanciful instances of interior styling, including cathedral-like ceilings and accoutrements, the picture palaces' interiors themselves, and often the very architecture of the organ console, would in their heyday have supported horror's gothic allusions. As famous American theater organist Gaylord Carter recalls, "going into the Million Dollar Theater in [the late 1920s], with its magnificent orchestra and wonderful organ, was like entering a cathedral."[10]

In some other respects, the way in which the organ is used in *Carnival of Souls* goes against type. Either that, or its reversal of the established genre conventions invites us to read the film in a particular way. The fact that *Carnival of Souls'* organist is a beautiful woman is the key instance of play with genre conventions. In horror movies the organist is typically a weird male loner, with plans to exert some sort of power. This topos has appeared in horror films since at least *The Phantom of the Opera* (Rupert Julian, 1925; re-released with sound 1929), which is based on Gaston Leroux's 1909–10 novella *Le Fantôme de l'Opéra*; and may partly exploit the solitariness of the typical church organist who commands his immensely powerful instrument from his usually hidden loft. Hiding underneath the Paris Opera the masked "phantom" has an organ in his lair (Figure 1.3).[11] *Dr. Jekyll and Mr. Hyde* has a similar image: a grand home with the quite unlikely installation of a full pipe organ—the addition that Rouben Mamoulian's version adds to Stevenson's story. This idea of making the organist an eccentric, dangerous genius probably originates

Figure 1.3 Christine being seduced by the phantom outside his bedroom in *Phantom of the Opera*

in Jules Verne's 1870 novella *20,000 Leagues Under the Sea* (*Vingt Mille Lieues Sous Les Mers*), in which scientist Captain Nemo lives an isolated life at the bottom of the sea in his submarine *Nautilus*, whose grand gentlemen's club-style salon contains a pipe organ (Figure 1.4).

The cinematic image of a man playing his organ at home or in some other secluded place is quite sexually suggestive. Indeed, it is hard not to conclude that from the earliest days of the establishment of genre horror movies, the long-established English-language organ pun has been an important part of the pipe organ's attraction.[12] In *Phantom of the Opera* Christine is seduced by the voice of the phantom who speaks to her through the walls of her dressing room. She goes in search of him, but he soon becomes the proverbial beast in his fantastical boudoir. The scene when she unmasks the phantom follows an overtly sexual trajectory. Christine follows him into his lair. He takes her into the bedroom then goes just outside the door to play his organ (see Figure 1.3): the title of the piece is "Don Juan Triumphant," as the pointed close-up of his score confirms. (It is after this that, having emerged from the bedroom and listened to him enraptured, Christine sneaks up behind him and pulls the string that will drop his mask.) The metaphor is similarly blatant in

Figure 1.4 Édouard Riou's drawing of the Grand Salon in the original
edition of *Vingt Mille Lieues Sous Les Mers*

Dr. Jekyll and Mr. Hyde. Organ-playing Dr. Jekyll's sexual and emotional
frustration is central to the film, whose plot dwells on his expressions
of (sexual) frustration at not yet being permitted by Muriel's father to
marry her; he turns himself into Mr. Hyde and disappears off to a music
hall essentially in order to satiate that sexual need. By the time of the
Dr. Phibes films—*The Abominable Dr. Phibes* (Robert Fuest, 1971) and
Dr. Phibes Rises Again (Robert Fuest, 1972)—the sexual connotation is
quite camp.

It might or might not be relevant to all this that the organ work most repeated in horror films is Bach's Toccata and Fugue in D Minor, a piece explicitly referring to "touch" and involving repetition and a relentless driving rhythm typical of many baroque pieces, and certainly toccatas—notwithstanding the fact that the date, title, and even Bach's authorship of this particular toccata and fugue remain disputed.[13] Though the phantom plays "Don Juan Triumphant," Dr. Jekyll and so many who followed him are associated with the Toccata and Fugue. *Dr. Jekyll and Mr. Hyde* opens with an orchestral transcription of the Toccata and Fugue as title music, though Dr. Jekyll does not himself play it. The opening credits are immediately followed by the famous point-of-view sequence of Jekyll at the organ playing the Chorale Prelude in F Minor, BWV 639, "Ich ruf zu dir, Herr Jesu Christ," and he returns again later to the Toccata and Fugue after Muriel's father finally gives him and Muriel the go-ahead to marry: Jekyll immediately rushes home triumphant, arms waving, to play his organ. *The Black Cat* (1934), *The Raven* (1935), and many other films follow *Dr. Jekyll* in using the Toccata and Fugue. It is even used in the 1954 film version of Jules Verne's *20,000 Leagues Under the Sea* (1954) and its sequel *Mysterious Island* (1961). In the Hammer horror film *The Gorgon*, James Bernard's score draws on the style of Bach's Toccata and Fugue on Hammond organ for the coffin lid moment.

If Bach's Toccata may in English connote the idea of auto-erotic "touch" in the context of the larger organ pun, it is also often associated with a kind of virtuosic inventive madness, of which Dr. Jekyll is cinematic archetype and Verne's Nemo key precursor. Though we do not actually see Dr. Jekyll playing the Toccata passage, the opening organ-playing scene constructs Dr. Jekyll as having a god-like outlook onto the world. The sequence is filmed strictly from Jekyll's point of view, and rendered quite optical by the iris shot: in this way we are given Dr. Jekyll's eyes, not just his approximate point of view. Other characters, notably his butler, a policeman, and colleagues, directly address the camera. This filming device helps us to recognize his high status and emphasizes the notion that he is controlling matters, even though we do not actually see him. An almost god-like aura attaches to him not only because of the respect he is paid by those around him but also as a result of his command of the three-manual organ, with all its religious connotations and implication of access to sonic power (Figure 1.5). In a later scene we see him confidently tossing his head back as he plays (Figure 1.6). Having succeeded in controlling this immensely powerful musical instrument, he immediately attempts, god-like, to control nature.

Such a reading of Jekyll follows a strain of the reception of Jules Verne's Captain Nemo. According to Jean-Paul Dekiss, director of the Centre International Jules Verne in Amiens and the writer of several books on the author:

Figure 1.5 Iris shot of Jekyll looking onto his organ keyboard in *Dr. Jekyll and Mr. Hyde*

Figure 1.6 Jekyll playing his organ in *Dr. Jekyll and Mr. Hyde*

Verne was the first modern mythmaker. He was the first writer to try to tell the story of what happens after God is de-throned, what happens when Man begins to fashion his own world, what happens when Man shrinks the globe and re-creates the terms on which he had existed for thousands of years.[14]

In this respect, organ-playing Nemo gave rise to a hundred enigmatic, hermit-like, megalomaniacal, scientific geniuses—many of whom in genre horror movies (Dr. Jekyll, *The Black Cat*'s Poelzig, Dr. Phibes, etc.) also play the organ or are underscored by organ.

Such a use of the organ locally as a genital symbol and more broadly as a phallic symbol is perfectly consistent with horror's use of monsters as a symbol of an unconscious content in the mind.[15] Given that horror usually involves something visual, as opposed to purely conceptual, the on-screen pipe organ is structurally similar to the monsters that surround it and serve as embodiments of the audience's worst fears. Not exactly embodied, the pipe organ nevertheless both visualizes and renders audible phallic power, making use of a similar distorting hyperbole.

In light of this genre convention, the different symbolic configuration in *Carnival of Souls* seems quite pointed. Mary is portrayed as a beautiful, independent, indeed, somewhat semi-detached young woman. She is a working woman whom we first encounter moving to a new town and a new job. She is single, with no husband or boyfriend (or desire for one), and succeeds in keeping her lascivious boarding house neighbor Mr. Linden at arm's length—notwithstanding a number of sequences involving his peeping through slightly open doors at her in a state of undress. The film constructs a homology between the idea of playing the organ soullessly and Mary as a somewhat soulless person (ultimately revealed as the result of her being a zombie). As she tries out an organ at Reuter's organ factory, the organ manufacturer compliments her on her playing:

> "Well Mary. You'll make a fine organist for that church. It'll be very satisfying to you, I think."
> "It's just a job to me."
> "Well, it's not quite the attitude for going into church work."
> "I'm not taking the vows. I'm only going to play the organ."
> "Why, you want more than that."
> " 'Course, it doesn't pay much, but, well at least it's a start . . ."
> "Mary, it takes more than intellect to be a musician. Put your soul into it a little. Okay?"

The film develops this theme of soulless organ playing. As Mary finds herself inexplicably drawn toward the abandoned pavilion, the organ music we hear is closer to that of a mechanical fairground organ: pipe organ in its most mechanized state.

In reading the significance of Mary's organist construction, it is important to bear in mind that the fact and the effects of difference are a key concern of horror.[16] For Raymond Durgnat, "the only films whose erotic content is as open as that of musicals are horror films . . . The kingpin of the horror film is the rendezvous of eroticism and violence."[17] He cites *King Kong* and James Whale's *Frankenstein*, noting that:

> Frankenstein's laboratory is a stone tower set on a hilltop, and the scene where the "embryonic" compendium of carcasses hoisted to the top of a tower while a storm rages is a crude but by no means unimpressive image for tumescence.[18]

Another obvious example is the almost pornographic slasher film, which usually involves a psycho killer slashing to death a string of mostly female victims. As Carol J. Clover has noted, one girl usually survives (*Halloween*, *The Texas Chain Saw Massacre*).[19] Despite their roots in *Psycho*, with its psychologically inflected *raison-d'être*, these films came not to bother with a story about bestial transformation, or otherworldly fantasy, thin though such premises usually are for horror's fantasies—often sexual fantasies of difference.

Mary Henry's sexless and soulless construction as "working woman" is therefore important, and may be read in the context of a wave of postwar 1950s horror movies. For Barry Keith Grant, horror movies of this era sometimes took a slightly new form, whereby women were being positioned by popular culture within domestic space.[20] Threats to masculinity, he argues, can be found in *The Incredible Shrinking Man* (1957) and *Attack of the 50-Foot Woman* (1958). Grant cites an interesting statement by director Don Siegel about *Invasion of the Body Snatchers*, suggesting that it betrays the nature of the fear expressed in a particular scene: Siegel observed that McCarthy tries "to kiss her awake in a delicious non-pod way but she's a limp fish and he knows immediately that she is a pod. In my life, I am sorry to say, I have kissed many pods."[21] Grant concludes, "Here the director, like so much of horror cinema generally, disavows the possibility of his own inadequacy and projects it onto woman as Other."[22]

Mary Henry in *Carnival of Souls* might be read as a projection of male fears of castration in a similar way: a fear that women were not functioning in the expected ways in society, were taking on traditionally male roles and as such seemed to have lost their souls. The opening scene visually connects this theme with her generically phallic organ playing. Mary and a couple of girl friends are in a car and are challenged to a drag race by a car full of young men. They lose at this very "boy's own" race when their car runs over the side of a bridge and plunges to a murky graveyard in the river. When, astonishingly, Mary emerges from the river and goes to drive off, the camera constructs a parallel between the boys' game of drag racing and the masculine business—certainly in horror movies—of playing a pipe organ, providing us with a close-up of her hand on the car choke and then on an organ stop at the Reuter organ factory. (Figures 1.7 and 1.8). Her business-like approach to her job, her independence, and the fact that she brushes off of her neighbor's advances all support this. Yet at the same time, she remains the object of male fantasy—albeit now a somewhat confused fantasy. As with so many horror films, we see her in more vulnerable moments—such as when she prepares for a bath—and is subject to the male gaze; in one scene she wears a nightgown, and the neighbor tries to force himself on her. As already mentioned, she is also presented as suffering from that archetypal female complaint, "hysteria." She emerges both as object of physical desire and as an independent, detached, emotionless, hysterical, and not only sexually unavailable but ultimate thoroughly undesirable woman ("off her rocker").

Cinematic form even seems to implicate itself on this point. She constantly sees a ghostly face staring at her, The Man, even though no one else can. At the end of the film, we learn that The Man is one of the undead calling her back to the world of death. His impersonal designation as "The Man"—as if a character in an expressionist "Ich drama" where characters are not given names but stand in for types—suggests that throughout the ostensibly realistic part of the film he stands

Figure 1.7 Mary Henry's hand on the car choke, in *Carnival of Souls*

Figure 1.8 Mary Henry's hand on an organ stop, in *Carnival of Souls*

for *all men*. In other words, The Man comes to stand for other characters—or rather, other male characters seem to become simply "Men" in Mary's eyes. The scene when Mr. Linden finally takes Mary out on a date and then brings her back to her room is one of several suggesting such a reading. Before they enter the room we see him flirting, putting his head on her shoulder. Inside we see him move toward her and do likewise, but when he looks up, we (and she) see not his, but The Man's, head reflected in the mirror. She screams. But the next shot reveals that Mr. Linden is still on the other side of the room. The implication is that Mary imagined Mr. Linden to have been even more forward than he was.[23] The fact that the director Herk Harvey played the role himself only makes the issue more intriguing. As The Man, a ghostly projection of All Men, the director seems to admit to his film director's role at this time of objectifying women.[24]

The Spectralization of the Cinema Organ

The pipe organ's potential to suggest readings of the film results not only from a twist on the usual casting of the organist but also from the way in which its music floats within the soundtrack as a whole. The fluidity with which diegetic, non-diegetic, and metadiegetic spaces are blurred renders the role of the organ music in *Carnival of Souls* truly fantastical.[25] It is constantly moving through what Robynn Stilwell has described as "the fantastical gap" between narrative functions.[26] Our confusion as to the narrative placement of the organ music we hear is critical to the disorientating effects the film generates. We are not always sure where it belongs within the soundtrack's "geography" (to borrow Stilwell's term), nor whether Mary Henry hears it or not. On the one hand, it is clearly linked with Mary's subjectivity by virtue of her fictive performance of most of the obviously diegetic music within the film. (The actress's terrible miming at the keyboard adds to, rather than detracts from, the fantastical effects.) When she thinks about the deserted entertainment pavilion, we hear echoes of mechanical "carnival" organ music. This could be construed as located (metadiegetically) in her head. Yet when she drives past the pavilion and finds herself unable to turn off the popular theater organ music apparently coming through her car radio, she is visibly spooked herself. She turns the radio dial but the music continues unaltered. Here, the film uses the organ music to play with the "fantastical gap," "fantastical" in the literary sense of a universe in which ordinary distinctions between fantasy and reality, mind and matter, subject and object, break down. Indeed, the repeated cross-fades that move from a close-up of her face (in her boarding house bedroom, or car), through the window and out toward the dark and distant pavilion, could be construed as a metaphor for the "fantastical gap" (Figure 1.9). Increasingly it is as if these organ intrusions into her mental space are ghostly calls from the pavilion to which she is drawn. Thus, when she is practicing in the church and suddenly finds carnival-style elements creeping into her anthems, she is spooked, wonders what is controlling her hands, and increasingly takes on the demeanor of one possessed. And not only mechanical organ elements creep in: atonal elements, what Donnelly calls the "cultural anti-matter"[27] so typical of horror film do as well (though to an audience educated in the musical avant-garde, it seems more like a Messiaen moment) (Figure 1.10). To Mary, however, the music her hands produce is clearly alien, a sonic construction of the fantastic, a subjective effect that extends to sequences when we hear no music, or dialogue, or sounds, but only Mary's footsteps, and Mary discovers that people are unaware of her physical presence. She is completely disassociated from reality. What at times seems a nuanced sonic construction of a subjective point-of-audition seems at others yet another manifestation of her inability to control her world. For most of the film the audience does not understand where the film is positioning her. The sonic construction of a fantastical world is a triumph.

The spectralization of the organ music in *Carnival of Souls* is a special case of what K. J. Donnelly has argued is a key characteristic of all film music, though of horror film music above all. For Donnelly, all non-diegetic film music functions within films:

Figure 1.9 Mary Henry seems drawn to the pavilion, in *Carnival of Souls*

Figure 1.10 Mary Henry's hands seem to have minds of their own, in *Carnival of Souls*

as a spectral presence, a celestial voice of God, seemingly appearing from nowhere, almost as if from heaven itself . . . [F]ilm music can rise up in divine power and possess the film and its audience at significant junctures. This "possession" is like a demonic force that is seemingly inexplicable, irrational and cannot be easily recuperated by the logic of film itself . . . [I]n horror films, film music customarily works ritualistically to *invoke* film demons.[28]

Being already visualized, the organs of horror are themselves able to assume an independently ghostly presence. When Mary's hands unwittingly produce "profane" (according to the priest) carnival music, the mystery of the moment stems partly from the question of who or what is possessed. Is it her or the organ itself—bearing in mind that the car radio had earlier seemed to be possessed. Or is the player of the organ a man after all? Does The (spectralized) Man who haunts her throughout, who rises up from the watery depths of the salty lake, sometimes control the organ—Phantom, Jekyll, and Nemo-like—after all?

In this respect, the organ helps to delineate one of the fundamental principles of the Freudian "uncanny." For Freud, uncanny feelings are partly accounted for as "surmounted beliefs"—this especially so in connection with belief in the ability of the dead to return to life. The carnival recalls Hoffmann's tales of automata impelled by their own uncanny force.[29] The fairground itself can even be considered one big animation: for Anna Powell it "is an animated Toyland or puppet theatre as well as an expressionist art exhibition."[30] Mary's ultimate fate in the home, and to the tune, of the carnival organ during scenes at the abandoned pavilion at the end of the film is suggestive. In the context of film, especially film music, the carnival organ is doubly uncanny. As an instrument seeming to play itself, the carnival organ is itself a musical manifestation of the uncanny. But mechanical organs are themselves also a thing of the past, essentially culturally dead, replaced in the popular musical imagination by other things, and in the specifically organ world by cinema organs and ultimately electronic organs. It is cinematically poignant that organist Mary finds her type and her fate at the abandoned pavilion, where zombies are dancing a grotesque dance of death to the sound of a carnival organ among the physical wreckage of a fairground-cum-entertainment pavilion, and does so using a visual style that owes more to German expressionist film than 1950s American film.

What is unique about *Carnival of Souls* is the fact that it is saturated with organ music. Though a function of the extremely low budget of the film, the choice of continuous organ music is a feature of the film that directly parallels Mary's liminal status. It is also one of several traits that links *Carnival of Souls* closely with the silent era and the early sound films of the early 1930s—when an organ might have provided continuous accompaniment to a silent film, only to emerge especially forcefully when a phantom appeared on the screen. Playing (more or less) in synch with the movement of on-screen hands, the "live" organ could distinguish itself as the "real" sound of the organ. The console might also have emerged phantom-like from its hideaway under the stage on an organ lift to play some "live" entertainment between the features, serving as a link between the cinematic "now" of synchronized music that draws us into a world of narrative fantasy, and a cinematic "then" of live pre-show music, musical interlude, and post-screening music.[31] The cinema organ was key to this culture. Indeed, those organ installations continued to do much exhibition work well into the sound era, even longer in Britain than in the United States.

We might therefore say that the pavilion haunts Mary Henry as some sort of entertainment ghost of the world to which she herself belongs in this film. To be haunted is, as Castle reminds us, "to find oneself possessed by spectral images of those one loves. One sees in the mind's eye those who are absent; one is befriended and consoled by phantoms of the beloved."[32] In *Carnival of Souls*, to be haunted is in one sense simply to be open to the history of horror films, though this goes further than a standard question of audio-visual intertextuality. Watching this film, the audience is haunted not only by Hitchcock, Cocteau, and Bergman, three directors whose traces many have detected. Its atavistic black and white shooting combined with the constant appearance of The Man means that it is haunted by traces of German expressionist film; but it is also haunted by silent cinema's organ accompaniment, and by silent film culture generally, including its fairground moment when films were exhibited alongside fairground rides and entertainments, and its musical dimension might have been as much the sound of a fairground organ as of a deliberately structured musical accompaniment. When we have the God's-eye-view of Mary Henry playing the organ, she echoes the Phantom of the Opera and Dr. Jekyll. But by emerging from the water itself, she links back to Captain Nemo himself, that loner who plays with his organ under water. No wonder Mary is herself haunted by organ music.

As cinema organs were dismantled from the picture palaces, as live performance disappeared from film exhibition culture, and as the cinema organ itself receded into distant cultural memory, on-screen organs have increasingly come to be specters of the cinema-variety days—as joyous and almost absurd as the carnival organs are in horror films such as *Carnival of Souls*. Like the Freudian uncanny, the on-screen pipe organ in a horror film looms up as a phantom of the most terrifying and "present" sonic aspect of the spectral form that was silent horror film and the beginnings of horror as a sound film genre.

Notes

1 K. J. Donnelly, *The Spectre of Sound: Music in Film and Television* (London: BFI, 2005), 21.

2 Steven Schneider, "Monsters as (Uncanny) Metaphors: Freud, Lakoff, and the Representation of Monstrosity in Cinematic Horror," in *Horror Film Reader*, edited by Alain Silver and James Ursini (New York: Limelight Editions, 2000), 168.

3 *The Daily Cinema*, n. 9345 (March 7, 1967): 5–6.

4 Terry Castle, "The Spectralization of the Other in The Mysteries of Udolpho," in *The Female Thermometer: Eighteenth-Century Culture and the Invention of the Uncanny* (New York: Oxford University Press, 1995), 125.

5 Audio commentary by Herk Harvey and John Clifford on the Criterion Collection DVD edition of *Carnival of Souls*.

6 Ibid.

7 Frederick S. Frank, "The Early and Later Gothic Traditions, 1762–1896," in *Fantasy and Horror: A Critical and Historical Guide to Literature, Illustration, Film, TV, Radio, and the Internet*, edited by Neil Barron (London: Scarecrow Press, 1999), 6.

8 For instance, *Frankenstein* (1931) opens with the tolling of church bells at a funeral, as does *The Devil Rides Out* (1968; *The Devil's Bride* in the US). *The Mummy*'s score includes an arrangement for orchestra and choir, a figure that is repeated in Don Banks's score for the Hammer horror *The Mummy's Shroud* (1967).

9 Edmund Burke, *A Philosophical Enquiry into the Origin of our Ideas of the Sublime and* Beautiful (original 1757), Oxford World Classics (Oxford: Oxford University Press, 1990).

10 Gaylord Beach Carter, *The Million Dollar Life of Gaylord Carter* (Oakland, CA: Paramount Theatre of the Arts, 1995), 43. The Million Dollar Theater was a huge picture palace in Los Angeles.

11 "For the 1929 sound version, Universal purchased a pipe organ from the Robert Morton Organ Company in Van Nuys, CA. It was installed on Stage 10, which was first used for filming and quickly converted for scoring music as well as doing Foley sound effects work. The organ was used for scenes where Erik plays the organ in his basement lair. It was used in several Universal feature film scores including, among other films, *Bride of Frankenstein* (1935) and *Ghost Story* (1981)." Available at: www.imdb.com (accessed August 10, 2008).

12 *Bride of Frankenstein* is often identified as the first genre horror film, the one that self-consciously repeats aspects of its precursors, above all the very early sound films *Frankenstein* (James Whale, 1931) and *Dracula* (Tod Browning, 1931). Earlier examples, such as German expressionist films *Nosferatu, The Cabinet of Dr. Caligari*, and *Orlac's Hands*, as well as *The Hunchback of Notre Dame* are among an array of even earlier precursors. Yet neither *Frankenstein* nor *Dracula* includes a diegetic organ; indeed, they have little if any music of any sort. *Bride of Frankenstein* does include organ music in its soundtrack, but no fictive organist.

13 The controversy was sparked by Peter Williams in "BWV 656: A Toccata in D Minor for Organ by J. S. Bach?," *Early Music* 9/3 (July 1981): 330–7. Williams's views are not shared by all.

14 Quoted in www.independent.co.uk/news/world/europe/jules-verne-mythmaker-of-the-machine-age-528338.html (accessed August 10, 2008).

15 See Schneider, "Monsters as (Uncanny) Metaphors," 169.

16 See Steve Neale, *Genre* (London: BFI, 1980), 43; also Constance Penley, introduction to *Close Encounters: Film, Feminism and Science Fiction*, edited by Constance Penley, Elisabeth Lyon, and Lynn Spigel (Minneapolis, MN: University of Minnesota Press, 1991), vii.

17 Raymond Durgnat, "The Subconscious: From Pleasure Castle to Libido Motel" (1958), in Silver and Ursini, *Horror Film Reader*, 39.

18 Durgnat, "The Subconscious," 40.

19 This is one of a number of norms of the slasher film identified by Carol J. Clover in "Her Body, Himself: Gender in the Slasher Film," in *The Dread of Difference: Gender and the Horror Film*, edited by Barry Keith Grant (Austin, TX; University of Texas Press, 1996), 66–115.

20 Barry Keith Grant, "Introduction," in Grant, *The Dread of Difference*, 2.

21 Quoted in Ibid., 4.

22 Ibid.

23 Consider also the following. The Man spooks her after a (male) mechanic has raised her onto a car hoist; a tiny creak of a door prompts terrible fear and a lengthy dream sequence involving imaginings of The Man coming after her. A male stranger waiting behind her to drink at a park fountain likewise seems to her like The Man, until a benign waiting stranger is revealed. The *coup de grâce* is when The Man replaces Mr. Samuel, the apparently friendly psychoanalyst. The mechanic's and Mr. Samuel's resemblance in her mind to The Man occur in a passage from the film that is retrospectively explained as a dream sequence.

24 Harvey claims that he played the central role of The Man for economic and egotistical reasons. On the retrospective DVD commentary Herk Harvey asks John Clifford what The Man stands for, as if he genuinely does not know himself. Clifford replies, somewhat evasively, "I don't know. I refuse to answer these things as a writer. What did *you* think you were?" Harvey: "I thought that I was the one questioning her ability to come back. I said: this is against the laws of nature, or this is against religion . . ." "Is that why you peeked in her bedroom?" interrupts Clifford, hinting that the male gaze into her bedroom—and into everything about her—is behind the concept of The Man. ". . . No, I agree with that. I don't know for sure. Except that I do know that I felt, in playing the part even, that he was a laid-back malevolent character, in the sense that you never see him—except maybe in the dance and in a couple of the looks—actually be aggressive to her, like many of the horror shows today that have a lot of physical horror in it. [sic] In *Carnival of Souls* I think one of the main attractions is that it's implied horror throughout." Clifford interjects, "He's an unexplainable threat, isn't he?" They both then draw a connection between this unexplainability and the fact that the things we worry about, as children and adults, from dreams to real life, are things we don't understand. Clifford wonders whether he could write a film like that now that he's older.

25 For Gerard Genette, metadiegetic is that level of narration involving stories-within-the-story. From this Claudia Gorbman derives the concept of metadiegetic music and sound: that which is imagined or perhaps hallucinated by a character, and which helps to construct the character's own reality within the diegesis. See Claudia Gorbman, *Unheard Melodies: Narrative Film Music* (Bloomington and Indianapolis, IN: Indiana University Press, 1987), 23.

26 Robynn J. Stilwell, "The Fantastical Gap between Diegetic and Nondiegetic," in *Beyond the Soundtrack: Representing Music in Cinema*, edited by Daniel Goldmark, Lawrence Kramer and Richard Leppert (Berkeley, CA: University of California, 2007), 184–202.

27 Donnelly, *The Spectre of Sound*, 44–6.
28 Ibid., 20–2.
29 See "Automata," in *The Best Tales of Hoffmann*, edited by E. F. Blieler (New York: Dover Publications, 1967), 71–103.
30 Anna Powell, *Deleuze and Horror Film* (Edinburgh: Edinburgh University Press, 2005), 28. Here she is writing about the German expressionist film *The Cabinet of Dr. Caligari*.
31 For more on the connection between the role of the cinema organ in the transition to the sound era, see Julie Brown, "The Phantom of the Cinema: The Coming of Sound Film and the Cinema Organ" (forthcoming).
32 Terry Castle, "Spectralization of the Other," 123.

Chapter 2

Mischief Afoot

Supernatural Horror-comedies and the *Diabolus in Musica*

Janet K. Halfyard

In terms of genre, the devilish and the supernatural find their usual home in horror films—but horror, like most genres, also has its comic equivalents, films that locate themselves in the same generic area but instead play the horror for humor more than terror.[1] Both horror and comedy, after all, draw attention to taboo topics, things that disturb us to the point of screaming or laughing. Music has a well-established role in interpreting the image for the audience in mainstream cinema, so we can logically assume that music will form part of the mechanism by which this transformation from the horrifying to the comic is also achieved. This chapter examines the strategies used in a range of supernatural horror-comedies and how the music manages to simultaneously locate the film within—or at least close to—the horror genre, while at the same time encouraging the audience to laugh instead of scream.

Capturing the overall tone of a film is often an important part of how a composer develops a scoring strategy: this tone—the overall character and identity of the film—may be achieved through the manipulation of musical elements including melody, tonality, tempo, rhythm, instrumentation, musical texture, and potentially any other aspect of the composition. Horror, for example, has particular musical gestures—the stinger to scare us, drones and sustained *tremolandi* strings to create suspense—that composers have long used to create the kinds of emotional responses required by the genre. Orchestral scores predominate, and with them come uses of some otherwise unusual instruments: harpsichords and church organs probably appear more in horror films than in any other genre, and the cultural association of the sound of these instruments with gothic horror has been discussed.[2] Other strategies for classic horror scoring focus on the use of atonal and dissonant harmonies. Neumeyer and Buhler examine the way that pitch relations work within film scores and observe that, although something of a generalization, we tend to read major keys as more optimistic. We read these more stable modes—minor keys possess a greater potential for chromaticism and thus for dissonance than do major keys—as expressive of positive emotions: "What is crucial in the major/minor distinction is affect, not scale form or the diatonic/chromatic dichotomy. In other words, major/minor is another aspect of [our] 'cultural musical codes' (Gorbman 1987: 3), a coded binary pair."[3] This allows major/minor keys and consonance/dissonance to represent different characters and ideas as mutual opposites along dichotomies of good and bad or positive and negative.

Atonality, however, effectively operates "outside the system," thereby leading to more specific ways of reading it in cinematic contexts:

> It is surely not a coincidence that atonality makes its deepest inroads in suspense, horror and science fiction films . . . [where] subjective crisis and psychological rupture are often prominent themes, with the character experiencing a debilitating loss of centre, which is figured musically by the absence of a tonal centre.[4]

Similarly, in horror films, the monsters are "Others" who are themselves outside the (human) system, so here we tend to find the humans represented by tonality, and the monsters by atonality, as, for example, in James Bernard's score for *Dracula* (known as *Horror of Dracula* in the United States) (1958), with its stridently atonal main title for Dracula himself.[5] By using atonal music, the destabilizing threat that the character represents gets coded in audible terms, even when the audience is unable to decode it or is not consciously aware that it is happening. It is these uses of dissonance and atonality, coupled with the stingers of fright, and the sustained musical gestures and silences of suspense that collude to scare the audience.

One of the specific challenges facing a composer writing for a film that blends comedy and horror arises from the potentially conflicting tones implied by these two genres. How does one write music that will simultaneously allude to both fear and humor? In conjuring up the idea of the devil, the devilish, and the supernatural in otherwise comic films, the most obvious connection to standard horror scoring is that using a full orchestral score is the most prevalent strategy, but after that the strategies diverge somewhat: this music, after all, wants to allude to fear without necessarily inspiring fear itself. Composers working in this genre have a pronounced tendency to use two specific strategies that are related if different to those of true horror, but that nonetheless tap into some longstanding cultural musical associations. One of these is an allusive strategy, namely, the use of specific devices that allude to the horrific and the devil: the organ does still appear in specifically ironic musical gestures, but the more important instrument is the violin; and there are also instances of composers making specific intertextual allusions to other music in order to draw in ideas of horror, the devil, and the supernatural. Second, we find a pitch-based strategy, in particular, the use of the tritone, a highly dissonant interval within the Western musical system and one of the few that has a profusion of names (tritone, augmented fourth, diminished fifth), stemming in part from the fact that it does not fit neatly in the normal system. Apart from the fact that both the strategies have the potential to parody classic horror, both also overtly reference mythologies associated with the devil, and so they use a subtly but importantly different set of associations to those of classic horror scores.

Since the devil stopped playing the bagpipes around the end of the medieval period, the violin has been his preferred instrument of choice, as heard most famously in Saint-Saëns's *Danse Macabre* (1874) and Stravinsky's *The Soldier's Tale* (1918). Both those pieces draw on the folklore of the devil as a fiddler who plays at a gathering of witches in the former, and who tricks a man out of his soul in the latter. While the violin of course sits as a mainstay of most orchestral music, its use in supernatural horror-comedy scoring alludes more particularly to folk music, and indeed to Saint-Saëns and Stravinsky. *Danse Macabre* also introduces the second, pitch-based strategy: it requires the use of *scordatura*, the technique of retuning one of the violin strings. In this case the E string is retuned to an E flat, thereby creating a tritone with the adjacent open A string.

The tritone's position within the medieval study of music caused it to acquire an interestingly specific musical symbolism. Its numerological characteristics oppose all that is defined as good in Western theology and music: six is the number of the devil, while seven is the perfect number, the divine number. The demonic tritone falls on the sixth semitone above (and below) the tonic as opposed to the perfect fifth, which falls on the seventh semitone. The tritone is the sixth step on the circle of fifths away from the tonic; it is, harmonically speaking, as far from grace as one can fall, associations that led to it being christened the *diabolus in musica*, the devil in music, and that have always made it exceptionally useful to composers who wish to convey the idea of evil, the Other, or the alien. One might therefore argue that this use of the interval to represent evil is nothing new and certainly nothing unique to the supernatural horror-comedy, but there are specific differences in the way that tritones are used here compared to other genres. Philip Tagg, for example, has examined the use of the tritone in relation to crime in thrillers and film noir, arriving at a very specific model for this scoring involving prominent use of tritones in association with minor keys, jazz influences, and chromaticism.[6] Scott Murphy, meanwhile, examines the use of the tritone in science fiction films, where he observes that a particular musical gesture, a chord progression consisting of two major key chords separated by a tritone, has come to be correlated with the presentation of images and ideas of outer space.[7] In non-comic horror, by contrast, the prevalent use of either discordant or entirely atonal music can render the tritone redundant as an interval specifically signifying disrupture or the supernatural in the context of so many other intervals and chords equally disruptive of tonal harmony. In supernatural horror-comedy the scoring is again specific in the way it tends to bring out the tritone itself as an important interval, very much as Saint-Saëns did, and for the same reasons.

The Devil has the Best Tunes: The Tritone in Supernatural Horror-comedy Scoring

The composer most associated with comic horror films is Danny Elfman, largely because of his work with Tim Burton, a director who often brings a comic twist to macabre subject matter and with whom Elfman has worked on several films that have some relationship to the horror genre, most notably *Beetlejuice* (1988), *Batman* (1989), *Edward Scissorhands* (1990), *The Nightmare Before Christmas* (1993), *Sleepy Hollow* (1999), and *The Corpse Bride* (2005). Most of these films are more idiosyncratic than strictly comic, and similarly they allude to, rather than actually are, horror—characters, sets, and narratives all borrow ideas from the horror genre (ghosts, living skeletons, lonely mansions, misty graveyards, a betrayed woman returning from the dead to seek justice for her murder, etc.) without ever really trying to scare the audience—and the characters who most clearly derive from horror (Edward, Jack Skellington, the Corpse Bride) are also the ones with whom we are asked to empathize.[8] *Beetlejuice*, the earliest of these, is the only one of these that sits unequivocally in the non-animated horror-comedy sphere. Later in his career, but still likely a result of his work on *Beetlejuice*, Elfman wrote the music for Peter Jackson's *The Frighteners* (1996), a ghost story about a psychic investigator aided by several deceased sidekicks on the trail of a murderous phantom.

Elfman's scoring strategy in these two films bears some of the distinctive hallmarks of the style he quickly established in his work with Burton, a style generally characterized by film music critics as a juxtaposition of the dark and the quirky,[9] and the main title of *Beetlejuice* is a good example. The dark element here stems from two main features, both of which are common to a great deal of his scoring for Burton: the use of a minor key, and the use of low-pitched, dark timbred instruments, especially brass, (although a mellow clarinet also takes a prominent role). Added to these elements is a melody with a sharp-edged contour, its sense of angularity created by the tortuous route taken from the first note to the last an octave below and by the insistent use en route of a tritone D sharp against the tonic A (Figure 2.1).

This tritone acts as a constant "wrong note," upsetting the melodic line with a dissonance that stabbing tritone chords from muted trumpets reinforce. The main title sets a sinisterly dysfunctional tone, offset by the

Tritone A - D♯

Figure 2.1 Elfman, main title theme from *Beetlejuice*

quirky side of the equation: the fast, dance-like rhythmic character of the piece sets a scurrying klezmeresque clarinet line against jauntily syncopated tritone chords from the trumpets.

The tritone performs the important work of introducing the idea of devilishness in the film's main title, at a point where the visual image— an aerial shot of the town and woodlands, which ultimately turns out to be a model—does not overtly suggest that anything is wrong. Gorbman established the idea of mutual implication as an important mechanism in the way that music and image interact to create meaning in a film.[10] In theory, any piece of music and any visual image or sequence has a set of potential meanings: but put a specific piece of music with a specific image and they will tend to imply mutually a particular meaning, one that they both have in common: "any music will do (something), but the temporal coincidence of music and scene creates different effects according to the dynamics and structure of the music."[11] Here, the neutrality of the visual image, an establishing shot of a mostly rural landscape, creates a familiar and unthreatening tableau—certainly the scene presents no obvious visible threats until the very end, when the appearance of a colossal spider causes us to realize that we are looking at a scale model. The music tells a completely different story: the minor key, driving rhythms, stabbing chords, angular melody, and the various tritones present in these latter two features all suggest something rather more sinister than the landscape indicates. The mutual implication of music and scene here strongly signals that some unknown danger lurks below the tranquil surface—which indeed proves to be the case, with the central characters dying in the first few minutes of the film and then unwittingly unleashing the appalling Beetlejuice on themselves and the new occupants of their home. Beetlejuice himself, therefore, lurks in the music: not yet visible, not yet unleashed, but foreshadowed by the dark and quirky music of the main title.

Similar melodic and harmonic techniques occur in *The Frighteners*. Elfman employs a great deal of discordant or entirely atonal music in the general scoring of this film, undercutting the ability of the tritone to signify supernatural threats in and of itself. The main theme, however, appears in a minor, albeit tonal, key and while it does not contain any tritones, when it occurs in the underscore, a tritone pedal quite often harmonizes the theme. For example, in the scene where the hero of the film, Frank Bannister, witnesses the choosing and subsequent murder of

Figure 2.2 Elfman, extract of "Victim 38" scene from *The Frighteners*

victim 38 in the restaurant restroom (Figure 2.2), Elfman juxtaposes the tonic A of the theme with an E flat in the violins. In the ensuing car chase, a dramatic tritone from the brass section accompanies the first sighting of the hooded, death-like figure perpetrating the crimes.

Both of these Elfman scores also contain a great deal of parodistic horror music, an effect created by writing in excess of what the image suggests, and thereby an obvious subversion of Gorbman's idea of mutual implication for comic effect. Enormous, full orchestral horror score stingers, set against an otherwise perfectly tranquil shot of their house, accompany the moment in *Beetlejuice* when Adam and Barbara realize they are dead. One of Elfman's own favorite examples of this type of parody, where he uses dramatic, full orchestral scoring, occurs in *The Frighteners* with the tiny rag doll that attacks Lucy when Frank's ghosts invade her home.[12] A similar moment occurs later, with a timpani roll and stabbing brass tritone chords for the moment when, having kidnapped Lucy and bundled her into his car, the deranged FBI agent Milton Dammers reaches into his coat and pulls out not the expected gun but rather a rubber hemorrhoid ring which he then carefully places on his car seat.

The Frighteners also contains another technique from Elfman's palette that again remains largely exclusive to him in horror comedy scoring: the use of the whole tone scale, a scale quite unlike a standard diatonic major or minor scale. First, while a diatonic scale has seven notes, the number of notes in the whole tone scale is only six (the devil's number). It is also completely symmetrical, in contrast to diatonic scales with their irregular patterns of whole- and half-tone intervals. As a result of this symmetry, every single note in the scale forms a tritone with one of the other notes, compared to a major scale, where only one pair of notes (the fourth and seventh degrees) form a tritone. The presence of so many tritones in the whole tone scale means that the moment one starts writing melodic runs of notes, one unavoidably produces large numbers of tritonal relationships, which can make the music sound extremely eerie: this scale does not sound natural to our Western ears in the way major and minor scales do, and as such it has the potential to cross into the areas Neumeyer and Buhler reserve for atonality and dissonance, the representation of the alien or Other. Elfman made particular use of the whole tone scale in the early years of his scoring career, especially in relation to characters or situations that might be thought of as demonic or hellish: in *Beetlejuice*, he uses it for the "hell dimension" of the worm-infested desert that the ghostly Adam and Barbara find themselves in every time they try to leave the house; he uses it again for the music associated with the demonically grinning, gargoyle-like Joker throughout *Batman*; and in *The Frighteners*, he uses it to represent Milton Dammers, the occult-obsessed FBI agent convinced that Frank Bannister is responsible for the series of murders in fact being carried out by the long dead Johnny Bartlett.

Milton Dammers's very name references the supernatural and the devil with its dual allusions to John Milton (*Paradise Lost*) and damnation, and the music at his first appearance uses the whole tone scale to reinforce just how strange and dangerous a character he is (Figure 2.3). His obsession with the supernatural (he has occult symbols scarred into his chest) makes him seem demonically possessed at times, and he is certainly the greatest threat, after Bartlett, to everyone's safety, coming close to killing both Lucy and Frank in his crazed attempts to prove that Frank is the murderer. The use of the whole tone scale when we first meet him allows for some subtle alluding to his evil characteristics at the same time as being strange and disturbing, rather than overtly frightening. Elfman then uses the same whole tone modality in a much more dramatic and threatening way when Dammers later asserts his superior rank as an FBI agent over the local police and starts questioning Frank after he has been implicated in a second murder.

Elfman's work, therefore, explores and exploits the tritone in two specific ways: as a dissonant interval in otherwise tonal (normally minor key)

Figure 2.3 Elfman, Milton Dammers's first appearance in *The Frighteners*

music; and as a consequence of writing in the whole tone scale. Elfman's work apart, the single most prevalent strategy employed by other composers for incorporating tritones into melodies results from the use of the Lydian mode. All seven-note scales and modes have a tritone in them somewhere, and in the major (Ionian mode) scale, that interval occurs between the fourth and seventh scale degrees. The tritone in effect gets buried because no note from the scale will form a tritone interval when played with the tonic. In the other modes (e.g. Dorian, Aeolian) there is also a tritone between two degrees of the scale; but it is only in the Lydian mode that there is a tritone in relation to the tonic, occurring between the tonic and the fourth degree of the scale (Figure 2.4).

In this one mode we find the *diabolus in musica* in a prominent and audible position; but because the Lydian mode otherwise closely resembles a familiar, tonal seven-note scale, its use allows composers to be altogether more duplicitous in writing music that superficially sounds quite innocent but that conceals (and ultimately reveals) the devil. There are a number of supernatural horror-comedies that use the Lydian mode in this manner. In *The Witches of Eastwick* (1987), John Williams's main title presents a jolly, rustic dance of a theme in the Lydian mode, a theme effectively masquerading as an innocent folk melody just as Jack Nicholson's character masquerades as something more innocent than he truly is for much of the ensuing film (Figure 2.5).[13]

Jerry Goldsmith's main title for *Gremlins 2: The New Batch* (1990) again uses the Lydian mode but, unlike the other two films, the composer

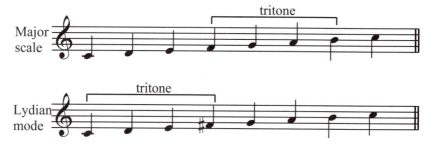

Figure 2.4 Tritones in the major scale and Lydian mode

Figure 2.5 Williams, main title theme from *The Witches of Eastwick*

does not obviously use it anywhere else in the score. With no hint of the folksy charm characterizing the other themes, Goldsmith writes a bold Lydian-mode fanfare (Figure 2.6) for the opening of the film.

Goldsmith's use of the Lydian mode for this opening alludes to the supernatural without pre-empting the thematic material that will be associated with the innocent Gizmo or the as-yet uncreated gremlins. There is nothing of the rural idyll suggested by the other films that might lead him into a folk-music theme; there is also nothing specifically frightening in the opening sequence, and the director may not have wanted to overstate or prefigure the film's supernatural narrative, so although the character of the melody is quite different, the Lydian mode again provides a subtle but none the less specific means of prefiguring the supernatural events to come.

In addition to melodic uses of tritones, supernatural horror-comedy scores also demonstrate some truly fiendish modulations that stand in direct contravention to all the classical rules of harmony in the ways they employ shifts between tritonally related keys. This particular strategy is employed exclusively in relation to the minor keys that are otherwise characteristic of horror scoring, and here the potential for comic effect stems from the exaggeratedly extreme distance that the music travels harmonically as it moves from one key to the next by way of various types of tritonal relationship. The harmonic movement itself descends into a parody of horror's dark and sinister harmonies by moving abruptly to new key areas that are so outlandish that they become ridiculous and so potentially more humorous than frightening.

Marc Shaiman's main title waltz-theme for *The Addams Family* (1991) follows this pattern (Figure 2.7). It starts in F minor and the first phrase

Figure 2.6 Goldsmith, main title theme from *Gremlins 2: The New Batch*

Figure 2.7 Shaiman, waltz theme from *The Addams Family*

remains resolutely over this tonic bass. The answering phrase, however, ends with a sudden shift to a chord of G sharp (enharmonically A flat) minor. Shifting to A flat *major* would have been harmonically consonant— A flat major is, after all, the relative major of F minor. However, the use of enharmonic G sharp minor introduces a B natural into the harmony that, with its tritonal relationship to the tonic F, creates an angular, disjunct, and harmonically unexpected move, set within the context of an elegant if melancholy waltz. The music here cleverly evokes the self-same suave elegance of Gomez and Morticia Addams—characters that specifically parody the mysterious and glamorous supernatural villains of early horror films such as vampires from Europe—at the same time as capturing, through a harmonically eccentric and non-conformist modulation, their charismatic parody of evil and eccentric non-conformity.

Something similar occurs in John Debney's score for *Hocus Pocus* (1993). The underlying harmony here sits very much in the same area as much minor key classic horror scoring, but the harmonic shifts it employs appear specifically to seek out and exploit tritones. Resolutely in minor keys, the opening passage of the main title starts with a sequence that simply alternates between the tonic chord on A minor and a version of the submediant, rendered somewhat chromatically in Figure 2.8 as an F minor triad.[14] There is, in fact, no such thing as an F minor triad in the key of A minor. Technically, the submediant chord in a minor key, like the dominant, should be a major chord: the third of the chord should be the tonic, A, but here it has been flattened. In the key of A minor, this is properly written as G sharp, the sharpened leading note, not A flat, a note that should not exist in the key of A minor at all. In short,

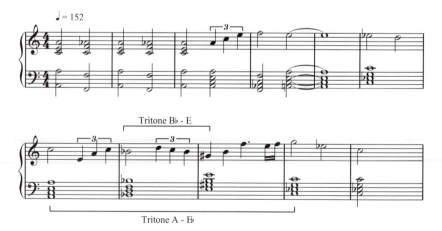

Figure 2.8 Debney, tritone shifts in the main title of *Hocus Pocus*

F minor is simply the wrong chord for this key, employed by the composer for chromatic effect. Debney then uses a series of highly unorthodox shifts to explore two principal tritone pairs, one between the tonic A (in the tonic chord) and E flat (in the chord of C minor), the other between B flat and E, both found toward the end of Figure 2.8 in their tonic chords, which are used as part of a chromatic modulation from A minor to C minor. Again, as with *The Addams Family*, were C minor to be rendered as C major, this would be a normal and expected modulation to the relative major, but instead we have less a modulation and more a deeply chromatic shift into a quite distant key area. The exaggerated harmonic shifts produce a parody of the genre by closely paralleling, yet exaggerating, the effect of earlier horror scoring.

Jerry Goldsmith's score for *The 'Burbs* (1989) presents further exploitation of tritones via the Lydian mode and minor-key harmonies. The main title happens in two parts: a nocturnal scene in which an opening aerial shot moves in from the Universal logo of the earth spinning in space to focus onto North America, then the specific community, and finally the actual house at the center of the narrative; and then a daytime scene of the same community the following morning. The night sequence is scored in the minor key, and as the camera finally reaches its shot of the mysterious, gothic-styled house, a series of minor chords, played on the organ, outlines two tritone relationships as the music shifts in unorthodox manner from F minor to E minor (Figure 2.9). Following this, the scene switches to daylight and the music likewise switches into an apparently contrastingly major key cue (which is in fact Lydian), the overly bright melody and manically cheerful pizzicato strings with their constant tritone C sharps against the tonic G acting as the composer's confirmation that all is not well in this apparently idyllic community (Figure 2.10). Goldsmith effectively employs these two quite different strategies for incorporating tritones into his music in two opening sequences; in both, he begins with a nod back to the earlier vocabulary of horror films before switching to the ironic undermining of an idyllic setting.

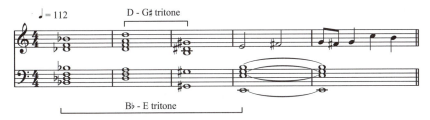

Figure 2.9 Goldsmith, tritone shifts in the main title of *The 'Burbs*

Figure 2.10 Goldsmith, Lydian mode theme in the main title of *The 'Burbs*

The Devil's in the Detail: Allusions to Horror and the Devil

The second part of the overall strategy in scoring these films is the intertextual allusion to other devices and music that themselves reference either horror or the devil. More than one instance happens in *Beetlejuice*. My earlier discussion of tritones in the main title concluded that the tritones here foreshadow the disruptive presence of Beetlejuice himself, but this foreshadowing also takes another musical form. Towards the end of the main title, there is a sudden break in the melody, a series of drum beats, and then a sudden burst of a new melody (Figure 2.11) which bears more than a passing resemblance to Grieg's theme in "In the Hall of the Mountain King" from *Peer Gynt* (Figure 2.12).

The melody deviates so strongly from what has been heard up to this point in Elfman's cue, and the theme sounds so readily identifiable as essentially the same as Grieg's, that it focuses attention on a significant intertextual connection. The Mountain King, after all, is a troll and Grieg's composition describes Peer Gynt being chased by trolls, so the theme might be seen as another representation of Beetlejuice (who certainly appears quite trollish) and the threat he represents: but the troll allusion gives another devil-like identity to the eponymous character via the music.

Figure 2.11 Elfman, passage from the main title of Beetlejuice

Figure 2.12 Grieg, theme from "In the Hall of the Mountain King"

This type of allusion, therefore, might be thought of as another kind of "devil in music," alluding to specific ideas of devils and demons (and trolls) as they appear in other musical works. There is also a specific allusion to the Tango from Stravinsky's *The Soldier's Tale* for Beetlejuice's first actual appearance in the film as he reads of Adam and Barbara's recent demise and starts to plot (see Figure 2.13 and Figure 2.14). To a listener whose ear is tuned to these allusions, the combination of the Troll King music and the Stravinsky effectively confirm Beetlejuice as acting "*in loco diabolus*": but even a listener unfamiliar with Stravinsky will likely understand the disjunct rhythms and chromatically sliding melody of the cue to indicate that Beetlejuice is a very shifty character indeed.

Another musical allusion that tends to crop up in film music (and concert music) with impressive regularity is the *Dies Irae*, a medieval plainsong chant to a text from the Requiem that describes the day of wrath of its title, the coming of the final judgment with the inevitable consequence that sinners will go to hell: the text prays for rescue from those fires (Figure 2.15). Stanley Myers uses a brief quote of the *Dies Irae* in *The Witches* (1990) at the point that Helga, the grandmother who knows the truth about witches, appears to have been vanquished; rather more comically, Goldsmith uses it in an elaborate set of musical allusions towards the end of *Gremlins 2*. The gremlins' main motif is a sprightly minor-key pair of alternating chords (Figure 2.16). At the climax of the film, the gremlins stage a song and dance musical extravaganza of "New York, New York" as they prepare to invade the city, but then the extravaganza transforms into a Busby Berkley-style routine set to Gershwin's *An American in Paris*, now remodeled as *A Gremlin in New*

Figure 2.13 Elfman, Tango for first appearance of Beetlejuice

Figure 2.14 Stravinsky, *The Soldier's Tale*, "Tango," bars 1–4

Di - es   ir - ae,   Di - es   il - la

Figure 2.15 Dies Irae plainchant

Figure 2.16 Goldsmith, "Gremlins" motif

York. At the end of this set piece, the gremlins find themselves defeated, and as the gremlin leader perishes, Goldsmith adds a single, *sotto voce* statement of the *Dies Irae*; it becomes apparent that the opening two notes of this melody have lain unnoticed but very appropriately (given their potential ability to bring about the end of the world as we know it) within the gremlins' main motif all along.

Beetlejuice and *The Witches of Eastwick* both make considerable use of solo violins, a general reference to the idea of the devil as a violinist. In *Beetlejuice*, the violins take a prominent role in the underscore to the film as well as in the main title—a violin plays the tango that introduces Beetlejuice, as it does in *The Soldier's Tale*, and we have jaunty, folk-style violins, with a dangerous smattering of tritone double stops, accompanying Adam and Barbara's fateful final journey to and from the village stores at the opening of the film, ending in their untimely deaths. In *The Witches of Eastwick*, the same folk-style violins are the most prominent instruments in the main title, distinctive for a non-vibrato, more strident timbre than would be expected from a classical violin-playing style. Not only this, but Daryl van Horn is a musician: we learn early on in the film that he bought the Lennox mansion in Eastwick because he needed all the space for his pianos, and when he seduces music teacher Jane he does so by playing the violin in virtuoso style, further reinforcing his devilish credentials.

Death Becomes Her (1992) almost loses itself as a film in its dense series of allusions, charting as it does the rise and fall of two friends and rivals, and their pursuit of eternal youth, a fairly common theme in supernatural horror and vampire narratives. Most of Alan Silvestri's score is a pastiche of 1940s melodramas in the Golden Age style of composers such as Erich Wolfgang Korngold and Max Steiner. The overblown gestures and searing, hyper-emotional chromaticism of the rather old-fashioned scoring creates comedy by parodying the extreme and self-indulgent emotions of the central characters, Madeleine and Helen. They are presented in the style of two glamorous rivals, a Joan Crawford versus Bette Davis construction in which they constantly try to outshine and outsmart the other. One other recurring motif is quite different, playing against this overly emotional, evocative music, and in doing so it again evokes Stravinsky's *Soldier's Tale*, both in the shape and character of the motif itself, but equally in the timbre of spiccato violins in the lowest violin register and the marching rhythm of the accompaniment (Figures 2.17 and 2.18).

This quirky, Stravinskian motif—with obligatory tritone accompaniment—appears mostly when the appropriately nicknamed Mad or Hel have dropped their histrionic fronts and are either plotting or carrying out their plots, mainly against each other. In the same way that Stravinsky's music itself stood as a more objective, less sentimental answer to late romanticism, so this motif reveals the objectively unattractive truth about the central characters instead of the glamorous and romanticized versions of themselves that they prefer to present to the world, and which the Golden Age scoring represents.

Finally, the tritone itself is in effect simply another form of allusion: a tritone is not innately devilish in any way, but alludes to the concept of the devil in a way that makes musical sense in the context of Western tonal harmony, its hierarchical ordering of pitches, and its concepts of consonance and dissonance, of right and wrong ways of behaving musically. The two strategies outlined here, of intertextual allusions and use of the tritone, are ultimately just one strategy, where the tritone's allusion to the devil is so well established and developed that it takes on a life of its own within a score. The tritone, it seems, is the devil in music because it is always wrong, it is the destabilizing force that upsets the status quo: but then, introducing a tritone F sharp into C major is what needs to be done in order to modulate conventionally to the dominant. As we leave the medieval period and move into the subsequent eras of music history, it seems that we position the tritone as the thing that makes music interesting, capable of change and development. That disruptive capability is ultimately what makes things fun: and if one thing is true of all the

Figure 2.17 Stravinsky, *The Soldier's Tale*, Scene 1, bars 2–4

Figure 2.18 Silvestri, "Stravinsky" motif from *Death Becomes Her*

devils, witches, imps, divas, and demons of the films discussed here, it is that they are the truly interesting characters. By contrast, the good characters, the ones being threatened, often appear as much more bland. This contrast may be why these musical strategies work so well and with such frequency in horror-comedies. Because you can use the tritone without abandoning tonal harmony, having it as the one disruptive interval tends to make it quirky rather than frightening, in the way that a more seriously tonally disrupted music might be; and the equally quirky allusions to Troll Kings, violin-playing devils, and medieval visions of hell juxtaposed with George Gershwin are more likely to amuse than scare. Horror and dread are never far away, but the techniques employed by composers—playfully parodied and exaggerated allusions to the harmonies, instruments, and textures of horror scoring, use of the Lydian mode to bring the merest suspicion of danger into otherwise idyllic images, and witty asides in the form of allusions to other music about the devil—all allow the composer to allude to horror while retaining a mischievous sense of comedy that draws the audience into a complicit understanding that none of these horror-comedy devils should actually frighten us.

Notes

1 William Paul explores the important convergence of the horror and comedy genres in the so-called gross out film in *Laughing, Screaming: Modern Hollywood Horror and Comedy* (New York: Columbia University Press, 1994). Vivian Sobchack notes that "*Carrie* has its comedic counterpart in *Revenge of the Nerds*" in "Bringing It All Back Home: Family Economy and Generic Exchange," in *The Dread of Difference: Gender and the Horror Film*, edited by Barry Keith Grant (Austin, TX: University of Texas Press, 1996), 161.

2 As with other genres, numerous types of non-orchestral scoring have been used in horror and horror-related genres, such as the muted synthesizer scores of vampire films such as *The Hunger* (1983) or *Near Dark* (1987), or the popular music scoring of the action-horror films of the *Blade* trilogy (1998–2004) and *Resident Evil* series (2002–08). See, for example, Janet K. Halfyard, "Love, Death, Curses and Reverses (in F Minor): Music, Gender and Identity in *Buffy the Vampire Slayer* and *Angel*," *Slayage* 17 (October 2001) at www.slayageonline.com (accessed December 16, 2008) and "Music of the Night: Scoring the Vampire in Contemporary Film," in *Terror Tracks: Music, Sound and Horror Cinema*, edited by Philip Hayward (London: Equinox, 2009).

3 David Neumeyer and James Buhler, "Analytical and Interpretative Approaches to Music (1): Analysing the Music," in *Film Music: Critical Approaches*, edited by K. J. Donnelly (New York: Continuum, 2001), 20. Within the quote "(Gorbman 1987: 3)" refers to Claudia Gorbman, *Unheard Melodies: Narrative Film Music* (Bloomington, IN: Indiana University Press, 1987).

4 Neumeyer and Buhler, "Analytical and Interpretative Approaches," 23.

5 See David Huckvale, *James Bernard, Composer to Count Dracula: A Critical Biography* (Jefferson: McFarland, 2006) as well as Randall D. Larson, *Music from the House of Hammer: Music in the Hammer Horror Films, 1950–1980* (Lanham, MD: Scarecrow, 1996), 22–27.

6 Philip Tagg, "Tritonal Crime and '*Music* as Music'," in *Philip Tagg's Online Texts* (1998) at www.tagg.org/articles/xpdfs/morric70.pdf (accessed December 16, 2008), 5.

7 Scott Murphy, "The Major Tritone Progression in Recent Hollywood Science Fiction Films," *Music Theory Online* 12/2 (May 2006) at http://mto.societymusic theory.org/issues/mto.06.12.2/mto.06.12.2.murphy_essay.html (accessed January 3, 2009).

8 The major exception is the Headless Horseman in *Sleepy Hollow*, by far the darkest and most potentially frightening of Burton's films of the ones listed.

9 For a more detailed discussion of Elfman's scoring techniques see Janet K. Halfyard, *Danny Elfman's Batman: a Film Score Guide* (Lanham, MD: Scarecrow Press, 2004).

10 See Gorbman, *Unheard Melodies*, 15–16.

11 Ibid., 16

12 Frederick C. Szebin and Steve Biodrowski, "Interview with Danny Elfman," *Soundtrack!* (March 1997): 6.

13 Very similar to the Witches theme, James Horner's main title theme for *Jumanji* (1995) (a fantasy film with some terrifying moments) again uses the Lydian mode on a tonic D to construct a charmingly innocent-sounding theme for the flute, whose embedded G sharp tritones nonetheless betray the supernatural trouble ahead (Figure 2.19).

14 Figure 2.8 is a bare reduction demonstrating the melody and underlying harmony: the original cue is much more fully orchestrated.

Figure 2.19 Horner, main title theme from *Jumanji*

Chapter 3

The Monster and the Music Box

Children and the Soundtrack of Horror

Stan Link

> When the voices of children are heard on the green
> And laughing is heard on the hill,
> My heart is at rest within my breast
> and everything else is still.
>
> William Blake

From *Songs of Innocence* (1789), Blake's "Nurse's Song" portrays the poet's emotions more enduringly than it does the sound of children. In 1973, *The Exorcist* had a child, Regan, howling "Let Jesus fuck you!" and exhorting a Catholic priest to "stick your cock up her ass, you mother-fucking worthless cocksucker!" Between Blake's reveries and Regan's blasphemies lie more than mere decades. Their stark contrast maps a mutation of how children are represented—a gulf of meaning. The bridge connecting Blake's idyll and a child-demon's gravelly exclamation that "your mother sucks cocks in hell" is the "voices of children." Although a young girl, Regan's speech sounds adult and male, effecting her identity's displacement by demonic possession. Sound is not merely symptomatic, but becomes the very site of the transformation from innocence to obscenity. If horror cinema such as *The Exorcist* fell into that gap of meaning, then sound pushed it.

That bleak metamorphosis cannot be written off as "vulgarization" within popular culture. Alban Berg's opera, *Wozzeck* (1925), for example, dimmed the lights on its dark tragedy not with horrendous musical intensity but with children's voices. Marie lies stabbed to death by Wozzeck, who later drowns retrieving the knife. In the final scene, the child they leave orphaned plays blissfully unaware among his friends. "Ringle-Ringle-Rosenkranz," they sing. Another child enters with news that the boy's mother has been found: "Hey you! Your mother is dead!" Chirping "hop-hop, hop-hop" the son spurs his imaginary horse to see the corpse. "When the voices of children are heard on the green"— laughing, speaking, singing—their expressive gravity may rival the most massive orchestral sonorities. Devastating in its alchemy of pathos from irony, Berg's understated ending affirms that children's expressivity echoes more than their own "innocence and experience." Holding a mirror to *our* knowledge of the world, "Ringle-Ringle-Rosenkranz" grows implicatively richer—a plot device drawing simple curves from complex equations.

The notion of simplicity indicating something beyond itself reaches into the Enlightenment aesthetic of "noble simplicity" to which Rousseau refers in his *Dictionnaire de musique* of 1768.[1] But already in 1737, Johann Mattheson had also idealized simplicity by admonishing his readers to understand it "not as something dumb, foolish, or low, but rather much more as something precious, unadorned and extraordinary."[2] By the late eighteenth and nineteenth centuries, simplicity represented emotional authenticity, with works such as Schumann's *Kinderszenen* (*Scenes from Childhood*), Tchaikovsky's *Album for the Young*, Humperdinck's *Hansel und Gretel*, and dozens of *Wiegenlieder* ("cradle songs") and berceuses ensconcing simple images of childhood in the romantic musical imagination.

Comparing Blake's "Nurse's Song" from *Songs of Innocence* to a poem bearing that same title in *Songs of Experience* (1794) extends the child theme to reflect adult fears:

> When the voices of children are heard on the green
> And whisp'rings are in the dale,
> The days of my youth rise fresh in my mind,
> My face turns green and pale.
> Then come home, my children, the sun has gone down,
> And the dews of night arise;
> Your spring and your day are wasted in play,
> And your winter and night in disguise.

The nineteenth century saw the child topos become a musing on mortality, and by the time of Gustav Mahler's biographically prescient *Kindertotenlieder* (*Songs on the Death of Children*, 1904), the romantic fruits of childhood ripen to death on a grand scale. Like most things romantic, the wager on children as a pretext for emotion was greater than any investment in the pleasures of childhood itself. And when profoundly negative emotions crouching beneath romantic longing seized hold of music in expressionistic works such as Richard Strauss's *Salome* (1909) and Arnold Schönberg's *Erwartung* (1909), "childhood" would not escape the spreading psychological gloom. *Wozzeck*'s finale bore a century's musical momentum. "Ringle-Ringle Rosenkranz" amalgamates romantic sentimentality with expressionist aesthetics of crisis, making innocence a nexus and victim of both.

The sound and music of cinematic horror were therefore latecomers to childhood's meeting with starkly intensified emotion, harvesting ground already tilled by European art music. Especially with Germanic music as guiding spirit, the classic film score migrated to well-charted territory. Vulnerability makes children an inevitable subject for horrors ranging from innocents *in* danger (i.e. *Poltergeist*) to "innocents" *as* danger (i.e. *The Omen*). In such memorable films the soundtrack not only underscores narratives, but extends and enacts them. Encompassing everything from simple a capella children's songs and lullabies to high musical modernism in a full orchestra, the counterpoint of music, child, and horror asks innocent but challenging questions: "How do we hear children?" "What do we hear *through* them?" Although a full roll-call of horror's children might produce its own subgenre, some familiar films suggest recurring answers.

Performing Innocence

Don't Look Now (1973)

A young girl in a red hooded raincoat plays near a pond while her parents work in the house nearby. She finds a rubber ball and tosses it into the pond. Inside, her father spills his drink on a photographic slide, making the pigments of an unknown figure also in red slowly ooze like blood. Suddenly struck by a premonition, the father runs outside to find his daughter has drowned.

Nicolas Roeg's film ambles into tragic death with benign non-diegetic piano music. But while the girl's drowning sets in motion a quasi-supernatural misadventure, its mellifluous musical introduction sounds disconnected from her fate. The piece and its performance, however, are vividly significant: beginners' piano music played with faltering inexperience. Simple music *plays* innocence, deepening our experience of it. The piece can be heard as a performance, both musical and symbolic, of youthful vulnerability. Such naive music makes defenselessness sensible—concretized in becoming audible. In its hesitancy, this music sounds inexperienced not only in its unassuming material, but in its execution, foregrounding the very notion of performance by way of uncertain dexterity. Bearing marks of developing ability, the music forces awareness of being *played* rather than *presented*, as a flawless performance might. Through its motoric immaturity, the beginners' piece makes clear that musical simplicity encodes physiology. Leaving its trail in narrow melodic ranges hewing to the singing voice, in the reach of small hands in "five finger exercises," and in regular rhythms affirming a palpable pulse, the young body imprints itself in childhood music. A sounding incarnation of her youth, musical simplicity fleshes out the girl's body. Audibly embodied, innocence now lies further exposed, amplifying potential dangers.

Although physical and psychological vulnerability dwell at the heart of any horror film, the image of the immature body haunts *Don't Look Now*. In Venice after his daughter's death, the father glimpses a short figure in a hooded red raincoat reminiscent of his daughter's. A recent rash of murders suggests the elusive figure somehow relates to his dead child and also faces potential danger. The father follows her and, upon catching up with her, the figure in red seems to sob as he approaches. But her small size has been mistaken for immaturity. The turning hood reveals not a child, but a dwarf whose older, deeply wrinkled face grins as she slices the father's throat. Musically, however, hope that the red raincoat was linked to the child was already dispelled. The faltering piano music has not been heard since the daughter's death, leaving the remaining music without an imprint of immaturity.

Their Mother's Voice

Melodic simplicity frequently implies singability. The voice it implies, however, may not remain an abstraction. The title sequence to Roman Polanski's *Rosemary's Baby* (1968) unveils another face of simple tunes— not only the child, but the mother. Beginning with a non-diegetic vocalise, a gentle, wordless lullaby, the film warmly anticipates birth and maternity. Central to bonding infant and mother, the maternal voice forms an enveloping auditory environment, as Michel Chion describes in *The Voice in Cinema*:

> In the beginning, in the uterine darkness, was the voice, the Mother's voice. For the child once born, the mother is more an olfactory and vocal continuum than an image. Her voice originates in all points of space, while her form enters and leaves the visual field. We can imagine the voice of the Mother weaving around the child a network of connections it's tempting to call the *umbilical web*. A rather horrifying expression to be sure, in its evocation of spiders—and in fact, this original vocal connection will remain ambivalent.[3]

The lullaby musically enacts the mother-child relationship, in effect performing their bond. The simple tune encodes the immature body intertwined with a maternal presence—connected by the "umbilical web."[4]

Rosemary's Baby, however, questions that bond. The soundtrack dramatizes its strength *and* ambivalence. As Rosemary first sees her newborn son, sired by Satan, the animalistic sound of a whinnying, muted trumpet registers her shock. Guttural rather than melodic, the cue must be heard for what it *isn't*. Namely, while gentle diatonic melodies may perform the maternal bond, withholding those values here intensifies separation.[5] Indeed, Rosemary's reaction and its music evoke Julia

Kristeva's "abjection" concept of encountering objects of disgust such as vomit, feces, or corpses, provoking forceful rejection or expulsion.[6] Just as simple music performs innocence, the music of Rosemary's initial encounter with her offspring enacts abjection—a performance of her retching retreat from what she bore. The child and motherhood itself have become repulsive, and the cue marks an audible absence of the lullaby. Shortly after Rosemary's initial rejection, however, the child cries while being clumsily rocked by a much older woman. Responding to the otherwise normal sound of a baby crying, Rosemary comes to accept him as her child. Her son's voice reattaches Rosemary to the umbilical web. Now caring for Satan's son—*her* son—a maternal smile crosses Rosemary's lips, and the film closes on the motherly lullaby with which it began.

Rosemary's Baby resolves its mother-child ambivalence most substantially in that final lullaby. Conversely, Bernard Herrmann's theme for Larry Cohen's *It's Alive* (1973) establishes ambivalence from the outset. "Brooding" in both senses of the word, the score casts an ominous shadow from the titles on to the opening scene of an expectant mother waking to realize "it's time." A prenatal prediction of doom, the weightiness of Herrmann's score dispels any joy in this moment. The mutant baby kills the delivery room staff, but Herrmann's score has already gone through the labor of establishing a music-emotional separation of the child from the mother by eschewing vocally oriented melodies of the sort in *Rosemary's Baby*. When simplicity encodes childhood, the body, and maternity through things such as voco-centric melodies, formal clarity, register, rhythmic certainty, and diatonic pitch material, then complementary musical values may represent opposite dramatic descriptions. Particularly within horror involving children, pitch and contour exceeding the voice, metric ambiguity, and chromaticism mark distance from maternity and innocence.

Stanley Kubrick's *The Shining* (1980) makes overpowering use of these values. Pedaling his tricycle alone through corridors of an empty resort hotel, a small boy, Danny, encounters specters of twin girls murdered at the hotel. They invite Danny to "Come and play with us . . . forever and ever and ever . . ." Danny's fear is devastating, musically registered by Krzysztof Penderecki's *De Natura Sonoris No. 1*. Deep, sonorous percussion, metrically and tonally nebulous, textural rather than melodic, the cue is musically distinct from values typically underscoring children's immaturity. It instead constructs the Kristevian abjection ensuing in flashes of the murdered girls lying in their own blood. And just as Rosemary's reaction to her son separates them from each other, the disorienting music here enacts Danny's isolation from what Kaja Silverman refers to as the "fantasy of the maternal voice."[7]

In exceeding the confines of that voice, musical body coding becomes amorphous. Such ambiguity may be especially pertinent to horror. As

Noël Carroll observes, the "categorically incomplete" frequently characterizes the monstrous. Defining "horrific impurity," he writes that "an object or being is impure if it is categorically interstitial, categorically contradictory, incomplete, or formless."[8] Not quite human, the *It's Alive* baby remains "interstitial." Both a newborn *and* evil incarnate, Rosemary's baby turns "categorically contradictory." We can hear the most effective soundtracks for horrific threat by way of musical analogues to Carroll's terms in the ambiguous superseding the defined, the fragment displacing the whole. Monstrosity resides in denying musical orientation toward the categorically complete human body, exceeding its limitation, avoiding simplicity, remaining aloof from rhythmic certainty, and so on. In short, like the monster, the music of the monstrous derives from its difficulty to apprehend with conceptual clarity. Thus the "innocent tune" and its musical antitheses, although found in any cinematic genre, becomes doubly effective in horror, and redoubled by interplay with children.

Poltergeist (1982) amalgamates these issues when malignant forces spirit a child, Carol Anne, into an invisible realm in her family's house. Composer Jerry Goldsmith represents Carol Anne with a simple diatonic lullaby, emphatically contrasting with the more chromatic musical material associated with the paranormal threats. In the film's most heartrending scenes, the family tries to prove Carol Anne haunts her own family home. As her family and a team of paranormal investigators gather in the living room, the score sounds thematically fragmented, amorphous and tonally uncertain. Carol Anne cannot be seen, but her voice comes through a television. Likewise, the child cannot see her family, but hears their voices. As her mother tries to communicate with her, the first hints of the lullaby emerge metallically on the vibraphone out of an orchestral ether. The full lullaby sounds in the oboe as Carol Anne's mother asks, "Can you say hello to Daddy?," to which the girl's disembodied voice responds, "Hello, Daddy." Torn to this point, the vocal web between mother and child tenuously reweaves itself through their speaking voices and Goldsmith's non-diegetic lullaby, reinforced when taken up by the orchestral strings.

But as her mother pleads, "Can you find a way home to us, baby?" Carol Anne responds, "I'm afraid of the light," and comes under attack in her realm. Goldsmith's music reflects this in abandoning the lullaby for a harmonically shifting passage undercutting the umbilical connection between the two worlds. Carol Anne's voice goes silent, and it becomes unclear if she can hear her family. Musical turbulence drives to the image of a nebulous vortex opening above the living room. Carol Anne's voice re-emerges with "Mommy, there's somebody here." The score recedes as heart-pounding footsteps from the ceiling accompany the girl's cries of "Get him away from me! Leave me alone!" The mother follows the sounds to the staircase as an ascending chromatic glissando in the strings evaporates into the sudden gong and high pitched metallic chimes accompanying a sudden gust of air blowing the mother's hair back, causing her to gasp. Carol Anne's voice evaporates, but the musical umbilicus is reattached briefly as the lullaby returns in the metallic sound of the vibraphone. The mother cries joyfully that "She just moved through me!" Moreover, the lullaby's return does not simply betoken Carol Anne's spiritual reality to her mother. It carries with it her physical reality and body as her mother exclaims, "I felt her. I can smell her. It's her! Smell my clothes! She's all over me." Music, voice, child, maternity, and body find each other again in a "simple" lullaby.

Musical Premonition and Irony

Jaws (1975)

In a widening circle of frothy, crimson water, a boy named Alex Kintner is quickly and completely devoured by a great white shark. As panicked swimmers scramble to safety, the boy's mother searches in vain for her son, looking out to sea as a torn, deflated life vest washes ashore.

Although unfolding suddenly, this bloody tableau arrives with an unlikely but clear musical warning. Before composer John Williams's famously menacing shark cue, our prescience arrives in a diegetic strain of "Do you know the muffin man?" This innocent overture from the voice of another boy playing safely on shore furtively sets a place for the gruesome feast. The simple tune and the orchestral cue play off of each other. As in *Poltergeist*, threatening music is categorically separate from the child. In *Jaws*, however, it is not only the material differences that matter, but differences in their relationship to the scene. While the Carol Anne lullaby expands on and takes us further into the narrative, "The Muffin Man" is a musical non-sequitur. The boy's singing is a distraction, misdirection even, from anxiety. We sense what is about to happen by pretending *not* to know.

The playground in which music and film see-saw between childhood and danger is irony, and the dramatic effect derives from music indicating the opposite of peril. "The Muffin Man" encrypts mortal threat by hiding it behind playful simplicity. Ultimately, the innocent tune amplifies the character of the mechanistic ostinato, which circles back to make that moment appear optimistic or foolish. "Do you know the muffin man?" Well, yes . . . but apparently he's a harbinger of death and dismemberment. At once an ingenuous and *dis*-ingenuous performance, in harrowing films such as *Don't Look Now* and *Jaws* the sound of innocence frequently announces its own end.

Anempathy: Musical Indifference and the Banality of Evil

The Omen (1976)

Still images of a happy early childhood transition to a boy, Damien, celebrating his fifth birthday at an elaborate party on the grounds of his parents' estate. A loving nanny holds Damien as he blows out the candles on his cake. His parents and some older children sing "Happy Birthday." The nanny carries Damien off to pose for pictures. Damien's mother takes him from the nanny, who then wanders alone to the edge of the party where she encounters a large dog. They exchange a prolonged stare. The scene continues with Damien riding a merry-go-round. While the carousel full of children revolves, the nanny calls, "Damien! Look at me! I'm over here!" "Damien, I love you!" Spotting the nanny, Damien's mother plucks him from the carousel into her arms. Damien points. His nanny has climbed out of a third-story window and stands on the roof with a noose around her neck. "Look at me Damien! It's all for you!" The nanny jumps, snapping her neck as she swings through the glass of the second-story window below. Swaying back outside, she dangles lifelessly. The merry-go-round continues to circle as everyone watches in horror. A photographer snaps pictures as Damien rests in his mother's arms. Looking over her shoulder, Damien sees the dog, giving it a slight smile and a wave.

This scene's soundtrack drastically intensifies its peripeteia. A non-diegetic music box rendition of "Happy Birthday" underscores the initial montage of stills, eliding with the diegetic "Happy Birthday." As the nanny encounters the dog, sounds of children fade into a menacingly pulsating non-diegetic synthesizer cue. Cutting away from the nanny and dog back to the party, the sound of children's play banishes the mastiff's cue. The rotating carousel becomes the diegetic source of a mellifluous metallophone (the characteristic sound of music boxes and ice cream trucks). Though briefly inaudible under the ensuing screams of horror, the carousel music continues throughout the nanny's suicide as it continues to spin with several children still aboard, turning in shocked silence. The faint sound of a creaking rope accompanies the twinkling music as the nanny sways gently. The mastiff's cue returns with a shot of Damien looking toward the dog.

The intransigence of the merry-go-round after the nanny's spectacular self-destruction is the scene's most compelling feature. Any musical acknowledgement of the nanny's death seems noticeably missing. No score wells up to reflect her grimly enthusiastic end. The nanny doesn't matter— musically cast aside like a child's toy that became uninteresting. Her end seems most poignant here in its very *lack* of significance, providing a memorable example of musical "anempathy" as described by Michel Chion:

> music can also exhibit conspicuous indifference to the situation, by progressing in a steady, undaunted, and ineluctable manner: the scene takes place against this very backdrop of "indifference." This juxtaposition of scene with indifferent music has the effect not of freezing emotion but rather of intensifying it, by inscribing it on a cosmic background. I call this . . . kind of music *anempathetic* (with the privative *a-*). The anempathetic impulse in the cinema produces those countless musical bits from player pianos, celestas, music boxes, and dance bands, whose studied frivolity and naiveté reinforce the individual emotion of the character and of the spectator, even as the music pretends not to notice them.[9]

Pretending "not to notice" something amiss with the child it celebrates, anempathy is at work with the music box "Happy Birthday" during the scene's beginning. Offering comparison with the "Muffin Man" prelude to death in *Jaws*, the juvenile piano in *Don't Look Now*, and most directly to the lullaby beginning *Rosemary's Baby*, music deliberately looks away as tragedy approaches. It is not that the musical narration doesn't know, but rather that it *does* know and won't tell. "Studied frivolity" cannot be completely innocent.

Far from inert, the ultimate expressivity of anempathetic music may derive from the cinematic medium itself. As Chion continues, anempathy emphasizes film's "automatic" quality:

> For indeed, all films proceed in the form of an indifferent and automatic unwinding, that of projection, which on the screen and through the loudspeakers produces simulacra of movement and life—and this unwinding must hide itself and be forgotten. What does anempathetic music do, if not to unveil this reality of cinema, its robotic face? Anempathetic music conjures up the mechanical texture of this tapestry of the emotions and senses.[10]

The film continues, *must* continue, regardless of how we feel about its events. Anempathy not only sensitizes us to emotions "against a cosmic backdrop," but requires us to experience film qua film. As with film's projection, the untroubled music box plays on and on regardless of what happens.

Music boxes and other mechanical music therefore become particularly effective in child-related horror. Their unknowing demeanor mimics innocence. Trailers for the *It's Alive* films featured music box frivolity in setting a mechanical "Happy Birthday" against the image of party favors and balloons just before a mutant claw tears through a birthday cake. "The *It's Alive* baby is back again. Only now there are three of them. *It Lives Again*," the voice-over intones before "Happy Birthday" continues. The seismic scare is not enough to shake music from its insistently naive detachment. Inevitable machines—film projection and music boxes among them—often lurk in the effect of anempathy.

The Omen makes a spectacular display of "mechanical texture" by weaving automatic images, music, and sound overtly into its narrative tapestry. Its still montage makes visible the film's status as photography, rupturing our immersion in a "motion picture." Momentarily ejected from the narrative world we are forced to acknowledge viewing a film. Mechanical music twice countenances the indifference of film's "automatic unwinding," first in the "Happy Birthday" still montage and then in the carousel music aftermath. Apart from its unceasingly benign music, the *image* of the merry-go-round embodies anempathy. Spinning in counterpoint with the nanny's pendulum swings, it renders visible the ineluctability of mechanization. Snapping dozens of pictures in just seconds, the photographer's rapid-firing shutter winds the scene back to where it began—the audibility of film as an automatic medium.

Music and the Expressivity of Filmic Automatism

The Birds (1963)

A woman sits by the playground outside a schoolhouse. Lighting a cigarette, she inhales and exhales in a leisurely rhythm. Inside, the class sings a song, "Risseldy Rosseldy." Gathering one by one at first, as if trying to be inconspicuous, crows flock unnoticed on the playground behind the woman. Watching an arriving crow, she sees it alight among an assemblage whose size suggests some dark sense of purpose The local community has suffered inexplicable incidents involving birds, and she goes to the schoolhouse to warn that the students should be evacuated to safety. As the class leaves the school, a sudden panic descends with the birds as they swoop and peck at the children, as though this was their plan all along.

As with *The Omen*, the scene features notable anempathy as children's music naively blankets danger. As in *Don't Look Now*, the children in Hitchcock's film are more exposed to hostile elements through their audibility. Keeping their off-screen bodies present, the children's voices make first contact with the adversary outside their window. The schoolhouse song becomes a performance of filmic automatism and inevitability. That the children themselves create the scene's anempathy ironically intensifies its suspense. As well as performing innocence, the victims here propagate the scene's indifference toward them and amplify the threat against the vulnerability they embody. Complicit in the "mechanical unwinding," the children perform simultaneously in the narrative world and in the very medium of film. This particular song seems a perfect meshing of the children into a "mechanical texture." "Risseldy Rosseldy" alternates lines about marital discontent with nonsense that expands and contracts, imparting a feeling of unpredictability. At the same time, the text maintains a jaunty iambic rhythm in the narrative lines and dactyls in the chorus, reinforcing a sense of motorized resolve:

> The butter came out a grizzle-y-grey.
> Ristle-tee, rostle-tee, Now, now, now!
> The cheese took legs and ran away!
> Ristle-tee, rostle-tee, hey donny dostle-tee,
> knickety-knackety, retro-quo-quality,
> willoby-wallaby, Now, now, now!

Giving an impression of inevitable unfolding, the insistently rhythmic nonsense of the song accompanying the purposeful flocking of birds reflects an obscure process threatening to become hypertelic—growing without goal or end. The effect is cancerous. With the children's song empowering the threat to their own safety, the unknowing body attacks itself. While nature appears to be the agent in *The Birds*, it is only the messenger. Film's "unbeatable slow machine that brings you what you get," to borrow an image from poet Philip Larkin, again reveals itself as the music's fundamental subtext.

"Risseldy Rosseldy" constructs suspense in *The Birds* with mirthful efficiency, making direct contact with automatism's core effect: powerlessness. In *The World Viewed*, Stanley Cavell describes automatism that "codes the experience of the work of art as 'happening of itself.'" Cinema serves as an "automatic world projection":

> In viewing a movie my helplessness is mechanically assured: I am present not at something happening, which I must confirm, but at something that has happened, which I absorb (like a memory). In this, movies resemble novels, a fact mirrored in the sound of narration itself, whose tense is past.[11]

Having unfolded on their own, events appear about which spectators can do nothing. In this regard, a fundamental experience of spectatorship lies in having desires *fail* to impact "the world viewed." Invited to look, contemplate, remember—but not touch—the world before us is "happening of itself." As Cavell suggests:

The explanation is not so much that the world is passing us by, as that we are displaced from our natural habitation within it, placed at a distance from it. The screen overcomes our fixed distance; it makes displacement appear as our natural condition.[12]

If we claim to feel absorbed, it has been film's power to make our true condition of remaining at a "fixed distance" invisible to us. Automatism inheres in every film, but insofar as it becomes *revealed* in "the *experience* of the work of art as happening of itself," musical anempathy makes automatism overt. By turning it audible, anempathy forces a confrontation with the invisible, "natural condition" of displacement. Refusing to reflect danger, "Risseldy Rosseldy" and "The Muffin Man" sing out loud cinema's promise to neutralize the spectator: *In watching, you exchange your own power for mine.*

Revealed fully at the nexus of musical anempathy, horror, and child, the spectator's nominal relationship to "automatic world projection" then becomes richly expressive. Film's "fixed distance" becomes a discomfiting powerlessness: parental anxiety. Of itself, an imperiled child is an unremarkable narrative situation, compelling spectators to assume quasi-parental concern. Ironic music, however, forces the spectator to experience the loss of power to intervene. Mellifluous non-sequiturs such as "The Muffin Man" or a beginning piano etude as preludes to death make us feel the limit of our ability to reach across our "fixed distance." Cavell's filmic "helplessness" has a pointed real-world analogue in parental fears about a child's well-being. Shark or Satan aside, the unbeatable power in cinema ultimately becomes film's automatism, nullifying our reactions with music often acting as a potently deliberate reagent.

The implication of anempathetic children's music exceeds a "mechanically assured" threat, however. Suggesting that while the film is present to us, we are not present to it, Cavell writes that "movies allow the audience to be mechanically absent." "How do movies reproduce the world magically?" he asks. "Not by literally presenting us with the world, but by permitting us to view it unseen."[13] The automatic world projection intensifies our sense that children are beyond our help, but it does so because it is *we* who cannot inhabit *their* world. We are powerless because as displaced spectators we are not *there*. Cavell concludes that:

> A world complete without me which is present to me is the world of my immortality. This is an importance of film—and a danger. It takes my life as my haunting of the world, either because I left it unloved (The Flying Dutchman) or because I left unfinished business (Hamlet).[14]

Left it unloved . . . unfinished business . . . complete without me—beneath its role in intensifying a child's death in film then, innocent music translates still more deeply into anxieties about our *own* deaths as spectator-parents. The inexorable rhythms of children singing "Risseldy Rosseldy" signal *our* remove from *their* lives. Doggedly playing on, *The Omen's* haunting carousel is haunted by *us*, watching from a position at once privileged and yet at a helpless remove. Seeing while remaining unseen, we also hear without being heard. We are "dead to the world." Assuring us of our inability to intervene, music marks our passage.

Here the force of anempathetic naive tunes, music box melodies, lullabies, and children's songs becomes clearly nostalgic. In *Jaws*, "In the Good Old Summertime" and other oom-pah-pah favorites emanate from a beachside carousel. The one-room schoolhouse of *The Birds* was largely a thing of the past. And that sort of classroom music making would remain for most spectators something recalled from their own past. The campy *Ice Cream Man* (1995) begins with a flashback to the traumatic shooting of the neighborhood ice cream man in front of his truck. The remainder of the film predictably sprinkles itself with the sound of an ice cream truck driven by a lunatic serving treats fouled by mice and eyeballs. While representing gruesome deaths, the sound of the truck attempts to excavate "simple pleasures" from a ruined, if imaginary, perfect past. By the same token, the "Happy Birthday" and carousel music in *The Omen* hearken back to pre-phonographic reproduction—mechanical rather than electro-magnetic or digital. So markedly out of date, such anachronisms mean as much as any more particular musical expressivity. Their "out-of-date-ness" *is* their affect. Thus temporal remoteness exaggerates the anempathetic musical construction of children in danger. Appearing as mere distraction, innocent music presents its own threat to render us powerless and lost in time.

Innocence as Horror

The Bad Seed (1956)

Mother: What happened to old Mrs. Post in Wichita?
Rhoda: There was ice on the steps and I slipped and fell against her. And that was all.
Mother: That was all?
Rhoda: No. I slipped on purpose.

Perhaps innocence itself is the illusion. On the surface, little about Mervyn LeRoy's *The Bad Seed* casts it within the horror genus. But Rhoda sprouts a monster—a "categorical contradiction" of a perfectly pretty blond child *and* remorseless sociopath. Pitilessly dispatched, Rhoda's victims stood between her and something she wanted. Particularly in its use of music to ends we might find in horror proper, however, the film carries monstrous genes. Indeed, *The Bad Seed* presents a wonderfully synoptic case study precisely because Rhoda's most hideous features stand unveiled most fully in the soundtrack, which fully dissects the recombinant anatomy of innocence, music, and horror: musical child, dreadful child, and dreadful music.

Coming first not as an image, but through the sound of her practicing "Au Clair de la Lune" at the piano, Rhoda's physical immaturity forms our initial impression. Complimenting the music, her father says "That's a mighty pretty piece," but Rhoda's playing of the classic beginners' piece is halting and awkward. The tune was thematically established in a frantic, distorted form during Alex North's orchestral score in the opening titles. The first diegetic performance, then, amplifies its own "purity" by way of contrast, reinforcing Rhoda's pre-adolescence as the film's primary conceit.

During the scene containing the dialogue excerpted above, Rhoda has just told how she came to murder another child. Her mother then seized the moment to ask about a previous "accidental" death. "I slipped on purpose," comes the answer. Alex North slips "Au Claire de la Lune" into the score as we understand Rhoda's awareness of her murderous intent. The simple tune now offers ironic acknowledgement—not that Rhoda's innocence has ended, but that it was an illusion. If anything, the melody has only constructed the wishful naiveté of Rhoda's mother.

The tune's climactic, ghastly appearance comes as the gardener, Leroy—who never believed Rhoda's innocence—burns to death in what merely appears to be an accident. Moments before a fire spreads in the cellar occupied by Leroy, Rhoda enters the apartment, going straight to her piano room and shutting the door. Playing "Au Clair de la Lune" again and again, Rhoda is accompanied by Leroy's horrifying screams as he burns to death outside. "That man is still screaming and the piano is going on and on while he's dying in the fire!," Rhoda's mother cries. But Rhoda doesn't stop, her piano stoking her mother's hysterical grief in knowing what Rhoda has done. Wailing sirens now join the tune. Still performing with ruthless, mechanistic insistence, Rhoda ratchets up the tempo, turning the tune to a grotesque parody of itself. Rhoda doesn't relent until her mother pounds on the door, tearfully pleading for her to "Stop that music!" Again, music becomes abjection as Rhoda repulses her own mother. The child calmly and "innocently" emerges with the word "Mommy . . ."

Reflecting the scene's emotional pitch, the climactic tempo devastates the simplicity of "Au Clair de la Lune." Rhoda cuts the umbilical web with a melody, silencing her mother's "fantasy of the maternal voice," now turned to screams. Synthesizing the complementary sets of musical values that usually describe the innocent and the monstrous, Rhoda transforms herself into a monster by mutilating the immature body implicit in the piano tune. Since its performance at the film's beginning, the tune has shed any pretense of innocence, now consciously performing the anempathetic indifference—Rhoda's indifference—toward a gruesome death. The piano not only expresses Rhoda's cruelty, but literally becomes its "instrument." Rhoda's simple music articulates her sociopathic disregard for the suffering she has caused.

Conclusion: Music and Children Post Childhood

In all, horror has fed on a steady diet of children. But comparing the birthday scene from *The Omen* of 1976 with its 2006 remake may suggest a changing metabolism. Musically, the child topos dims considerably. There is no music box "Happy Birthday," and the carousel remains musically, sonically, and dramatically in the background. At the point where the original draws attention to the carousel's insistent music, the remake lets Marco Beltrami's score deliver the more literal shock of the suicide. There are, naturally, differences between directors, composers, and so on, to acknowledge. Both cinema and horror have changed a great deal in thirty years. If the remake of *The Omen* indicates any musical trend, it could simply be that naive tunes became inexpressive clichés. The musical introduction to the young girl in *The Tooth Fairy* (2006) comes by way of tinny music leaking from her iPod headphones. The film's subsequent use of a music box playing "Three Blind Mice" while someone is rendered alive in a threshing machine makes that mixture of innocence and irony feel like a cinematic and musical throwback.

But if horror constitutes a "cultural history," as David Skal suggests, there may be a more interesting story in differences between musical strategies.[15] *Children of the Corn* has become a twenty-five-year franchise, beginning with a 1984 feature, continuing with six sequels and a television remake for 2009. Although the first installment of *Children of the Corn* is full of both, Jonathan Elias's score avoids "innocent" music. The film promises not simply the eradication of adults by children, but the eradication of childhood itself as children form their own murderous religious society, complete with leaders and prophet. The musical imprint of children is confined to wordless voices of children in a quasi-choral chant, sounding more cultish than childish. In many ways, the score correctly registers the absence of "childhood" even as children abound.

Without even a preliminary survey it would be hasty to draw conclusions from such brief examples. Further, earlier films such as *It's Alive* and *The Exorcist* also provide scant musical articulations of childhood. Distinctions between films bearing musical markings of their childhood elements and those without feel more significant than arbitrary. What could be at stake in those differences? For horror at least, we might wonder whether the musical nineteenth century has at last run its course. But through changing music, might we be encountering changing views of childhood? As Jacques Attali suggests:

Music is prophecy. Its styles and economic organization are ahead of the rest of society because it explores, much faster than material reality can, the entire range of possibilities in a given code. It makes audible the new world that will gradually become visible . . .[16]

If rejecting musical innocence is not merely to abandon clichés, but serves as harbinger of something becoming visible, then what is that "new world?"

To Attali, "music makes mutations audible."[17] Comparing the narratives and musical strategies of *Poltergeist* and *The Sixth Sense* (1999), we can understand them as inversions. *Poltergeist* dichotomizes musical values, audibly differentiating between the child and paranormal threats. The narrative conceit of *The Sixth Sense*, on the other hand, requires James Newton Howard's score to integrate the music-emotional representations of the boy, Cole Sear, with all the film's other characters whether mundane or other-worldly. Goldsmith's lullaby constructs Carol Anne's immaturity while her dramatic role consists of being looked for and heard. Cole Sear's young age remains musically unmarked, while his dramatic import resides in seeing, listening, and bearing witness: "I see dead people." *Poltergeist*'s Carol Anne disappears into the spirit realm. Spirits visit Cole Sear in *his* world. As such, *The Sixth Sense* draws no distinction between the material world, the afterworld, and the child's world. But separateness has traditionally been the very definition of "childhood." As Howard P. Chudacoff describes colonial childhood in *Children at Play: An American History*, children "created spaces and activities in which to amuse themselves independent of the domestic and social worlds created by parents and other adults."[18] He argues that adults' and children's worlds have now come to blur their distinctions. Perhaps Attali's "herald" announces a future in which "childhood" ends as a discrete category. A music-topical childhood of the type grounded in nineteenth century musical representations loses descriptive power if both musically and socially children and childhood go their separate ways. It becomes easy to understand a proliferation in cinema of monstrous children as reflecting their categorical ambiguity. Perhaps Herrmann's score for the mutant film, *It's Alive*, was indeed prophetic in enacting the audible mutation of a musically, socially, and physically disappearing childhood. "Children should be seen and not heard," but in both being heard and being silent, they say far more than meets the ear. Children in horror become a way of hearing other tales. Musically, "childhood" has its own story to tell—and not just "one day there was a little girl who . . .", and not just about innocence and its end. Whether silent or singing, horror's children tell about the world outside their world, voicing things innocence cannot know.

Notes

1 Jean-Jacques Rousseau, *Dictionnaire de musique* (New York: Johnson Reprint Corp, 1969), 277.
2 Johann Mattheson, *Der vollkommene Capellmeister*, translated by Ernest C. Harriss (Ann Arbor: UMI Research Press), 149. I am indebted to Melanie Lowe for locating these first two citations.
3 Michel Chion, *The Voice in Cinema*, translated by Claudia Gorbman (New York: Columbia University Press), 61.
4 Kaja Silverman, *The Acoustic Mirror: The Female Voice in Psychoanalysis and Cinema* (Bloomington, IN: Indiana University Press, 1988), 72–100. Silverman gives a detailed reading of the maternal voice dealing explicitly and critically with Chion's "umbilical web."
5 Lucy Fisher, "Birth Traumas: Parturition and Horror in *Rosemary's Baby*," in *The Dread of Difference*, edited by Barry Keith Grant (Austin, TX: University of Texas Press, 1996). Fisher refracts the spectrum of birth-related themes into "false labor," "multiple births," "hysterical pregnancy," "afterbirth," and so on.
6 Julia Kristeva, *The Powers of Horror: An Essay on Abjection* (New York: Columbia University Press, 1982). The reader will also find useful Barbara Creed, "Horror and the Monstrous-Feminine: An Imaginary Abjection," *Screen* 27, 1 (1986): 44–70.
7 Silverman, *The Acoustic Mirror*, 73.
8 Noël Carroll, *The Philosophy of Horror or Paradoxes of the Heart* (New York: Routledge, 1990), 32.
9 Michel Chion, *Audio Vision*, translated by Claudia Gorbman (New York: Columbia University Press, 1994), 8.
10 Ibid., 9.
11 Stanley Cavell, *The World Viewed*, enlarged edition (Cambridge, MA: Harvard University Press, 1979), 26.
12 Ibid., 41.
13 Ibid., 40.
14 Ibid., 160.
15 David J. Skal, *The Monster Show: A Cultural History of Horror* (New York: Faber and Faber, 1993), 287–305. In particular, Skal gives a useful outline of the ways in which horror films of the 1960s and 1970s reflected shifts in attitudes toward pregnancy and birth.
16 Jacques Attali, *Noise: The Political Economy of Music*, translated by Brian Massumi (Minneapolis, MN: University of Minnesota Press, 1985), 11.
17 Ibid., 4.
18 Howard P. Chudacoff, *Children at Play: an American History* (New York: New York University Press, 2007), 20.

Chapter 4

The Strange Case of Rouben Mamoulian's Sound Stew

The Uncanny Soundtrack in
Dr. Jekyll and Mr. Hyde (1931)

Neil Lerner[1]

From a vantage point in the twenty-first century it may be difficult to imagine a horror film soundtrack without the dissonances and narrative telegraphing that have been a characteristic part of the horror genre for several decades; yet an archeology of the soundtracks of early horror films has only recently begun, even though the rise of this particular genre seems to have been intimately tied to the drastic advances connected to sound reproduction technologies (as well as having been a genre that was and is simultaneously profitable and disreputable). Robert Spadoni argues convincingly of the link between the coming of sound film and the rise of horror as a genre in 1931, positing that the strangeness of the synchronized soundtrack would resonate especially well in *Dracula* (Browning, 1931) and *Frankenstein* (Whale, 1931), two films whose transgressive stories complicated notions of life and death just as the technical advances of the new sound cinema confused reality and artifice for its shocked audiences.[2] Spadoni's understandable emphasis on *Dracula* and *Frankenstein*—Universal Pictures' important building blocks of the horror cycle that Spadoni has ending in 1936[3]—overlooks (and underhears?) Rouben Mamoulian's remarkable version of *Dr. Jekyll and Mr. Hyde*, released in the US only five-and-a-half weeks after *Frankenstein*, at the end of 1931. The occasionally epistolary nature of Robert Louis Stevenson's 1886 novella, *The Strange Case of Dr. Jekyll and Mr. Hyde*, which gradually reveals (in the manner of a mystery) the connection between Jekyll and Hyde, provides another reason to link *Dr. Jekyll and Mr. Hyde* together with *Frankenstein* and *Dracula*, two works that also unfold their stories in part through letters written by characters in the novels. Numerous stage versions (most famously those starring Richard Mansfield) preceded the early films based on Stevenson's novella, with the 1920 rendition featuring John Barrymore generally regarded as the most distinguished cinematic version before Paramount Pictures returned to the story in 1931.[4] With Mamoulian's version of *Dr. Jekyll and Mr. Hyde*, sound design and music took on an enhanced role in the film's creation of dread and revulsion for the audience, as the soundtrack worked together with the point-of-view shots to form a groundbreaking sense of embodied subjectivity; elements of sound and music help to put the audience eye to eye (and ear to heart, as will become clear) with their own mortality.[5]

While the 1920s saw remarkable uses of live, continuous music at many of the large movie palaces in urban areas, those traditions ground to a halt in the late 1920s. The 1931 horror films that preceded *Dr. Jekyll and Mr. Hyde*, *Dracula* and *Frankenstein*, made sparse use of music, as was typical at that time. In the early sound films, music often found itself relegated to opening and closing credits along with scenes that showed music-making or dancing; the use of music as underscore only gradually picked up momentum through the first part of the 1930s (perhaps most notably with Steiner's score for 1933's *King Kong*). *Dr. Jekyll and Mr. Hyde* follows those conventions of rather sparse use of music with two important exceptions: during the first transformation scene of Jekyll into Hyde, Mamoulian accompanies the visual special effects with a groundbreaking sound collage that Irwin Bazelon described as "pre-musique concrète," and when Jekyll breaks up with Muriel, a non-diegetic version of a waltz from earlier in the film reappears.[6] Production records show that "music and sound effects" accounted for $3,405.00 of the $557,000 estimated budget; the largest part of the $3,405 went to "musicians' salaries on score" ($1,608.34).[7] George Turner identifies Nathaniel W. Finston as the musical director for the film, and he also names Sigmund Krumgold as the performer of the organ solos that in the film are attributed to Fredric March's Dr. Jekyll character; neither Finston nor Krumgold received a screen credit (typical before 1936 at Paramount, according to Clifford McCarty) nor are they named in the production records, and McCarty attributes the main and end titles (arrangements of music by J. S. Bach) to Herman Hand.[8] A cue sheet from the American Society of Composers, Authors and Publishers (ASCAP) lists, in addition to Hand, Rudolph G. Kopp, John M. Leipold, and Ralph Ranger as additional composers and arrangers who worked on the film, although presumably the only composing that happened was for stock music such as "Old English Ditty #4." The organ solos constitute but one of several moments in the film where music performing occurs by on-screen characters; the other appearances are an orchestra accompanying dancing, some singing and instrumental music in a music hall, and a piano played in a parlor. In each instance the musical selections resonate with the broader theme of imminent mortality running throughout film, and rereading the film with the ear together with the eye opens up the possibility for understanding the entire narrative as the organist's dream.

Stevenson's novella says nothing about the possibility of Henry Jekyll as a musician, and while it seems likely that the idea of having Jekyll play organ may have originated with screenwriters Percy Heath and Samuel Hoffenstein, the early versions of their screenplay do not specify particular works, apart from describing that the opening credits are to be accompanied by a Bach prelude played on an organ.[9] The opening credits as ultimately realized in the film open with Bach, but instead of the requested prelude, it opens with the famous Toccata from the Toccata and Fugue in D Minor (BWV 565), and instead of sounding from an organ, Herman Hand's orchestrated version stabs out the stinger-like mordent and descending figures of the opening measures.[10] Even later versions of the screenplay contain general requests for types of music (e.g. a Strauss waltz is requested for the dance scenes), and Mamoulian's own shooting continuity script calls for "Organ: Air for G String Bach," although a Chorale Prelude ("Ich ruf zu dir, Herr Jesu Christ," BWV 639) is actually what Jekyll plays.[11] Mamoulian, Heath, and Hoffenstein's calculated introduction of music to Stevenson's narrative taps into a wealth of existing codes and meanings; the characters' involvement with music in the film deepens the audience's sense of shared interiority with on-screen characters while also bringing a dream-like quality to the film.

Mamoulian—who as a director achieved his first successes on stage and on Broadway, most famously with his 1927 version of Dorothy and Du Bose Heyward's *Porgy*, which ran for 367 performances for the Theatre Guild in New York City—saw Stevenson's original story as one of good versus evil and morality versus immorality, but he preferred the exploration of the tension between lofty spirituality and base animalism:[12]

> We have animalistic, fleshy desires, basic instincts; and we also have higher instincts. So I thought if the conflict were Dr. Jekyll's trying to liberate the good and free it from the animalistic, to control the baser instincts, that he would really give man freedom. . . . And that's what he's trying to do. Actually, some people refer to *Jekyll and Hyde* as a horror film. It isn't because there is no monster; he is the primeval man. Actually in his make-up we tried to duplicate as much as we could the Neanderthal man, who is our common ancestor. So he's just a primitive man. And the whole struggle is between the spiritual and the animalistic instincts. And also it elevates the motivation of Hyde; it makes him more interesting. At least, after all, his goal is high; his purpose, the purpose for the film, is a noble one. But he fails. He does not achieve it. And therein is his tragedy.[13]

Mamoulian often complained that the film was not a horror film, but his argument stems more from the perceived illegitimacy of horror as a genre rather than any proof that Hyde is not a monster: "It is not a horror story because I think it's more legitimate, it's based on a very valid psychology, a very valid human condition."[14] By introducing two female romantic interests for Jekyll, as had happened beginning with the staged versions of the story in the late nineteenth century (the novella does not specify any particular women in Hyde's life), the film balances Mamoulian's notions of the spiritual and the animalistic on libido: Jekyll's frustrated sexual desire for Muriel Carew, which leads him to unleash Hyde's sadistic domination, presumed rape, and eventual murder of Ivy, a prostitute. Ultimately the question of sexual desire becomes subsumed under the larger conundrum of human mortality, something that both S. S. Prawer and Virginia Wright Wexman explore in their astute readings of the film.[15] Like its more iconic partners *Dracula* and *Frankenstein*, *Dr. Jekyll and Mr. Hyde* powers its sense of dread through continual reminders of death. As Hyde says to Ivy in the film, "but pleasure is brief in this world," an exclamation that fits with the various shots of the skeleton hanging in Jekyll's laboratory: each serve as a *memento mori*.

A Cinematic Reverie for Organist, or, "Was it a Vision, or a Waking Dream?"

As the practices for incorporating music in film were just beginning to move towards standardization in the early 1930s, the choices of personnel now known usually to be responsible for making musical decisions (such as music editors, composers, and musical directors, along with, of course, directors and producers) cannot be known with much certainty. None of the individuals documented to have worked on music for the film (Nathaniel Finston, Sigmund Krumgold, Herman Hand, Rudolph G. Kopp, John M. Leipold, and Ralph Rainger) received any screen credit. With Mamoulian, two further things complicate the picture: his propensity to claim credit for group innovations (Mamoulian and cinematographer Karl Struss, for instance, differ on who came up with the technique to produce the edit-less transformation) together with his exceptional background in opera and theater. No documents have yet surfaced that demonstrate with any clarity just who made particular musical decisions for the soundtrack in *Dr. Jekyll and Mr. Hyde*. While Heath and Hoffenstein's later drafts begin to request generalized musical accompaniments (as in the request in the Second White Script that a "Bach prelude played on a pipe-organ by a skilled performer" should accompany the main title credits), there is no documentation to explain how a Bach prelude became the now infamous—through its overuse in horror films—Toccata and Fugue in D Minor.[16] Evidence exists that suggests Mamoulian may well have played a key role in choosing particular pieces. In 1937 Mamoulian was quoted by Bruno David Ussher on the topic of choosing music for a film:

> Aside from the caliber of music used, R. M. is very particular as to when music should be heard, how loudly, or when the spoken voice alone suffices. In principle he believes that music's chief function in

pictures is to "tell" what the human language, the human tongue cannot convey. "From there on music must voice and portend what the author wishes to convey at this moment," he said one day. He helps with the script and often rewrites entire portions "because music, and particularly songs, must be originally part of the action.[17]

Mamoulian also liked to tell the story of how, when directing *City Streets* (1931), he requested that the music department provide him with some Wagner (the *Meistersinger* Overture), but was told that even better music could be originally composed for him; he insisted on having Wagner instead.[18] Mamoulian relayed a sense of frustration with the way music was used in films coming out of the 1920s—that "fitting" or "synchronizing" of music that James Lastra discusses in connection to the emergence of cinema "sound"—and Mamoulian explained that "most of the music in the studio at the time was in small labeled boxes, as in a pharmacy; fire music, moonlight music, and so on. Different bits from hackneyed themes, mostly."[19]

Mamoulian's background in theater and, especially, opera, had prepared him well for his work in film. He was sometimes involved with the commissioning of new music, such as when he had Otto Luening compose an original score for a 1926 version of Maeterlinck's *Sister Beatrice* that Mamoulian directed in Rochester, New York.[20] Mamoulian was also part of a New York production of Arnold Schönberg's *Die Glückliche Hand*, sponsored by the League of Composers and conducted by Stokowski, which took place in 1930.[21] Whether it was Mamoulian, musical director Nathaniel Finston, or screenwriters Heath and Hoffenstein, someone made a series of subtle and informed musical choices for *Dr. Jekyll and Mr. Hyde* (see Table 4.1).

The music follows normative 1920s practices in the ways that it is used to situate time, place, and mood and also in the close connection between action on screen and the musical borrowing. In addition to the Bach organ works, the soundtrack makes use of two nineteenth-century waltzes (*Abendsterne* by Joseph Lanner and *Il Bacio* by Luigi Arditi), several nineteenth-century music hall songs ("Champagne Charley" becomes "Champagne Ivy" in the film), and a piano piece by Robert Schumann ("Aufschwung" from *Fantasiestücke*). Furthermore, three of the four major characters perform music: Jekyll plays the organ, Ivy sings, and Muriel plays the piano. That Hyde does not create music himself may be read as another way, together with make-up, that the film positions him as a kind of alien apart from or not yet fully human.

Hyde's lack of his own musical impulse (along with many other things) sets him in strong contrast to Jekyll, whose opening moments of organ playing in the film immediately bond the audience with his character through the famous point-of-view shots that open with hands playing

Table 4.1 Music used in Dr. Jekyll and Mr. Hyde

Timing	Title	Composer	Diegetic	Comments
0:00–1:07	Toccata and Fugue in D Minor (BWV 564)	J. S. Bach	no	orchestra; mm. 1–3, 12–19, 29–30
1:07–2:09	Chorale Prelude "Ich ruf zu dir, Herr Jesu Christ" (BWV 639)	Bach	yes	organ played by Jekyll; transposed down a minor third; mm. 2–8
10:16–12:07	Abendsterne (op. 180)	Joseph Lanner; the script specifies "Strauss waltz"	yes	
12:19–15:45	Il Bacio (The Kiss)	Luigi Arditi	yes	instrumental only
38:12–40:00	several music hall pieces (works like "Old English Ditty #1, 3, & 4," or "I'll Strike You with a Leather," all of which are mentioned on the cue sheet)	Kopp, Leipold, Lloyd, Rainger	yes	
40:02–45:02	"Champagne Ivy"	adapted from "Champagne Charley" by H. J. Whymark (words) and Alfred Lee (music)	yes	sung by Ivy
52:26–52:39	"Champagne Ivy"	same as above	yes	sung by Ivy
59:52–1:00:15	Toccata and Fugue in D Minor	Bach	yes	organ played by Jekyll; mm. 121–27
1:21:44–1:23:11	"Aufschwung" (from Fantasiestücke, op. 12)	Robert Schumann	yes	piano played by Muriel; mm. 1–55
1:24:22–1:25:00 1:26:07–1:26:39 1:27:04–1:27:19	Il Bacio (The Kiss)	Arditi	no	
1:35:13–1:35:25	Tocata and Fugue in D Minor	Bach	no	orchestra; mm. 142–44
1:35:26–1:35:50	"Shipyard Music"	Bernard Kaun	no	

the organ. An orchestral arrangement of the Toccata and Fugue in D Minor runs through the opening title cards, transitioning directly into Bach's Chorale Prelude "Ich ruf zu dir, Herr Jesu Christ." In order to move even more discretely from the D minor cadence at the end of the Toccata into the Chorale Prelude, someone (presumably Herman Hand, who is credited on the cue sheet with arranging the main title music) transposed it from its original F minor into D minor. That raises the question of why they did not simply choose a work in D minor. Perhaps the words implied in the prelude, from the hymn tune borrowed by Bach, possess some meaning relevant to the film?

Figure 4.1 shows the transposed melodic line from the prelude, along with the words that would have accompanied this part of the melody in its original version as a sung hymn: "I beg, hear my complaint; the true faith, Lord, I aspire to, which you wish to give me."[22] The film positions Jekyll, after all, as a saintly figure who works medical miracles in the "free wards," and the narrative conceit of splitting one's evil nature from the good one demands a certain piety on the part of Jekyll, something the Protestant church music and this particular hymn provide. Towards the end of the film, after Hyde has murdered Ivy and Jekyll has promised Lanyon that he will break off his relationship with Muriel, Jekyll grasps a book (presumably a bible) and gazes upward in prayer: "Oh god, this I did not intend. I saw a light, and I did not see where it was leading." Here Jekyll makes overt through his dialogue the religious conviction implied with the opening organ music.

Music naturally accompanies the early dance sequence in the Carews' drawing room, and we see a small dance orchestra performing waltzes. According to Mamoulian's Shooting Continuity script, the scene should have a "Strauss waltz played by small orchestra," but in fact the waltzes that occur in the soundtrack are by Joseph Lanner (*Abendsterne*, op. 180, 1841) and Luigi Arditi (*Il Bacio*, 1860).[23] Besides being appropriate for the time and setting, their extra-musical associations suggest that these particular waltzes were chosen for their allusive potential.[24] The argument works less well for *Abendsterne*, or "Evening Star," because the music here occurs indoors, without any mention of the evening or of stars in the dialogue. Yet in an earlier version of the screenplay, an unused scene has Jekyll referring to Muriel as a star ("Because I want so to be alone with you—because I couldn't have endured seeing you shining like a star among

[Ich ___ bitt er - hör mein __ Kla - gen den rech - ten ___ Weg, __ O__ Herr, ich mein, den wol - lest du mir ge - ben,]

Figure 4.1 Excerpt (main melody only) from "Ich ruf zu dir, Herr Jesu Christ," as heard in the soundtrack (transposed down a minor third), and with the words implied by the original hymn tune

your father's stuffy friends and not plucking you out of your heaven").[25] Perhaps then Muriel's earlier description as a star, and the role that metaphor was to play in her relationship with Jekyll, might have motivated the decision to use Lanner's *Abendsterne*.

Arditi's famous waltz-song *Il Bacio* ("The Kiss") leaves little question as to why it was used, as it accompanies a sequence between Muriel and Jekyll as they kiss in a garden. Given that Mamoulian's motivation for using his heartbeat in the first transformation scene was spontaneous (at least according to his accounts), it may simply be a coincidence that *Il Bacio* has a line that refers directly to heartbeats: "Ed i palpiti udirei/Che rispondo no al mio cor," or "And the heartbeats you feel/That answer to my heart."[26] Regardless, it provides yet more evidence in the text of the film itself that hearts and heartbeats constitute an important thematic motif. That the music begins not with *Il Bacio*'s introduction but rather starts right at the part, when sung, that contains repeated urgings to kiss may demonstrate that this specific piece was chosen for its overt meanings in the words. *Il Bacio* functions in the score similarly to how a theme song would work in a 1920s film accompanied by music: as a musical theme that is meant to indicate the romance of two characters, and that returns at appropriate moments. *Il Bacio* returns later in the film, in a manner reminiscent of the visual dissolves (e.g. the lingering dissolve of Ivy's swinging leg and Jekyll's departure from her apartment, a dissolve meant to indicate Jekyll's obsession on that image; and the lingering dissolve as Jekyll looks up in prayer and Muriel begins to play piano), and it recurs three times non-diegetically in the scene where Jekyll tells Muriel that he must leave her. Such non-diegetic uses of music were still uncommon at that time, yet here Mamoulian does even more than simply not providing an on-screen source for the music. Mamoulian explained his fondness for generating ironic effects with music:

> I find myself using either the terms of painting or the terms of music. For instance, I love the use of counterpoint. The orthodox way of scoring any motion picture is that a happy scene has happy music, a tragic scene has sad music. I don't think this is as dramatically expressive as using the music in counterpoint to the scene. When Jekyll comes and tells Muriel that he is going to give her up, a completely tragic scene, the music heard is the waltz when they were happy, waltzing around the room. The music goes against the mood which, of course, makes the despair much more poignant.[27]

To the already powerful counterpoint created just by the return of such peppy, major music during an emotionally grinding scene, someone cleverly decided to transpose the melody up a step for each of the three times it occurs. Each use of the waltz uses the same "kiss me, come and kiss me" part of the waltz, with it first sounding in D major, then E major, and finally F-sharp major. Presenting the melody in successively higher keys serves to ratchet up the suspense in a scene, even when done in such a subtle manner.[28]

The music performed by the two main female characters also establishes setting, locale, and social class. When Hyde goes to the Variety Music Hall in search of Ivy, he first notices her when she sings a short song, "Champagne Ivy," which is based on a nineteenth-century music hall song, "Champagne Charlie." In a later scene in Ivy's apartment, Hyde sadistically forces Ivy to sing "Champagne Ivy" for him, and she complies. While a music hall song efficiently defines Ivy's social stature for the audience, so too does piano playing by Muriel in her father's house. Muriel performs Robert Schumann's "Aufschwung" from his *Fantasiestücke*, op. 12. Often translated as "soaring," the title literally means "upswing," and again, Mamoulian (if indeed he made that decision) has set music that cuts against the grain of the scene, for we know Jekyll is about to end their relationship as she plays, and the joyousness of the emotion in not merely the title but especially as suggested in the music itself resonates in painful counterpoint with the break-up that is just about to happen. An even more subtle connection might be drawn between the title ("upswing") and the fact that it had been Ivy's swinging leg that had proved to be so distracting for Jekyll; Muriel also swings, but within the confines of her domestic gender role and the controlled upswinging of playing Schumann at the parlor piano. Mamoulian alerts us to Jekyll's fixation on Ivy through an extended dissolve of her leg, and just as that superimposition soon after finds the release of Hyde (and Jekyll's libido), this final superimposition of Jekyll and a woman (here, Muriel and her upswinging piano playing, as seen in Figure 4.2) marks Jekyll's final, albeit unsuccessful, attempt to tamp down his sexual and romantic desire by terminating his relationship with Muriel. That Robert Schumann was himself involved in a protracted struggle with a father over the right to marry a daughter—to say nothing of Robert's propensity for imagining different personalities within himself—brings yet more significance to the presence of Schumann's music in this scene.

The simplest explanation for all of these musical choices may be that the works were selected merely for their chronological proximity to the time period of the film, and so their presence works to support an illusion of realism just as period authentic costumes or scenery do. Yet the film's richness in intertextual allusions works against that possibility, given the complexity behind the literary and artistic quotations. One of the more striking uses of an existing work of visual sculpture occurs in the scene when Hyde murders Ivy. Here, Mamoulian adroitly moves the camera away from Hyde's violent actions, settling it instead on a copy of Antonio Canova's *Cupid and Psyche* in Ivy's room; as Mamoulian explains, "these

Figure 4.2 Jekyll prays as Muriel plays

things sharpen the situation and make it much more interesting."[29] In an earlier scene, Jekyll expresses his joy at being granted permission to marry Muriel by playing organ at his home. He announces, "if music be the food of love, play on," directly quoting the opening line of Shakespeare's *Twelfth Night*. Duke Orsino's exclamation, comparing as it does appetites, vomiting, and music, bears interesting connections to Jekyll's situation here and his continuous struggle to be in control of his emotional impulses. Most directly, Jekyll here feeds his romantic impulse with the organ music, allowing himself an unmeasured moment of emotional exuberance, even though quite soon the music will become "not so sweet now as it was before" (I.i.8).

Another tangled intertextual web forms around Jekyll's utterance of lines from Keats's "Ode to a Nightingale." On his way to the Carews', Jekyll pauses to sit in a park, whereupon he listens to a nightingale and pronounces that "thou wast not born for death, immortal bird, no hungry generations tread thee down, thou wast not born for death." Jekyll then watches in horror as a cat creeps along the tree's limb and kills the bird, despite his protests.[30] Upon repeating "thou wast not born for death" with a sneer, Jekyll finds himself spontaneously transforming into Hyde, and the line of Keats, together with the cat's murder of the songbird, both provide ominous foreshadowing for Ivy's imminent death. Keats's poem explores profound questions of mortality, and thus it fits well with the overall emphasis on life's fragility in the film. An unused bit of dialogue, typed on a blue piece of paper glued to the back of one of the pages of the Second White Script, has Jekyll speaking even more lines of the seventh stanza in Keats's ode (ll. 68–70: "The same that oft-times hath/Charm'd magic casements, opening on the foam/Of perilous seas, in faery lands forlorn.").[31] Set in a "Devon garden by the seas," listening to the song of a nightingale, Jekyll follows his recitation of the poem with the lines "Weren't we right not to wait, my love? This beauty is ours—ours—this beauty . . . beauty that must die, and Joy, whose hand is ever at his lip bidding adieu . . . adieu . . ." The five lines in the middle of Keats's seventh stanza that were not used in this draft of the screenplay include a brief discussion of the biblical Ruth, a character whose widowed fidelity to her in-laws has a certain resonance with Muriel.

Particularly relevant for this film, however, are the last two lines of the poem: "Was it a vision, or a waking dream?/Fled is that music:—Do I wake or sleep?" Beyond functioning as a metaphor for life and death, probing the boundaries between being awake and asleep connects directly with the medium of film and its ability to entrance us with dreams and—as is the case here—nightmares. Bringing these Keatsian questions (of waking or sleeping) into this film comes back to the film's music in two important ways. First, the poem grants special status to song (here, that of the nightingale) in ways similar to the function of music in the film; the three main characters who perform music do so as an expression not simply of their emotions but of their life. Second, the closing question of the "Ode to a Nightingale," together with the particular parts of the Bach Toccata and Fugue that get used in the film, open the possibility of reading the entire film as a dream. The film opens with measures 1–3, then 12–19, and finally 29–30 of the Toccata, arranged for orchestra. After Jekyll has been granted permission to marry Muriel and returns to his home to tell Poole, his butler, he launches into an exuberant performance of measures 121–27 of the Fugue. After Hyde's death, and his posthumous transformation back into Jekyll, the orchestra returns to play the final three measures from Bach's organ work. The film quotes from the beginning, middle, and end of the piece, matching those parts of the music with the beginning, middle, and end of the film. Such a subtle reading of the film, triggered by unspoken words of a poem and a rigorous attention to the organ music, may well rest on evidence too slight to be immediately persuasive, but it may become more difficult to dismiss when considering another Hollywood film that might similarly be confusing the narrative arc through the implication of a shift to a character's dream: *Laura* (1944). In that film, the titular murder victim unexpectedly shows up after the detective who had been investigating her death—and who seems to be falling in love with her—falls asleep to the accompaniment of a dolly shot and David Raksin's haunting score, shifting the film from that point forward into (at least possibly) the point of view of his dream.[32] That the film never clarifies when or even if that dream ends makes it, according to Kristin Thompson, "extremely transgressive in relation to the tradition of classical Hollywood cinema."[33] Considerable documentation exists that demonstrates that at least some of those involved in making *Laura* knew they were branching the narrative into one character's dream.[34] No such documentation has surfaced for *Dr. Jekyll and Mr. Hyde*, apart from two important threads connecting the two films: Rouben Mamoulian, who originally was *Laura's* director, and Samuel Hoffenstein, who co-wrote the screenplay. Even if the only organist's reverie that the film gives us is Jekyll's blissful eruption in the middle of the film, *Dr. Jekyll and Mr. Hyde* nonetheless executes a remarkable blending of poetry, art, and music that does more than simply drop names or suggest shallow connections. By employing the organist as a central conceit in the film, the creators of *Dr. Jekyll and Mr. Hyde* pulled out all the stops to demonstrate that even a commercial horror film could wrestle with serious topics in complicated ways that extended and developed the ideas of earlier poets, sculptors, and musicians.

The Dreadful Heartbeat: Examining the Ingredients in Mamoulian's Sound Stew

Erika Greber argues that with Mamoulian's version of the story, *Jekyll and Hyde* was from that point onward a movie and no longer a literary work; the astonishing visual and acoustic special effects bring the audience into the experience of a transformation from Jekyll to Hyde in a far more visceral way than was possible with words on a page.[35] The film offers seven transformation scenes—five from Jekyll to Hyde, two from Hyde to Jekyll—and with each successive metamorphosis into Hyde, the make-up becomes more grotesque. The exterior here signals the interior, with a frightening face meant to parallel an ugly or at least animalistic personality. Paramount sought to capitalize on the shock value of the Hyde make-up in the press book that accompanied the film's 1931 release, with one entire section titled "March Develops Seven Distinct Character Types"; that information surfaced in later newspaper stories such as the one in the Fort Wayne *News-Sentinel* of October 27, 1931, with the elaboration that "[March's] final appearance as Mr. Hyde is enough to make chills run up and down the spine of a polar bear."[36] Several early reviews noted the power of the make-up to distress an audience. Clark Rodenbach, in the Chicago *News*, wrote that:

> Paramount out-horrored its competitors in making a picture of this kind, but at the expense of good taste . . . the horrors of the Stevenson

story may make you a little stick at your stomach. If they hadn't made Hyde such a hideous, revolting creation they'd have a swell picture.[37]

Carol Frink, writing in the Chicago *Herald-Examiner*, found similar fault with Hyde's presentation:

The handsome Fredric March turns from a debonair, clean-cut scientist to a hideous, snarling, buck-toothed, hair-faced Neanderthaler before your outraged eyes, not once but time and again. It is like being hit with a hammer—it does feel good when it stops.[38]

Some reviewers, however, gave hints that not all audiences responded with fear:

To be concrete about it, the dialogue lines placed in Mr. Hyde's evil-looking jaws and some of the incidents didn't often always impress as they were undoubtedly intended. The audience at the Rivoli the night the picture was caught must have felt partially the same way because, while the unwarranted titter of laughs that ripple through the house might have been hysterical, we don't believe they were.[39]

Carroll Carroll described in verse another instance of laughing instead of screaming: "Too bad the love scenes rang so hollow/The audience I sat with laughed./(Perhaps they simply couldn't follow/Such trains of thought—or just went daft).”[40]

Those complaints notwithstanding, a consensus quickly emerged that the special effects in the film were indeed remarkable and pushed the medium of cinema into new territory. Mamoulian carefully guarded the secret to the visual transformation for decades. The first metamorphosis occurs without an edit, with Jekyll looking into a mirror in a point-of-view shot that works to situate the audience squarely in Jekyll's perspective. Without even so much as a dissolve, March's hands and face darken in what was a true milestone of cinematic fantasy. Cinematographer Karl Struss claimed to have had the idea to use a technique he had used earlier:

So that's what we used back in Culver City on the healing of the lepers in *Ben-Hur*, and it was a simple thing to think of doing when I had the situation of changing Fredric March from Dr. Jekyll to Mr. Hyde in the 1931 Paramount film with Rouben Mamoulian. Nobody else had any ideas on the subject—I seemed to be the only one. It was done by using a red filter on strong red makeup, so that when you photographed red with a red filter the object was white. In front of the lens you put a two-inch square red "A" filter that had the same speed as a green "B" filter so that when you went from one exposure to the other, the density remained the same. The filters were gelatins hooked together in a little holder with the red on top and the green below. They were done as close to the 2-inch focal length lens as you could get them. When the transition started it would slowly change and with the green filter you could see the image, the face, become quite dark, with lines and so forth, depending on how much makeup we had put on in the first place. I controlled the makeup with the makeup man.[41]

Interestingly, while guarding the secret to the visual aspects of the transformation, Mamoulian (and even Paramount) began talking about the sound as soon as the film was first released. The Paramount press packet contained a section titled "March's Heart-Beats Heard in Tense Scene," and it makes clear the importance of sound and in particular the sound of the heartbeat in the promotion of the film:

> The beat of the human heart recently was recorded in Hollywood for talking pictures for the first time.
>
> The sound effect was secured by Rouben Mamoulian, Paramount director, for a scene in "Dr. Jekyll and Mr. Hyde," in which Fredric March plays the dual personality role and Miriam Hopkins and Rose Hobart have the leading feminine roles. This remarkable picture dramatization of Robert Louis Stevenson's weird story is the feature picture at the . . . theatre for . . . days the . . . part of next week.
>
> To obtain the "boom, boom" of the heart-pump, the microphone was held over March's heart. The sensitiveness of the instrument boosted the sound past that which one naturally hears while holding an ear over a heart to the quality attained by listening through a stethoscope.
>
> The heart-beat was conceived by Mamoulian as one of his novel effects in the Stevenson story; by use of this, the director will obtain the sensation of one's own heart pounding in one's ears as he chronicles the experiences of Jekyll in transforming for the first time into Hyde.[42]

Paramount's hyping of the heartbeat went further than just pointing to the novelty of hearing a heartbeat, as it reached into the discourses of science and medicine to advise exhibitors to use amplified heartbeat sounds (having a "doctor, scientist, or electrical genius to give it dignity" or "an interne [sic], doctor, or medical student could be assigned to your lobby for the run of the attraction") as ballyhoo to draw patrons into the theater: "Invite and intrigue them with some such copy as: 'Is your heart in good shape? Have it examined, hear it beat before you see 'Dr. Jekyll and Mr. Hyde,' the biggest thrill classic of all time.'"[43] The heartbeat motif was clearly thought to be an important component to what made this film tick, as becomes clear when seeing how it returned in the 1941 MGM version directed by Victor Fleming (and MGM had purchased the rights to Paramount's version so as to monopolize the Jekyll and Hyde market): Daniele Amfitheatrof's music that accompanies Spencer Tracy's Jekyll as he first transforms into Hyde contains musical gestures that simulate heartbeat sounds, as orchestral instruments attempt to simulate what Mamoulian achieved through non-orchestral means.[44]

Mamoulian accompanies the change with images of the room rapidly spinning around before presenting a series of dissolves that feature characters speaking lines of dialogue, most of which we have already heard in the film, but some of which we either were not privy to hearing or which Jekyll has imagined (see Table 4.2).[45] These spoken words all refer back in some way to Jekyll's state of chastisement, sexual frustration, and hostility.[46] As we watch the transformation through Jekyll's eyes, we begin to hear a heartbeat, and the scene is set up to be heard and read as Jekyll's heartbeat becoming our heartbeat before becoming Hyde's heartbeat.[47] Yet other sounds occur during this pivotal scene: mysterious,

Table 4.2 Description of the first transformation scene

26:41	We (audience/Jekyll) look at glass with the potion
26:44	We move closer to the mirror
26:53	We drink
26:59	Clutching throat, start to gasp
27:05	Transformation becomes visibly obvious
27:10	Heartbeat begins
27:17	Drop to floor
27:18	High-pitched metallic sound as room starts to spin
27:28	Jekyll and Muriel in the garden: "Marry me now. I can't wait any longer."
27:33	General Carew: "Positively indecent!"
27:35	Ivy's hand pointing to the garter on her leg: "Look where he kicked me."
27:37	Lanyon: "Your conduct was disgusting!"
27:38	General Carew: "It isn't done. It isn't done!"
27:40	Jekyll in top hat: "I could strangle him. Strangle him!"
27:43	General Carew: "Indecent. Indecent."
27:46	Jekyll: "Can a man dying of thirst forget water?"
27:50	Lanyon: "Disgusting. You're mad. Mad."
27:53	Ivy: "Come back soon, won't you? Come back. Come back. Come back. Come back."
28:04	Dissolve away from Ivy's leg back to spinning
28:09	Room stops spinning
28:17	High-pitched metallic sound stops
28:24	Heartbeats stop
28:25	Return to mirror and see yourself as Hyde

high-pitched, metallic sounds that resist verbal description. The overall sound collage here has an uncanny quality, in part because of the vaguely familiar yet unidentifiable sounds. Mamoulian frequently discussed what went into the sound mix in this scene, although there are variations in his story that leave some ambiguity as to just what went into it. As he told Thomas R. Atkins in a 1973 interview:

> With such a fantastic transformation what sound do you use? Do you put music in here? God, it's coming out of your ears, the scoring. I thought the only way to match the event and create this incredible reality would be to concoct a mélange of sounds that do not exist in nature, that a human ear cannot hear. I said, "Let's photograph light." We photographed the light of a candle in various frequencies of intensity directly transforming light into sound. Then I said, "Let's record the beat of a gong, cut off the impact, run it backwards." And we recorded other things like that. But when we ran it, the whole thing lacked rhythm. I'm a great believer in the importance of rhythm. I said, "We need some kind of a beat." So they brought in all sorts of drums, a bass drum, a snare drum, a Hawaiian drum, Indian tom-toms. But no matter what we used, it always sounded like what it was—a drum. Finally in exasperation I got this wonderful idea. I ran up and down the stairway for a few minutes, and then I put a microphone to my heart and said, "Record it." And that's what is used as the basic rhythm in the scene—the thumping noise which is like no drum on earth because it's the heartbeat, my own heartbeat. So when I say my heart is in *Dr. Jekyll and Mr. Hyde*, I mean it literally.[48]

He singles out three elements here that resurface in nearly all of the various explanations: first, candlelight photographed directly to the soundtrack; second, the sound of a gong's reverberations (and not its initial attack), played in reverse; and third, his own heartbeat. In a nearly identical interview with Raymond Rohauer from 1968, he adds that "this aural concoction became known in the studio as 'Mamoulian's sound stew.'"[49] The recipe for his stew stays consistent except for one interview from 1961, where Mamoulian changed the action of photographing candlelight directly onto the soundtrack into "we painted on the sound track."[50] Tom Milne's monograph on Mamoulian copied the description from the Robinson interview, and a series of sources then quote Milne.[51] While it may be possible that this single outlier description is correct, it may also be possible—if not probable—that it was a single slip of the tongue that has gone unnoticed. Regardless of whether or not the sound was created by photographing candlelight or by drawing directly onto the film, Mervyn Cooke rightly observes that "with commendable restraint,

Mamoulian used this extraordinary effect only once in the film."[52] None of the other six transformation sequences employ those sounds, using instead heavy breathing, gasping, and grunting—or nothing at all, in the case of the last metamorphosis, right after Hyde has been shot dead, and his corpse reverts back to Jekyll.[53]

Besides putting his heart into his film, Mamoulian's innovative sound design in the first transformation scene draws the audience into a more visceral connection with the film and the character. Finding such a link between sounds and an audience's perception of a kind of embodiment lends support to K. J. Donnelly's argument that:

> music in horror films often attempts a direct engagement with the physical: for example, through the use of the very high (like the stabbing strings in the shower scene in *Psycho*) or the low (deep stingers or drones). These are not merely extremes of pitch, but are also tied to the intrinsic sounds of the human body: the high buzz of the nervous system and the deep throb of the bloodstream and heart.[54]

That dichotomy, of the high and low, echoes John Cage's oft-repeated description of his 1951 encounter with an anechoic chamber:

> I entered [an anechoic chamber] at Harvard University several years ago and heard two sounds, one high and one low. When I described them to the engineer in charge, he informed me that the high one was my nervous system in operation, the low one my blood in circulation. Until I die there will be sounds. And they will continue following my death. One need not fear about the future of music.[55]

In two important ways, then, Mamoulian's sound stew looked ahead to Cage's activities in the 1950s. First, his non-traditional use of sound for its intrinsic qualities, his openness to experimenting with recording techniques, with using the recording studio as a compositional resource, may be seen as a pre-figuring of the sorts of compositional experimentation associated with Cage and others (such as Pierre Schaeffer and Pierre Henry) by mid-century. In 1931, in the early days still of sound film, deploying such an imaginative use of sound to underscore an important scene (instead of more predictably accompanying it with some sort of melodramatic music) bears a resemblance to the reconfiguring of ambient sounds into music that Cage engineered with 4'33''. Second, Cage's epiphany of the ubiquitous high and low sounds resulting from being alive may match those of a viewer of *Dr. Jekyll and Mr. Hyde* in the ways that, like Cage's sudden realization of the bodily origin of some ambient sounds, the audience may (likely) not be initially aware that Mamoulian has brought into his sound stew both high buzzes (Jekyll's nervous system) and low, throbbing heartbeats. Hollywood's early sound films were beginning to find ways to bring verisimilitude to the experience of what it meant for a character (and an audience) to be alive in a film, an important technological and industry advance, to be sure, but also a key thematic element in a film that stakes so much of its horror in the fragility of life.[56]

Finally, Donnelly has also pointed to the tradition in horror films of music and sound effects being more holistically connected than in other genres:

> the horror film is often seen as a coherent atmospheric package that embraces both music and sound effects. In many cases, horror film music follows less the traditional leitmotif symphonic structure of the classical film score than creates a sound architecture combining a concern for ambience with intermittent shock effects.[57]

Those vague boundaries between music and sound effect come sharply into focus in *Dr. Jekyll and Mr. Hyde*. Mamoulian's sound design for the first transformation scene marks a watershed moment in the history of horror film music, experimenting as it does with acoustic materials in a radically different way from contemporaneous horror films such as *Dracula* or *Frankenstein*, which are characterized far more by their large chunks of silence and lack of non-diegetic music than by any imaginative uses of sound. Could it be possible that the sound stew suffers from being too far ahead of its own time, appearing decades before electronic music and the manipulation of sound in a studio became a merit badge for the mid-century avant-garde composer in the university and concert hall?

Conclusion: The Uncanny Subjectivity of *Dr. Jekyll and Mr. Hyde*'s Soundtrack

Sigmund Freud famously discussed the idea of the uncanny in a 1919 essay; Freud observes the disturbing quality that *Doppelgängers* can cause.[58] Such doublings, and their concomitant ambiguities, can generate feelings of uncanny dread by confusing the status of being alive and being dead. Mamoulian's *Dr. Jekyll and Mr. Hyde* creates a feeling of the uncanny in numerous ways, not the least being through its unsettling blending of wakefulness and dreaming, but also through its numerous allusions that each has a certain familiarity that can be disguised through their recontextualizations. Hyde's physical appearance, meant to be reminiscent of an earlier species of human, provides one instance of something that appears vaguely familiar. Inanimate objects appearing to be alive were uncanny to Freud, and in *Jekyll and Hyde*, the mechanized illusion of motion, the film, gets imbued with a living quality through the addition of the heartbeat sounds. The first transformation scene, with its accompanying "sound stew," creates a central encounter with the uncanny through its hauntingly familiar sounds, its curious mix of heartbeats, gongs, and candlelight. In other contexts, and without the sonic manipulation, these things would be banal and unremarkable, but in connection to the metamorphosis they assume the qualities of the kind of uncanniness that Freud defines as "that species of the frightening that goes back to what was once well known and had long been familiar."[59] Despite the greater attention given to *Dracula* and *Frankenstein* as the progenitors of the horror genre in Hollywood, the elaborate and layered use of sound and music in *Dr. Jekyll and Mr. Hyde* highlighted and opened up the possibilities of the soundtrack for creating fear and dread in the horror film.[60]

Notes

1 This essay benefitted tremendously from the assistance of Jim Buhler, Frank Dominguez, Daniel Goldmark, Burkhard Henke, Carole Kruger, and Andrew Oster.

2 Robert Spadoni, *Uncanny Bodies: The Coming of Sound Film and the Origins of the Horror Genre* (Berkeley, CA: University of California Press, 2007).

3 Ibid., 2.

4 For a broad history of various performative versions of *Dr. Jekyll and Mr. Hyde*, see *The Definitive* Dr. Jekyll and Mr. Hyde *Companion*, edited by Harry M. Geduld (New York and London: Garland, 1983), especially Pau Wilstach's "Richard Mansfield and Jekyll and Hyde," 159–61. A careful study of the adaptations of the story into stage, film, radio, and television appears in Brian A. Rose's Jekyll and Hyde *Adapted* (Westport, CT and London: Greenwood, 1996). The question of whether or not the work's genre falls within the category of horror versus science fiction gets careful treatment in Donald Lawler, "Reframing *Jekyll and Hyde*: Robert Louis Stevenson and the Strange Case of Gothic Science Fiction," in *Dr. Jekyll and Mr. Hyde After One Hundred Years*, edited by William Veeder and Gordon Hirsch (Chicago, IL and London: University of Chicago Press, 1988), 247–61.

5 Robert Winning notes the technical innovations of Mamoulian's film, drawing a connection between the extended subjective cinematography at the opening of the film and the later use of the similar effect in John Carpenter's *Halloween* (1978) as well as pointing to the "early example of a complex sound mix" in "Dr. Jekyll and Mr. Hyde," in *International Dictionary of Films and Filmmakers*, edited by Sara Pendergast and Tom Pendergast, vol. 1 (Detroit, MI: St James Press, 2001), 332.

6 Irwin Bazelon, *Knowing the Score: Notes on Film Music* (New York: Van Nostrand Reinhold, 1975), 147.

7 From the production records for Paramount Pictures kept at the Margaret Herrick Library, Beverly Hills, CA. The six expenses constituting the "music and sound effects" line were "compilation of score," "musicians' salaries on score," "musicians' salaries on sets," "mechanical sound effects," "music dept. supervision salaries," and "distribution idle time permanent musicians."

8 George Turner, "Two-faced Treachery," *American Cinematographer* 80/3 (March 1999): 196. Clifford McCarty, *Film Composers in America: A*

Filmography, 1911–1970 (Oxford and New York: Oxford University Press, 2000), 12, 127.

9 In the first draft of the script by Heath and Hoffenstein, dated June 23, 1931, the film opens not with Jekyll at the organ but with two men talking in the street outside a hospital. (These scripts are part of the Paramount Collection at the Margaret Herrick Library.) The August 3, 1931 version (called the "Second Script") opens with the organ. Among the other things initially in early drafts but not included in the final filmed version are two instances of Hyde's cruelty: first, an encounter Hyde has with a kitten (he hears it stuck on a high bridge, rescues it, then drops it into the river below) and second, an incident involving a blind beggar (Hyde offers to help the man cross the street, but midway through, Hyde jerks away his cane and leaves him stranded).

10 See Julie Brown's essay in this collection for further discussion of the organ music in this film.

11 In the folder "Shooting Continuity, ca. 1931," part of the Rouben Mamoulian collection at the Library of Congress (henceforth LC-M).

12 Mamoulian's direction of *Porgy* included a famous effect known as the "Symphony of Noises," a building up of naturalistic sounds into a highly stylized and rhythmical whole:

> The curtain rose on Catfish Row in the early morning. All silent. Then you hear the Boum! of a street gang repairing the road. That is the first beat; then beat 2 is silent; beat 3 is a snore—zzz!—from a negro who's asleep; beat 4 silent again. Then a woman starts sweeping the steps—whish!—and she takes up beats 2 and 4, so you have: Boum!—Whish! —zzz!—Whish! and so on. A knife-sharpener, a shoemaker, a woman beating rugs and so on, all join in. Then the rhythm changes: 4/4 to 2/4; then to 6/8; and syncopated and Charleston rhythms. It all had to be conducted like an orchestra.

As recounted by Mamoulian to David Robinson in "Rouben Mamoulian: Painting the Leaves Black," *Sight & Sound* (Summer 1961): 124. See also Mark Spergel, *Reinventing Reality: The Art and Life of Rouben Mamoulian* (Metuchen, NJ: Scarecrow Press, 1993), 55–68. Mamoulian revisits this idea in the opening of *Love Me Tonight* (1932), with the awakening of Paris.

13 Harry A. Hargrave, "Interview with Rouben Mamoulian," *Literature Film Quarterly* 10/4 (1982), 263–4. Mamoulian makes similar claims in an earlier interview: "I didn't want Hyde to be a monster. Hyde is not evil, he is the primitive, the animal in us, whereas Jekyll is a cultured man, representing the intellect. Hyde is the Neanderthal man, and March's makeup was designed as such." From *The Celluloid Muse: Hollywood Directors Speak*, edited by Charles Higham and Joel Greenberg (Chicago, IL: Henry Regnery, 1969), 134.

14 Bill Thomas, "Mamoulian on His *Dr. Jekyll and Mr. Hyde*," *Cinefantastique* (Summer 1971), 38.

15 See S. S. Prawer, "Book into Film I: Mamoulian's *Dr. Jekyll and Mr. Hyde*," in *Caligari's Children: The Film as Tale of Terror* (Oxford and New York: Oxford University Press, 1981), 85–107, and Virginia Wright Wexman, "Horrors of the Body: Hollywood's Discourse on Beauty and Rouben Mamoulian's *Dr. Jekyll and Mr. Hyde*," in *Dr. Jekyll and Mr. Hyde: After One Hundred Years*, edited by William Veeder and Gordon Hirsch (Chicago, IL: University of Chicago Press, 1988), 283–307. Both Prawer and Wexman recognize the racialized aspects to Hyde's make-up. Prawer sees it as "the stereotype of the black rapist" (95) while Wexman brings in the contemporary prohibitions in the Motion Picture Production Code of 1930, which among

other things forbade miscegenation, as she points to the ways Hyde is portrayed as a particular threat of primitive beastiality against "white womanhood." (289)

16 Peter Williams provocatively questioned the authenticity of this work in "BWV 565: A Toccata in D Minor for Organ by J. S. Bach?" *Early Music* 9/3 (July 1981): 330–7.

17 From a document titled "Bruno David Ussher Asks: Have you Met Mr. Mamoulian," dated June 1937, from the "Music in Film" folder (LC-M). Ussher, trained by German musicologists Arnold Schering and Hugo Riemann, was a Los Angeles music critic; see Catherine Parsons Smith, *Making Music in Los Angeles: Transforming the Popular* (Berkeley, CA: University of California Press, 2007), 188. Further proof of Mamoulian's keen sensitivity to the music in Hollywood films can be found in some handwritten notes Mamoulian prepared for a talk on film music; while undated, it is clear that he was well informed about the film composers active in the 1930s. After a list of Hollywood composers ("Al Newman, Max Steiner, Korngold, Stothart, V. Young, Waxman, Kurt Veil [sic], Rosza [sic]") he has, in parentheses, "style of Rich[ard] Strauss, Debussy, Ravel & Scriabin." Then there are three French composers listed ("Milhaud, Honegger, Auric"). A third list has what seem to be the more experimental composers in Hollywood at the time ("A. Copland, G. Antheil, Bernard Herrmann, Al Tansman, Ernst Toch"), while a final list gets a title ("Documentaries") and has the names Copland, Thomson, Blitzstein, and Eisler. From the "Music in Film" folder (LC-M).

18 Among other places, see Spergel, *Reinventing Reality*, 115–16.

19 James Lastra, *Sound Technology and the American Cinema: Perception, Representation, Modernity* (New York: Columbia University Press, 2000), 111–18. The Mamoulian quote appears in Higham and Greenberg, *The Celluloid Muse*, 133–4.

20 See Otto Luening, *The Odyssey of an American Composer: The Autobiography of Otto Luening* (New York: Charles Scribner's Sons, 1980), 271–3.

21 See Carol J. Oja, *Making Music Modern: New York in the 1920s* (Oxford and New York: Oxford University Press, 2000), 188, and Claire R. Reis, *Composers, Conductors, and Critics* (New York: Oxford University Press, 1955), 94–5. According to Reis, Mamoulian declared Schönberg's work not to be an opera, but "a whimsey" (95).

22 Peter Williams discusses this work as well as provides this translation of the hymn in *The Organ Music of J. S. Bach*, second edition (New York: Cambridge University Press, 2003), 307.

23 The ASCAP cue sheet lists another Lanner waltz (*Die Vorstädtler*); none of the waltz titles has a composer or arranger name following it, leaving it unclear who actually made the arrangements heard in the film. The Shooting Continuity script is part of LC-M.

24 In this respect, the use of these waltzes both follows and deviates from the admonitions given by George W. Beynon in *Music Presentation of Motion Pictures* (New York and Boston: Schirmer, 1921). Beynon on the one hand encourages the use of waltzes, stating that "waltzes are pleasing to the lay ear and are, at present, better understood by the picture patrons than some of the heavier forms of music" (27), while at the same time he strongly exhorted against musical puns, writing that "a chronic joker is loved by few, and the musician who thinks it clever to show his musical erudition by inflicting upon the public piece after piece linked to scenes by means of titles, only becomes offensive" (57).

25 From the Second White Script (August 7, 1931), pages E-2 and E-3 (LC-M).

26 I am grateful to Greg Snyder for assistance with this translation.

27 Thomas R. Atkins, "Dr. Jekyll and Mr. Hyde: An Interview with Rouben Mamoulian," *The Film Journal* 2/2 (January-March 1973): 36–44; this quote is from page 42. He also revealed his musical conception of film in the 1982 Hargrave interview: "In fact I find myself always in working on a film using musical terms because they apply. As you know music is made out of rhythm and measures. And I feel a film should have a strict structure: a measure, a flow, a harmony—counterpoint as music has" (Hargrave, "Interview with Rouben Mamoulian," 259).

28 Donnelly has noted the efficacy of "tension of rising pitch (transposition by sequence—simply moving the whole repeated unit of music up a semitone in pitch)" in horror film soundtracks, and the technique (e.g. an augmented triad rising by half steps) also gets used in other genres where building suspense is required. See K. J. Donnelly, *The Spectre of Sound: Music in Film and Television* (London: British Film Institute, 2005), 100.

29 Atkins, "An Interview with Rouben Mamoulian," 42.

30 After failing to find an actual nightingale to provide the birdsong, Mamoulian's assistant brought him an English woman whose whistling provides the nightingale's song on the film's soundtrack (Atkins, "An Interview with Rouben Mamoulian," 43).

31 In the Second White Script, LC-M. The other blue additions to this script are also marked in red as "special" and appear to have been planned for use in dissolve shots (the lines of dialogue that appear in Jekyll's first transformation, indeed more than were ultimately used, occur as "special" additions in this script).

32 Kathryn Kalinak argues for the significance of Raksin's score in the creation of the dream effect in *Settling the Score: Music and the Classical Hollywood Film* (Madison, WI: University of Wisconsin Press, 1992), 159–83. The process of "Len-A-Toning" that Kalinak discusses (181) (and which occurs at a pivotal moment indicating the dream) bears a similarity to the way the gong sound was treated in Mamoulian's sound stew; both involved the removal of the sound's initial attack.

33 Kristin Thompson, "Closure Within a Dream: Point-of-View in *Laura*," *Film Reader* 3 (1978): 90.

34 Besides Kalinak and Thompson, Chris Fujiwara discusses the production history of *Laura* in *The World and Its Double: The Life and Work of Otto Preminger* (New York: Faber & Faber, 2008), 35–54.

35 Erika Greber, "Mediendoppelgängereien: Dr. Jekyll and Mr. Hyde verwandeln sich in Film," *Poetica: Zeitschrift für Sprach- und Literaturwissenschaft* 36/3–4 (2004), 429–52:

> Mamoulians Opus ging es als ein Meisterwerk des frühen Horrorfilms in die Geschichte ein und stiftete einen Kinomythos: von nun an war "Jekyll und Hyde" ein Movie. Erstmalig hatte die Tricktechnik die Verwandlung sinnlich audiovisuell erlebbar gemacht. Zu den für damlige Verhältnisse verblüffenden Verwandlungsszenen kamen innovative Toneffekte und eine außergewöhnliche Kameraführung hinzu (gleich anfangs subjektive Kamera; schwindelnde 360-Drehungen und Herztöne begleiten die erste Metamorphose). (435) [Mamoulian's work became a masterpiece of early horror film and laid the foundation for a cinematic myth: from that point onward, "Jekyll and Hyde" was a movie. Thanks

to its special effects, viewers were able, for the first time, to experience the transformation audio-visually with their senses. Not enough that the transformation scenes alone were astonishing for their time, Mamoulian added innovative sound effects and extraordinary camera work to boot (subjective shots from the very beginning, dizzying 360 turns, and heartbeats accompany the first metamorphosis).]

I am grateful to Burkhard Henke for his assistance in this translation.

36 The press packet is in the folder "Dr. Jekyll and Mr. Hyde, Miscellany, ca. 1932–1934, 1968" (LC-M) while the newspaper clipping comes from "Scrapbook 1931" (LC-M).

37 Clark Rodenbach, "Critic Says Horror Film, 'Dr. Jekyll and Mr. Hyde,' Shows Birth of Bathtub Gin," December 30, 1931, from "Scrapbook 1931" (LC-M).

38 Carol Frink, "'Dr. Jekyll and Mr. Hyde' in New and Lavish Film," December 26, 1931, from "Scrapbook 1931" (LC-M).

39 No author or title given, *Motion Picture Daily*, January 6, 1932, from "Scrapbook 1931" (LC-M). Especially provocative among these varying receptions across the country is this reminder that even in 1932, live music was still connected to the screening of motion pictures, as becomes clear in the announcement of a famous jazz band and live organists who would be at the Brooklyn Paramount Theatre: "Duke Ellington and his band pep things up on the stage. Merle Clark and Elsie Thompson continue to please at the twin consoles. Paramount Sound News features Santiago 'quake flashes and several shorts round out the bill." From "The Screen" by B. R. in the Brooklyn *Times*, February 6, 1932, from "Scrapbook 1931" (LC-M).

40 Carroll Carroll, "Cine-Metric Reviews," New York *Sun*, January 14, 1932, from "Scrapbook 1931" (LC-M).

41 From an interview transcribed in *Karl Struss: Man with a Camera*, edited by Susan Harvith and John Harvith (Bloomfield Hills, MI: Cranbrook Academy of Art/Museum, 1976), 13.

42 From the folder "Dr. Jekyll and Mr. Hyde, Miscellany, ca. 1932–1934, 1968" (LC-M); this excerpt appears on page 8. In all further discussions on the topic, Mamoulian asserts that the heartbeat recorded on the soundtrack was his own, and not March's.

43 Titled "Heartbeats in Amplified Ballyhoo: Attendant and Loud Speaker Used," this article comes from the folder "Dr. Jekyll and Mr. Hyde, Miscellany, ca. 1932–1934, 1968" (LC-M); this excerpt appears on page 15. The heart as a central thematic element can also been discerned in Hyde's vicious pun to Ivy, right before he murders her, as he asks, "Isn't Hyde a lover after your own heart?"

44 Cue sheets and a conductor's score at the Franz Waxman Papers in the Syracuse University special collections department reveal that, although neither was credited, both Amfitheatrof and Mario Castelnuovo-Tedesco contributed cues to *Dr. Jekyll and Mr. Hyde*. Amfitheatrof wrote cues titled "Evil Montage, Parts 1 & 2," "Sex Montage" (these cues accompany the first transformation scene) and "Ivy Alone," while Castelnuovo-Tedesco collaborated with Waxman on "The Missing Key."

45 *Dr. Jekyll and Mr. Hyde*, DVD, directed by Rouben Mamoulian (1931; Burbank, CA: Warner Home Video, 2004).

46 At one point as the film was being produced, other lines were going to be added and repeated in this scene. For instance, Lanyon was to have repeated the line "There are bounds beyond which one should not go" five times as well as to repeat the word "control" several times, according to blue pages

with the word "special" in red glued to the script (the Second White Script, dated August 7, 1931, LC-M).

47 Ben Winters astutely argues that heartbeat sounds in a number of film scores help audiences experience a kind of fear in "Corporeality, Musical Heartbeats, and Cinematic Emotion," *Music, Sound, and the Moving Image* 2/1 (Spring 2008): 3–25.

48 Atkins, "An Interview with Rouben Mamoulian," 42–4.

49 On a page titled "National Film Theatre Programme Notes," from an interview with Rohauer that "is taken from the Gallery of Modern Art programme schedule on their Mamoulian Season," in the folder "Dr. Jekyll and Mr. Hyde Miscellany, ca. 1932–1934, 1968" (LC-M). Mamoulian took several pages of notes after his meetings with Rohauer in 1967 (see the folder "Speeches & Writings Screenings Film Festivals 1967" (LC-M).

50 David Robinson, "Rouben Mamoulian: Painting the Leaves Black," *Sight & Sound* (Summer 1961): 123–7; this phrase appears on page 125. Among the numerous sources that describe the stew without graphic animation, see the following two from the "Scrapbook 1931" folder at LC-M: Philip K. Scheuer, "A Town Called Hollywood," *Los Angeles Times*, January 3, 1932; Florabel Muir, "Megaphoner Puts His Heart Beats Into Jekyll-Hyde," *New York News*, January 4, 1932. The "Press miscellaneous" folder at LC-M has an untitled French interview titled "Un conte de fées sur l'écran" from *L'intransigeant*, September 3, 1932. Arthur Knight has Mamoulian photographing light and not drawing in *The Liveliest Art: A Panoramic History of the Movies* (New York: Mentor Books, 1957), 158, as do Charles Higham and Joel Greenberg in *The Celluloid Muse: Hollywood Directors Speak* (Chicago, IL: Henry Regnery, 1969), 135 (this interview specifies, as several do, that the light was coming from a candle). Another statement by Mamoulian, this time a transcription of a seminar at the Center for Advanced Film Studies held in 1970, clearly states that part of his process was to "light the candle and photograph the light—high frequencies, low frequencies, directly from light into sound." (From the folder "Misc. talks," LC-M, 31.)

51 Tom Milne, *Rouben Mamoulian* (Bloomington, IN and London: Indiana University Press, 1969), 49. Royal S. Brown cites the excerpt from the Robinson interview via Milne in *Overtones and Undertones: Reading Film Music* (Berkeley, CA: University of California Press, 1994), 182, and Mervyn Cooke, without pointing to a particular source, states that Mamoulian used "animated sound" in *A History of Film Music* (Cambridge: Cambridge University Press, 2008), 60 and in "Film Music," *Grove Music Online, Oxford Music Online*, at www.oxfordmusiconline.com/subscriber/article/grove/music/09647 (accessed January 14, 2009).

52 Cooke, *A History of Film Music*, 60.

53 Heavy breathing and gasping accompanies the first transformation together with the sound stew, and it is important to consider, as Barbara Flueckiger does, that "breathing and heartbeats also have a symbolic dimension. They represent automatic bodily functions, without which no life is possible. They thus indicate not only nearness but, especially in the extremely threatening contexts in which they are most frequently used, life as a value to be protected and as the opposite to death." From "Sound Effects: Strategies for Sound Effects in Films," in *Sound and Music in Film and Visual Media: An Overview*, edited by Graeme Harper, Ruth Doughty, and Jochen Eisentraut (New York and London: Continuum, 2009), 176. In providing an audible (if subtle) marker of life, these sound effects help to set up the stakes for the meditation on mortality that will follow in the film.

54 Donnelly, *The Spectre of Sound*, 105.

55 From John Cage, "Experimental Music" (1957), in *Silence* (Middletown, CT: Wesleyan University Press, 1961), 8.

56 As Mary Ann Doane has observed, "sound itself is often described as adding life to the picture. And the life which sound gives is presented as one of natural and uncodified flow." See "Ideology and the Practice of Sound Editing and Mixing," in *Film Sound: Theory and Practice*, edited by Elisabeth Weis and John Belton (New York: Columbia University Press, 1985), 57.

57 Donnelly, *The Spectre of Sound*, 94.

58 Sigmund Freud, *The Uncanny*, translated by David McLintock (New York: Penguin Books, 2003), 123–61.

59 Freud, "The Uncanny," 124. Originally, it was "das Unheimliche sei jene Art des Schreckhaften, welche auf das Altbekannte, Längstvertraute zurückgeht." From Sigmund Freud, *Gesammelte Werke*, volume 12 (London: Imago, 1947), 231.

60 *Dr. Jekyll and Mr. Hyde* nonetheless became a conventional trope with the genre as demonstrated by the myriad adaptations of Stevenson's story, with a reach that extends deep into the twentieth century. For example, the television series *Buffy the Vampire Slayer* makes frequent use of stock conventions from horror—from vampires, Frankensteinian creations, werewolves, demons, mummies, zombies, and so forth to even relatively obscure horror tropes such as the disembodied hand—and numerous stories that involve characters split into good and evil, or strong and weak, selves (see Tanya Krzywinska's "Hubble-Bubble, Herbs, and Grimoires: Magic, Manichaeanism, and Witchcraft in *Buffy*," in *Fighting the Forces: What's at Stake in* Buffy the Vampire Slayer, edited by Rhonda V. Wilcox and David Lavery [Lanham, MD: Rowman & Littlefield, 2002], 179). In the episode called "The Replacement," (2000, written by Jane Espenson) the character Xander finds himself divided into two selves, one comprised of his strong qualities, the other of his weak ones. In the *Star Trek* original series episode called "Mirror, Mirror" (1967, written by Jerome Bixby), a fluke accident creates an encounter with the characters' parallel, but barbaric, doubles. At the end of the episode, a line spoken by the character Mr. Spock ("May I point out that I had an opportunity to observe your counterparts here quite closely. They were brutal, savage, unprincipled, uncivilized, treacherous—in every way splendid examples of homo sapiens, the very flower of humanity.") suggests a direct homage back to Heath and Hoffenstein's 1931 screenplay, as Spock's wording reflects a line uttered by March's Mr. Hyde in his first meeting with Ivy: "I'll grant you I'm no beauty, but under this exterior you'll find the very flower of humanity."

Chapter 5

Voices That Lie Within

The Heard and Unheard in *Psycho*

Ross J. Fenimore

Psycho begins with a theft. Marion, our protagonist, is in the midst of a moral quandary. Having fled Phoenix with money stolen from her boss, she is forced off the highway by a torrential downpour but not before imaginary voices crowd her head, recalling elements of the story we never see. Marion stumbles upon the Bates Motel where she decides to spend the night and wait out the storm. She meets Norman, the rather attractive—if quirky—manager of the family motel. And she hears, but never sees, the voice of Mrs. Bates calling from the eerie house on the hill. What Marion does not know is that this voice is one of many imagined in the film. This voice has been stolen.

Psycho is haunted by phantom voices. Such acousmatic sounds (sounds one hears but is unable to locate on-screen) are a hallmark of horror film—the dislocation between what we hear and see creates a fundamental tension that blurs the known and the unknown, what we hear and what we do not (or what we think we hear, but quickly deny).[1] These cracks in the world of synchronized sound, where voices must match with lips lest they break the illusion of continuity, are then manipulated to play on the possibilities of resolution—when will we ultimately learn what is "real," and thus embodied, and what is not? Can we trust what the protagonist hears from these disembodied voices? And what can we hear that the protagonist cannot?

The imagined voice is the most frightening sound of all. Its visual presence on the screen is often difficult to locate, and its very diffuse nature makes its relation to what Michel Chion calls the *acousmêtre* essential.[2] The confusion between the real and the unreal in film is intimately related to what is heard and unheard. So long as the audience is left in between, there can be no realignment of the synchronized sound apparatus, and thus no security in receiving the illusion of film as just that. It is the very danger of recognizing the imagined voice as real that terrifies the audience the most. *Psycho* manipulates this fear with both Marion and Norman—both hear voices that have no immediate source on screen. Though Marion hears Mrs. Bates, it is not always clear when we hear Mrs. Bates herself or when she exists only within Norman's own mind.

Much of what creates the illusion of horror in *Psycho* hinges on a fundamental sonic disconnect: who is Mrs. Bates and when will she enter the foreground? As an audience, we cannot always reconcile the voice (or voices) we hear to a particular place of resonance. Alfred Hitchcock deliberately misleads us. He does so most famously with the voice of Mrs. Bates creeping into our ears from off-screen, but also with the voices Marion creates in her own head as she is on the run from Phoenix. These voices haunt us throughout the narrative, but they do so with both sound design and sound editing as well as with embellishment from the depths of the orchestral score. This is, of course, the illusion at the core of *Psycho*'s narrative turn: the audience is unable to fully place Mrs. Bates's voice with her body until we learn that we have always been looking in the wrong place.

There is equal confusion, initially, with the function of the score. No one hears any music at all in *Psycho*; that is, no one but the audience. The apparent lack of any crossover between the scored music and the diegetic world suggests that what we hear underneath the film emanates entirely from the subjective world of Hitchcock's characters themselves. Could this, however, be a lie?[3] To whom does this music belong—our guilt-ridden short-lived protagonist, Marion, or the dark shadows of the quietly lurking Norman Bates? To what degree does the orchestral score shift the film's window of subjectivity? The score persists as another voice within the film itself; often, this voice is tasked with the portrayal of physical characteristics of the main characters: paranoia, anxiety, rage, and insanity. The ability to peer into subjective states provides the only counter-balance to a voice we cannot locate. This essay will contend with this array of voices, both in sound design and score, as well as how they shape the narrative development of *Psycho*: how does a careful ear reveal the fractured subjectivities within the film? The voices that lie within the body, imagined and realized—unheard and heard—are at the heart of what makes *Psycho* so thrilling.

Aural Fragments: Severing Voice from Body

Michel Chion's work on the voice in cinema provides a useful means to explore the narrative work of the horror film. His mode of analysis gives careful attention to sonic detail and structure, especially how audiences perceive voices that emanate on-screen and off. Chion's argument derives from what he frames as the emancipated ideal:

> Contemporary Western culture resolutely claims to be monistic, fiercely rejecting the dualistic idea of man split down the middle.

The liberal, "emancipated" ideal becomes to reconcile the fragments of the self all within the body, considered as the homogenous and unsplit habitat of the individual.[4]

Chion recalls the fundamental tension within synchronized sound: though film attempts to hide this dualism, there always remains a tension propagated by the incision between body and voice. How the director threads this seam demonstrates the degree to which the apparatus of film hides the dualism. It is exactly this unearthing of the seam and the tearing of the parts that constitutes the thrill of horror film. The audience comes to expect the dismemberment of the apparatus and thus the pulling apart of the filmic body itself. It becomes critical, then, that the parts do not necessarily reconcile or, if they do, that the reconciliation remains fraught with this tension-in-common.[5] Resolution comes, as it does with *Psycho*, the moment when the audience realizes this rupture is not an illusion but an inherent contradiction of the apparatus; maintaining a narrative that feels out of place throws continuity off balance.

Psycho succeeds in building this tension because these fragments are not entirely reconciled. Marion Crane's death just before the first hour creates a fundamental imbalance in the film. With no protagonist, the audience must wonder how Marion's anxiety over immorality, brought to the forefront through her imaginary conversations, will be resolved, or even if they will be at all. Where once the underscore had served to frame Marion's emotional states—her love of Sam Loomis, temptation to steal the money, and the anxious escape from Phoenix—it soon betrays her at the pivotal shower scene with the sound of strings tearing into the acoustic space with great violence and forcefulness. Bernard Herrmann slams shut the music's subjective window and the score provides, instead, the aural kinetics of her death.

Hitchcock's public campaign to keep the surprise twist a secret generated significant word-of-mouth for the film.[6] Audiences were prohibited from entering the theater after the start time as a means of telling the public that something awful might happen at any moment. Hitchcock's proclamation of a viewing contract with the audience assured that they would adhere to the belief of cinema's continuity (that you should see the whole film in one sitting), despite the unconventional narrative structure of the film. Hitchcock has been attributed with changing audience decorum in the cinema. The quick building of suspense allows the film to easily envelope the audience.[7]

The motif of burial is central to *Psycho*. The "impossible embodiment" of Mrs. Bates's voice condemns her to float throughout the film.[8] This aural sense of disembodiment conjures the figure of the ghost; without a clear indication of the voice's source, the effect on film colors a picture of the soul outside the body, but trapped by this sense of eternal wandering.

The etymological link Chion outlines of embodiment to entombment, and entombment to interment, reaffirms the desire for the wandering soul (in the demotic sense) to find its place of rest. Here, the soul becomes the double—its separation from the body also maps onto the filmic split between recorded voice and filmed body, and Norman Bates's split between himself and his mother. If, as Chion argues, the audience's desire for the film is to witness the reunion of voice to body—to demystify the *acousmêtre*—then how might sound design and the score serve to amplify this possibility?[9] At what point might we be able to locate the emergence of her voice in the film prior to its revelation in the final scene? Chion's questions about voice are powerful, but fail to take Herrmann's role into account.

Norman Bates represents the tension-in-common crucial to horror narratives.[10] Noël Carroll reads Norman's tension as emblematic of the horror genre:

> He is *Nor-man*: neither man nor woman but both. He is son and mother. He is of the living and the dead. He is both victim and victimizer. He is two persons in one. He is abnormal, that is, because he is interstitial.[11]

Carroll finds *Psycho* itself difficult to classify within horror; curiously, this probably comes from the film's nods to neo-noir, documentary film, and suspense. Though Norman's dualism is hidden from us for much of the film, the audience continually suspects him of hiding something—his nervous mannerisms around Marion Crane suggest a discomfort with his own body that is both sexual and *indicative of* the presence of his mother within him.

The Unheard: Imagined Voices

Imagined voices set the entire plot of *Psycho* into motion. Although we do not hear them until Marion's flight from Phoenix, we are aware, nonetheless, that they have been haunting her from the moment we first peer through the window of the hotel room and discover her affair with Sam in a hotel room. Hitchcock makes these silent thoughts painstakingly loud with the role of the camera and the recurrent motif of "looking": the camera wanders away from our protagonist to settle on certain objects of importance. As Marion packs her suitcase to leave Phoenix, the camera peers down to the envelope on the bed, leaving, for a moment, the objective frame of the scene to cue Marion's subjective thoughts. The shot sequence establishes the voices within Marion's head, which appear later as she drives out of the city. Hitchcock's visual cues allude to clues within the plot, but also tie the camera especially to the subjective world of the protagonist (or, at least, what the audience should be thinking that the main character is thinking). Musically, the score realizes these tensions. The orchestra does not embellish the visual world of Phoenix. Instead, it channels the moral conundrum within the protagonist.

The music accompanying the escape is pivotal in setting up the multiple voices within Marion's head. Robin Wood considers the alliance between the audience and Marion Crane:

> With [Marion], we lose all power of rational control, and discover how easily a "normal" person can lapse into a condition usually associated with neurosis. Like her we resent, with fear and impatience, everything (the policeman, the car salesman) that impedes or interferes with her obsessive flight.[12]

Hitchcock gains our trust by quickly moving through the range of affects playing out within Marion's head. The further Marion gets from Phoenix, the more her moral character unravels before her. At first, she imagines her escape as something hopeful. She hears Sam's surprised voice and delight at her unexpected arrival. But even Sam's tone becomes suspicious, and his cadence on the line "What is it, Marion?" fails to arrive on the steady ground she had hoped her imagined arrival would provide. At the outset, Marion cannot even imagine a safe haven for her deeds; she is already fraught with guilt. In the second conversation, her morality comes directly into question. She imagines the car dealer asking "She look like a wrong one to you?" followed by an affirming "Acted like one" from the highway patrol officer who had earlier found her asleep on the side of the road. These conversations put into play the beginnings of an investigation that we never see on-screen. And yet, we know that something approximating these conversations likely happened.

This sequence pushes aside the other characters in the film. By placing their narrative within Marion's mind, Hitchcock brings her further into the forefront. On scoring this scene Herrmann writes, "We [Herrmann and Hitchcock] both agreed to bring back the music we'd related to the opening of the film, which again tells the audience, who don't know something terrible is going to happen to the girl, that it's got to."[13] The obsessive phrase repetition approximates the claustrophobic space of the car—the desire to escape the vehicle heightens as Marion drives through the rain unable to see anything but the sharp back-and-forth cutting of the blades across the windshield.[14] Furthermore, the phrase repetition mirrors the claustrophobia within Marion's own mind.[15] Here the elements of sound design and score composition join. Marion's decision to stop running is a means of shutting out the voices in her head. These are both the voices she imagines and the voices from the underscore that Herrmann creates to mirror anxiety. The effect of claustrophobia enhances the speed of the narrative. Hitchcock rushes Marion's imagined narrative, as well as the line of events not corroborated until later in the film when pieces of her conversations tie to actual events in the plot (her sister comes to look for her; the private detective investigates the hotel; the police have been investigating her). The use of strings to perform the entire score collapses the timbral canvas from the classical Hollywood style.[16] The timbral homogeneity of the orchestration shrinks the perception of space in the music. This sense of running out of space, even running out of time, is pivotal to setting up Marion's demise.

Herrmann's score establishes the principal imagined voice for the audience. Just as Marion believes what she hears, so does the audience; we trust in the score to relay affect honestly. The audience does not realize that this reliance will become the crucial trapdoor. Herrmann highlights the rhythmic dexterity and wide range of special effects available to the string orchestra instead of depending on its well-established lineage with early Hollywood's epic features (through melody and leitmotif) and melodramatic orchestral writing, a genre whose success hinged on overwrought emotion inhabited by the string player's prowess in wide vibrato and glissandi placed high in the instrument's register.[17] These effects heightened the role of the score as a voice sympathetic to the audience, whether providing a narrative map through the use of leitmotif or sustaining a performer's affect in a pivotal scene.

When the musical ideas of the prelude return to accompany the flight from Phoenix, Herrmann locks the muted string orchestra into five motivic units that wrestle against one another. I have outlined the units with some deference to Fred Steiner's own formulation: the opening chords (Figure 5.1); a semitone figure initially in the viola (and later appearing with the second violins) (Figure 5.2); a principal triplet motive that begins with the first violins (Figure 5.3); a dotted secondary motive (Figure 5.4); and the arrival at a brief arching theme (Figure 5.5).[18]

Figure 5.1 Opening chords (transcription from soundtrack)

Figure 5.2 Semitone figure (transcription from soundtrack)

Figure 5.3 Principal motive (transcription from soundtrack)

Figure 5.4 Secondary motive (transcription from soundtrack)

Figure 5.5 "Flight" theme (transcription from soundtrack)

The rapid shift through these metrically disparate motives illustrates the powerful rhythmic play at work as the first few minutes of music establish the out-of-control spiraling of Marion's morality. The juxtaposition of mechanical sounds frames the opening titles and Marion's "flight" music. Though the opening chords do not finish until the third measure, the C-sharp–D semitone rhythm propels itself from the final chord and sets up the rhythmic drive of the triplets in the following motive. The shift back and forth between slurred and dotted notes mimics the physical effect of cutting, frequently with the slur coming to an abrupt halt. A staccato eighth note follows each slurred triplet in the principal motive just as the short slurs in the semitone motive break on the second note. Alongside the dotted-eighth motion in the secondary motive, this articulation interrupts the run of the bow. Indeed, the only time the string player does not face impediment comes with the falling melodic line, though the melody plays above the same abrupt string features that begin the prelude as dynamic swells from piano to fortissimo shape its run. This line may be the one fleeting moment that allows for melodic expansion of the phrase; it is the longest of the phrases at twelve measures. The chords from the introduction, however, interrupt the line in its third appearance.

The emphasis for the scene is on the mechanical (short, jagged repetition); dense phrasing limits the melodic possibility and focuses the energy on rhythmic drive rather than melodic development. With only the suggestion of a theme in the twelve-measure violin line, the melodic development does more to mark a contour of falling motion than develop. The distinction between something automated, rather than human, is crucial. Herrmann emphasizes this persistent, circuitous drive as emblematic of Marion's moral trap but also to prepare the audience aurally for the musical tearing that will mark the plot's startling turn.

The Audience Screams

Linda Williams's study of excess in film gauges the degree to which certain genres of film—melodrama (specifically, the "woman's film" or "weepie"), horror, and pornography—push outside the conventions of classical Hollywood narrative cinema. Williams deems these aberrations "body genres" to describe the value in thinking about the oft understudied "form, function, and system of seemingly gratuitous excesses" that have profound effects on the body of the spectator.[19] Indeed, these are genres that can make us feel overcome in some fashion; their very success depends on how well they elicit signs of excess in the viewer. The difficulty in accounting for how to interpret this excess often relegates body genre films to a lower status. This derision occurs precisely because body genre films make explicit an affect of revulsion that depends on intense feelings of shame that surround these signs of excess: shame that comes after crying (in melodrama), after shock and nervous laughter (in the horror film), and after orgasm (in pornography). Shame allies each body genre in the way it colors the emotional and physical afterglow at moments of climax. In horror there is a repulsive response to the moment of death, but also an undercurrent of desire to see the act of violence through, and almost certainly a bout of laughter afterwards that relaxes the tension between repulsion and desire. The power of a moral contract with the viewer channels this undercurrent: immoral, sexually active "bad" girls must die so that the moral, non-sexual "good" girls can survive.

Psycho, though, complicates this contract.[20] The one good candidate for a good girl is Marion Crane's sister Lila, but because she enters the film in the second act her ability to channel the audience's sympathy is significantly lessened. Her character serves mostly as an auxiliary figure in the film's narrative, a kind of shadow of Marion herself.[21] Without a well-defined good girl, the moral universe of the film feels completely corrupt; from the opening scene of Marion and Sam's affair, Cassidy's sexual advances on Marion, and Caroline's drug dependence, the film creates a world where there are few good moral models. The quasi-documentary scene that appears at the end of the film balances *Psycho*'s dislocation from the model of traditional horror. This nod to the teen morality documentaries of the 1950s attempts to rationalize what has been consistently irrational throughout *Psycho*'s narrative (and will ultimately remain unresolved).[22]

In Williams's formulation of film genre, she outlines the features of bodily excess that "body" genres share:

1   The spectacle of the body caught in the grip of intense sensation or emotion.
2   The focus on what could probably best be called a form of ecstasy.
3   Visually, each of these ecstatic excesses could be said to share a quality of uncontrollable convulsion or spasm—of the body "beside itself" with sexual pleasure, fear and terror, or overpowering sadness. Aurally, excess is marked by recourse not to the coded articulations of language but to inarticulate cries of pleasure in porn, screams of fear in horror, sobs of anguish in melodrama.
4   In each of these genres the bodies of women figured on the screen have functioned traditionally as the primary *embodiments* of pleasure, fear, and pain.[23]

The shower scene from *Psycho* represents each characteristic. The scene provides the most prominent display of raw emotion in the film; the scoring matches the coarse tearing of the narrative's trajectory. As Williams writes, Marion's murder happens too early, not just within the expected dimension of horror film—clearly the placement of the scene before its expectation is necessary for the kinetic effect—but also due to the sudden shift of the score's role in the narrative. What we have heard up to this point has emanated from Marion's subjective world. The frenetic rhythmic motives of the opening title sequence accompany the chorus of voices in her head. The music in this scene, though, betrays Marion. Herrmann pulls far outside the expectation of classic Hollywood film scoring so that he can directly assault the audience. What remains is the sonic rupturing of flesh; the fierce string glissandi reveal what Hollywood censors would not.[24] When Hitchcock asked Janet Leigh what she thought of the scene, *Psycho*'s novelist Robert Bloch recalls Leigh responding: "When that knife went into me on the screen, I could feel it!" Bloch notes Hitchcock's response: "My dear, the knife *never* went into you."[25] And yet, following Leigh's response, the audience very much does hear it that way. The sharp cutting of the scene startles, but the music, together with a casaba melon in the sound design, amplifies the act of penetration. The jagged visuals map precisely onto the musical texture. The affect of repeated, violent penetration topples the audience from its voyeuristic stool prized only moments ago.[26]

Though some, including the composer, have argued that the strings represent birds screeching or the sound of a human scream, I believe that the effect is significantly more corporeal.[27] The effect of Herrmann's orchestration establishes a musical aura that signifies on both Marion and the audience. Stan Link's reading of the scene observes that:

A single musical cue such as Herrmann's shower scene plays a triple role in evoking the doomed woman's alarm, her killer's uncontrollable fury and the spectator's rocketing anxiety. As these various emotional perspectives wrap around each other—become *intimate*—boundaries of individual identity vanish. As characters, objects and spectators fuse, dramatic opposition tends to coalesce into a kind of unity: "*he*" becomes "*she*" becomes "*I*." Momentarily at least, there is an amalgamation of emotional experiences.[28]

Link's formulation, that the audience becomes part of the drama, reminds us of the tenuous balance between narrative and reality at work. Both sides of the screen feel the betrayal of the score etched into their flesh.[29] Placing this spectacle on the body, as Williams argues, is crucial, and Herrmann accomplishes the moment of corporeal inscription by continuing to play on the mechanical effects of string instruments.

Hitchcock painstakingly shot the scene around any explicit representation of nudity and violence that the production code would have vehemently rejected. Herrmann, though, can allow us to perceive the explicitness through hearing. Although we may not be allowed to witness the penetration of the knife itself, we can hear it. This rupture of illusion comes from the music itself. The audience is shocked not simply because Marion has died; the audience is shocked not simply because of the elaborate sequence of cutting Hitchcock employs; the audience is shocked because the score itself violates the rules of continuity by dislodging the spectator from the seat of observation. The music takes the side of neither the audience nor the protagonist. The music has enabled an independent voice within the film and leaves us wondering whose subjective state the music signifies, if any at all. Not only must the audience contend with a voice they are unable to locate and the loss of the principal character in the film, but the floor of the theater has dropped out from beneath our very feet. The filmic structures we come to depend on, especially as they are found in the score, have torn apart and we are left only to ride out this rollercoaster.[30]

The Heard: Mother's Voice

Mother's voice is a lie.[31] Furthermore, her voice is not the product of vocal manipulation by Anthony Perkins or any actor featured in the film itself. The voice of Mother is inherently contradictory: it is male and female, inflected with the sounds of old age (despite its source being young), and never reliant on a singular source. Mother's voice, surprisingly, is the conglomeration of three voice actors who themselves did not know when and how their voices would be used in *Psycho*.[32] The idea of initially cross-gendering the voice as Perkins had suggested, however, did stick and the actor ultimately convinced Hitchcock to use the voice of a young, unknown actor from Montana named Paul Jasmin.[33] Hitchcock had to balance the very difficult task of creating a voice that *sounded* like Perkins, but only vaguely, and without the slippage, and thus betrayal, that Perkins's own voice would have caused. Jasmin recalls, "[Hitchcock] really didn't tell you very much and volunteered *nothing*. He just wanted those voices he kept hearing in his head ... The woman's voice was really shrewish. That's the quality Hitchcock liked."[34] Hitchcock used Jasmin to voice Mother's lines on set; the effect of sonic cross-gendering was particularly essential to the final scene in the film where Hitchcock juxtaposes Norman's face with the fleeting ghostly appearance of Mother's skull. In post-production Hitchcock took a few additional steps. In order to better confuse the aural timbre of Mrs. Bates, he hired two actresses, Jeanette Nolan and Virginia Gregg (who provided the voice of Mother in two of the sequels).[35] Nolan also provided the screams for both the shower scene and the revelation in the basement. The film's sound editors, Walden O. Watson and William Russell, stitched the three voices together. Jasmin recalls:

> In post-production, [Hitchcock] spliced and blended a mixture of different voices—Virginia, Jeanette, and me—so that what Mother says literally changes from word to word and sentence to sentence. He did that to confuse the audience. I recognize my voice before Tony carries Mother down the stairs. But the very last speech, the monologue, is all a woman, Virginia, with probably a little of Jeanette spliced in.[36]

The sound design of Mother's voice fractures the construction of subjectivity—she speaks not with one voice, but three, and none of them belongs to the actor on screen. Watson and Russell subtly use this sound design to form a crucial marker of Norman's identity. They splice Mother's words as a collage of both gender and timbre. The slight timbral shifts between phrases belie the expectation that Mother exists objectively within the film world. We hear something fundamentally off about her voice that demands investigation. This shifting builds the suspense on both occasions when we think Mother will be revealed: the first attempt at revelation fails when Mother murders Detective Milton Arbogast on the steps to her room; the second attempt, when Marion's sister Lila ventures into the basement, reveals Mother's body rocking back and forth. In neither instance does Hitchcock reconcile Mother's voice.

And yet, we do know Mother's identity long before her revelation. The scene in the parlor accentuates the fractured subjectivity of Norman Bates. Anthony Perkins's virtuosity in this scene evidences his ability to balance both the boy-next-door qualities of Norman alongside an increasingly unstable inner turmoil. James Naremore marvels on the visual rhymes that enhance Norman's multiplicity: "Norman sometimes looks feminine and avian (the double of Marion Crane), sometimes like a dark-haired leading man (the double of Sam Loomis), and sometimes like an angular stick figure (the double of Mrs. Bates's skeleton)."[37] Taxidermic subjects adorn the room as they peer down on Marion. Herrmann reveals subtle clues of Mother's presence within Norman. We do not hear her vocally, but the underscore signals a stark subjective shift, and Anthony Perkins accentuates his performance to reveal a second voice speaking from within. Hitchcock's camera, alongside Herrmann's deft scoring, increasingly devotes more screen time to Norman (especially between 40:32 and 42:20).

The music in the "madhouse" scene begins with what Graham Bruce has coined the "madness motif" (see Figure 5.6).[38] We have heard a relative of this motive before. The first appearance came in Phoenix as Sam and Marion discussed their future, though it returns to the parlor scene mutated from its romantic origins. The scene begins somewhat innocuously, as Norman extends an invitation to dine in the parlor. Marion, upon suggesting that Norman send his mother to a psychiatric ward (using the euphemism of "institution"), sets off Norman's tripwire and we hear Mother for the very first time through her son. Perkins dramatically shifts his performance to match possession as his boy-next-door charms slip away.[39] Musically, the "madness" motif appears in the lower strings with a repeated emphasis on E-flat. The initial appearance rises to E-flat as the motive moves in octaves in the celli and bass (f. 6). When the violas enter, however, the "madness" motif creeps upward beyond an octave from F to F-sharp before sliding down to an E-flat; the violas attempt the leap once again, this time to F-natural, but stall out on E-flat (Figure 5.7). The cello returns underneath the viola to set its E-flats in syncopation, though this line, too, stalls out on a D-natural and accentuates the semitone dissonance Bruce emphasizes. Herrmann's

Figure 5.6 "Madness Motif" (transcription from soundtrack)

Figure 5.7 "Madness Motif" in the viola and cello lines (transcription from soundtrack)

imitative melodic writing, built on the "madness motif," further distorts the motive's relationship to the romance theme we associated earlier with Marion and Sam. The score signals a new romance at work, though not one Marion desires.

Herrmann's placement of the E-flats in juxtaposition with the dialogue signals an important parallel between Marion and Norman. Marion's line "Wouldn't it be better . . . if you put her . . . someplace . . . ?" is echoed by Norman moments later when he says "People always call a madhouse someplace, don't they? **Put her** in **someplace**." The boldface type indicates Herrmann's placement of the E-flats as they occur in the dialogue.[40] It is not just Norman who mocks Marion; the score begins to turn on her by highlighting certain words as Norman realizes that she has lied to him. This play occurs twice more: once on Marion's apology, "I'm **sorry**," and then at the end of the phrase when Norman asks, "What do you know about **caring**?"

The music in the "madhouse" scene does not reappear in the movie save only briefly in the "porch" scene and at the film's conclusion. What makes this scene unique in the film is the placement of the melodic lines high in the register. We have yet to see Herrmann call for such stratospheric scoring in *Psycho*. After Norman delivers the line "people always mean well" (as Mother), the violins crawl upward (Figure 5.8). The second violins land on an A-flat and descend for six measures, while the first violins rise to an A-natural. The violas return in syncopation with the violins as all three instrumental groups move back down. The "madness" motif returns again, three times, and descends the orchestral palette. The key moment arrives in the penultimate measure. The first

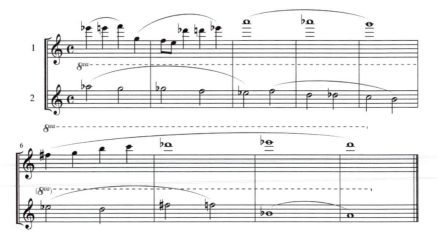

Figure 5.8 Melodic motion in the first and second violins (transcription from soundtrack)

violins arrive on an E-flat (the highest pitch) as Norman says "We all go a little mad sometimes."

Though this E-flat resolves down to D-natural and, with the rest of the string ensemble, gives us one of the most harmonically stable moments in the film (the perfect fifth of D to A), the note should not be forgotten. It is the very same E-flat that will return to assault our protagonist only a few moments later. Herrmann sharpens Norman's knife.

Mother's Voice, Unresolved

Psycho devotes a significant amount of time to silence.[41] We are left alone with Marion or Norman and their struggles within. Both of them lie to themselves. And both lies reconcile by the end of the film—one in death, the other in mental imprisonment. In the film, we hear Marion's imagined voices, and although the source fails to surface, we have the visual evidence of Marion driving alone in the car, in close-up, to assign these conversations to her. With Norman, though, the connection remains unclear. The audience is not immediately aware that Mother, too, is an imagined voice. Her acousmatic quality blurs the identification of voice with body, but even when we have the final realignment, her voice exists much in the same way Marion's inner voices appear in the car chase. The film moves from a voice clearly audible in the narrative soundscape (Marion: "If anyone ever talked to me the way I heard she spoke to you . . .") to a place locked deeply within Norman's fractured interiority ("I hope they are watching . . . they'll see. They'll see and they'll know, and they'll say: 'Why, she wouldn't even harm a fly . . .'" [the *acousmêtre*]). This final clue reveals itself when Mother (now in Norman's body) thanks the officer for giving her a blanket. But even then, the source of the voice remains unclear. Hitchcock leaves us standing in the hallway unsure if we hear Mother's voice in the soundscape (as Mother says "thank you" to the officer, does the officer hear her?) or whether, at this moment, the film pulls us into Norman's subjectivity completely. As Herrmann's score draws the film to its conclusion with the same material from the "madhouse" scene, we now hear only voices that lie within.

Notes

1 From the ancient Greek *akousmatikos*, the term referred to students of Pythagoras who listened silently to his lectures as their teacher stood behind a screen to improve their concentration. More recently, *acousmatique* was used by French composer Pierre Schaeffer, pioneer of *musique concrète*, a form of experimental music that began in Paris, *c.*1948.

2 Simply defined, the *acousmêtre* is the voice that is "heard without its cause or source being seen." Michel Chion, *The Voice In Cinema,* translated by Claudia Gorbman (New York: Columbia University Press, 1999), 18. He

elaborates on the definition in his chapter on *Psycho*. Here the *acousmêtre* becomes the "yet unseen voice, one that can neither enter the image to attach itself to a visible body, nor occupy the removed position of the image presented" (140). For further discussion see Michel Chion, "Phantom Audio-Vision," in *Audio-Vision: Sound on Screen*, edited and translated by Claudia Gorbman (New York: Columbia University Press, 1990):

> We may define [the *acousmêtre*] as neither inside nor outside the image. It is not inside, because the image of the voice's source—the body, the mouth—is not included. Nor is it outside, since it is not clearly positioned off-screen in an imaginary "wing," like a master of ceremonies or a witness, and it is implicated in the action, constantly about to be part of it.

3   The division is never absolute. For a discussion of the space between diegetic and non-diegetic music see Robynn J. Stilwell, "The Fantastical Gap between Diegetic and Nondiegetic," in *Beyond the Soundtrack: Representing Music in Cinema*, edited by Daniel Goldmark, Lawrence Kramer, and Richard Leppert (Berkeley and Los Angeles, CA: University of California Press, 2007), 184–204.

4   Chion, *The Voice In Cinema*, 125.

5   Royal S. Brown sees this tension further replicated in Bernard Herrmann's score and its use of bitonality. In Royal S. Brown, "Herrmann, Hitchcock, and the Music of the Irrational," *Overtones and Undertones: Reading Film Music* (Berkeley and Los Angeles, CA: University of California Press, 1994).

6   A detailed documentary, *The Making of Psycho*, can be found in the extras alongside newsreel footage from the period in the collector's edition of *Psycho* on DVD (Universal City, CA: Universal Studios, 1999). The footage recounts how movie theaters advertised Hitchcock's rules for attendance (often with a recording of the director's own voice playing).

7   On the opening music in the film, Herrmann writes: "The climax of *Psycho* is given to you by the music right at the moment the film begins. I am firmly convinced, and so is Hitchcock, that after the main titles you know that something terrible must happen." In *Sound and the Cinema: The Coming of Sound to American Film*, edited by Evan William Cameron (Pleasantville, NY: Redgrave Publishing Company, 1980), 132.

8   Chion, *The Voice In Cinema*, 140.

9   Carolyn Abbate writes on Chion:

> *Acousmêtre*, referring to the voice-being not grounded in an object, becomes in many cases a sonic cousin to the phantom, condemned to eternal wandering like the unburied dead, to float in the sound track. In Chion's most disturbing cases, such voices never find their final resting place.

From Carolyn Abbate, "Debussy's Phantom Sounds," *In Search of Opera* (Princeton, NJ: Princeton University Press, 2001), 155–6.

10 I refer here to the tension between synchronized sound and the image detailed earlier in Michel Chion's discussion of voice.

11 Noël Carroll, *The Philosophy of Horror or Paradoxes of the Heart* (New York: Routledge, 1990), 39.

12 Robin Wood, *Hitchcock's Films Revisited* (New York: Columbia University Press, 1989), 145.

13 Quoted in Steven C. Smith, *A Heart at Fire's Center: The Life and Music of Bernard Herrmann* (Berkeley and Los Angeles, CA: University of California Press, 1991), 239.

14 Susan Smith observes:

> Yet as an aspect of film rhetoric that usually exists outside of the narrative world, a movie score is inevitably equipped with distancing, not just identificatory powers. This is particularly so in the case of suspense music. As Richard Dyer has pointed out (again in relation to Herrmann's scores), such music does not simply encourage us to "feel that we're going along with a particular character," so, "that we feel *with* that character," for its ability to privilege us with advance warning of future narrative dangers also prompts us to feel something *towards* and *on behalf* of a character.

Smith goes on to discuss how music can represent characters that are no longer present in the film (due to distance or death). In Susan Smith, *Hitchcock: Suspense, Humor, Tone* (London: British Film Institute, 2000), 105. Smith draws from Richard Dyer's radio interview "Thrillers and the Music of Suspense," *Cinema Now* (series produced by BBC Radio 4). No dates available.

15 David Cooper discusses an alternate use of the ostinato in the opening sequence of *Vertigo* (1958) where the device is combined with several simultaneous tempi as a means of pulling the listener into Scottie's vertigo through rhythmic disorientation. Cooper emphasizes Herrmann's connection to Charles Ives, Charles Seeger, and Ruth Crawford as composers who experimented with polyrhythm. From David Cooper, *Bernard Herrmann's* Vertigo (Westport, CT: Greenwood Press, 2001), 83–6.

16 For a discussion of Herrmann's use of orchestral timbre see Fred Steiner, "Herrmann's 'Black and White' Music (Part I)," *Film Music Notebook* 1/1 (Fall 1971): 28–36.

17 "One of the hallmarks of [Herrmann's] compositional style is a predilection for the use of short motives which are often of an individual rhythmic character" (ibid., 34). Also, "But when one thinks of strings, one usually thinks of romance—above all, in film music" (ibid., 32).

18 Fred Steiner, "Herrmann's 'Black and White' Music (Part II)," *Film Music Notebook* 1/2 (Winter 1974–1975): 29.

19 Linda Williams, "Film Bodies: Gender, Genre, Excess," *Film Quarterly* 44/4 (Summer 1991): 3.

20 Williams, "Film Bodies," 8.

21 As Carol J. Clover writes, Lila only prefigures the final girl rudimentarily:

> The *Psycho* scene turns, after all, on the revelation of Norman's psychotic identity, not on Lila as a character—she enters the film midway and is sketchily drawn—and still less on her self-defense . . . She [the final girl] is the girl scout, the bookworm, the mechanic. Unlike her girlfriends (and Marion Crane) she is not sexually active.

In Carol J. Clover, "Her Body, Himself: Gender in the Slasher Film," *Representations* 20 (Autumn 1987): 187–228. Robert Bloch's novel, on which the film was based, complicates the good/bad dichotomy by emphasizing Marion's altruistic qualities: Marion drops out of school to support her younger sister after their parents are killed in a car wreck.

22 William Rothman argues that the film's allusion to documentary signifiers— the use of black and white film, the labeling of a precise time and location to open the film (Phoenix, Arizona on Friday, December 11, at 2:43 p.m.), and the role of the psychologist—is precisely *Psycho*'s fiction (or internal lie): that the world we enter is perceived as real (in William Rothman, *The Murderous Gaze* [Cambridge, MA: Harvard University Press, 1982], 251).

The use of black and white film also recalls *Psycho*'s debt to early sound film horror cinema. Stephan Pennington pointed me to the 1961 documentary *Boys Beware* (director Sid Davis, Davis Productions) that warns young teen men about the dangers of "homosexuals" (all of whom are child predators). The Inglewood Police Department and school district assisted with the film's production. Earlier documentaries include: *How to Say No: Moral Maturity* (Coronet Instructional Films, 1951), *Good Table Manners* (CIF, 1953), and *Social-Sex Attitudes in Adolescence* (Crawley Films, 1953).

23 Williams, "Film Bodies," 4; emphasis in original. The key phrase here is embodiment. Indeed, music's role in *Psycho*, with particular regard to the shower scene, is to accentuate the experience of bodily revulsion.

24 Jane Gaines and Neil Lerner hear a link between the tearing sounds of Herrmann's cue and Joseph Carl Breil's music for "The Rape of Flora" from D. W. Griffith's *Birth of a Nation* (1915). See Jane Gaines and Neil Lerner, "The Orchestration of Affect: The Motif of Barbarism in Breil's *The Birth of a Nation* Score," in *The Sounds of Early Cinema*, edited by Richard Abel and Rick Altman (Bloomington, IN: Indiana University Press, 2001), 267.

25 Stephen Rebello, *Alfred Hitchcock and the Making of Psycho* (New York: Dembner Books, 1990), 143.

26 Caroline J. S. Picart and David A. Frank discuss the crucial role of complicity Hitchcock establishes in the shower sequence in their article, "Horror and the Holocaust: Genre Elements in *Schindler's List* and *Psycho*" in *The Horror Film,* edited by Stephen Prince (New Brunswick, NJ: Rutgers University Press, 2004), 213. This scene is read against the role of voyeurism in the shower scene of Steven Spielberg's *Schindler's List*:

> *Schindler's List,* while employing similar cinematic tactics, reverses the narrative, indulging in the murderous propensities of the voyeuristic gaze, and yet withdrawing from it at the last moment, replacing a moment of confrontation with one of survival and ultimate redemption. With Norman Bates, Hitchcock explicitly implicates the viewer in voyeuristic gaze and murder.

27 Graham Bruce writes:

> This harsh discord spreading its parameters gradually through the whole orchestra has the effect of a scream; however, particularly in the glissando section, the mimetic point of reference, as Herrmann himself suggested, is the shriek of birds, reinforcing the bird associations previously established in both image track and music.

In Graham Bruce, *Bernard Herrmann: Film Music and Narrative* (Ann Arbor, MI: UMI Research Press, 1982), 210. See also Susan Smith: "The Herrmann score for the shower murder scene in *Psycho* pushes these anti-melodic tendencies to their farthest extreme by juxtaposing the female scream with a form of music that itself becomes a series of discordant *punctums* or shrieks." In Smith, *Hitchcock: Suspense, Humor, Tone*, 112.

28 Stan Link, "Sympathy with the Devil? Music of the Psycho Post-*Psycho*," *Screen* 45/1 (Spring 2004): 3; emphasis in original.

29 Carol J. Clover is poignant here:

> At least one director, Hitchcock, explicitly located thrill in the equation victim = audience . . . Not just the body of Marion is to be ruptured, but also the body on the other side of the film and screen: our witnessing body. As Marion is to Norman, the audience of *Psycho* is to Hitchcock.

See Clover, "Her Body, Himself," 213.

30 The rollercoaster metaphor is a recurring descriptor in writings on horror. Isabel Cristina Pinedo locates the parallel between the two experiences in the commingling of fear and pleasure or what she calls "recreational terror." The tension between stress and arousal plays off of the denied elements of control (and conviction) that produce pleasure and the resultant biochemical reactions within the body. See "Postmodern Elements of the Contemporary Horror Film," in *The Horror Film*, edited by Stephen Prince (New Brunswick, NJ: Rutgers University Press, 2004), 106.

31 For a fascinating discussion of another notable vocal falsity in film, see Katherine Bergeron's discussion of the 1994 film, *Farinelli*: "The Castrato as History," *Cambridge Opera Journal* 8/2 (July 1996): 167–84.

32 For a detailed accounting of the sound design that created Mother's voice, see Rebello, *Alfred Hitchcock and the Making of* Psycho, 131–5. The details of production in this essay come from his history of events.

33 Ibid., 131.

34 Ibid., 132.

35 Ibid., 132.

36 Ibid., 133.

37 James Naremore, "Remaking *Psycho*," in *Framing Hitchcock: Selected Essays from the* Hitchcock Annual, edited by Sidney Gottlieb and Christopher Brookhouse (Detroit, MI: Wayne State University Press, 2002), 387–95.

38 Bruce, *Bernard Herrmann*, 194.

39 The failure of Perkins to nab an Oscar nomination has become something of Hollywood lore; the actor went on to film three *Psycho* sequels (the fourth was made-for-TV), none of which involved Hitchcock. His sole nomination, for supporting actor, came in 1956 for the film *Friendly Persuasion*.

40 I do not mean to argue that Herrmann composed the scene intending to create these relations between pitch and dialogue. The music for this scene is not new material as it was originally composed for Herrmann's *Sinfonietta for Strings* (1935) (see Smith, *A Heart at Fire's Center*, 240). The mutations of the "madness" motive, however, and the emphasis on E-flat nevertheless inflect the narrative.

41 By using the term "silence," though, I intend to invoke a certain amount of suspicion, because at no moment in *Psycho* do we truly have complete silence.

Chapter 6

Pop Goes the Horror Score

Left Alone in *The Last House on the Left*

Joe Tompkins

Originally conceived by director Wes Craven and producer Sean Cunningham as nothing more than a pointed, low-budget experiment in bad taste, an "outrageous cinematic prank on a culture . . . reeling out of control in Vietnam,"[1] *The Last House on the Left* (1972) plays out like a modern-day Brothers Grimm fairy tale for the hippie generation—a piece of folklore spiked with bad LSD. Commencing in the idyllic backwoods of rural Connecticut, the movie tracks two teenage hippie girls as they giddily make their way from the country to the city on a quest to attend a rock concert in New York City's East Village. Looking to "score on some good grass," the girls stray from the beaten path, only to encounter a band of degenerate criminals who proceed to abduct, torture, rape, and eventually, murder them in their own backyard. Seeking refuge, the killers inadvertently wind up at the home of one of the dead girls' parents. After the parents discover what has happened to their daughter, they effectively carry out an elaborate but no less heinous revenge scenario. The film ends with each fugitive dead, and both parents bloodied and in shock.

Setting out to reveal "the dark underbelly of the Hollywood genre film,"[2] Craven's *Last House* breaks with a number of established horror film conventions—including conventional horror scoring techniques—in a deliberate effort to confront and agitate reified sensibilities. In particular, the film's unrepentant, intensely graphic depictions of torture and rape run directly in the face of traditional stylistic codes for representing screen violence. What's more, the film's modern-day setting, along with its focus on the middle-class family unit as a site of potential violence and aggression, deviates sharply from traditional horror cinema's preoccupation with purely exogenous evil and fantastic monsters. For this reason, a number of critics regard *Last House* as marking a turning point in the genre's evolution as a whole—a key index of the "postwar transition of the horror film from its classic to modern phases, when all too human threats replace gothic, otherworldly monsters, and graphic violence replaces suggested mayhem."[3]

Yet amid general discussions of modern horror's various formal and thematic transformations—as well as the particular ways *Last House* fits into this genre history[4]—scholars have largely neglected the issue of corresponding shifts in horror scoring practice. For example, *Last House* is one of the first modern horror films to rely extensively on contemporary pop music idioms as part of an original, purposefully composed score. While pop-oriented horror film scores began to emerge in Britain during the 1960s and 1970s with Amicus Productions and Hammer Studio films such as *Horror Hotel* (1963), *Lust for a Vampire* (1970), and *Dracula A.D.* (1972), these would typically consist of one or two songs added during post-production.[5] In these films, the incorporation of pop style (typically jazz or rock) arises mainly as an afterthought, part of a larger effort by these studios to update or "modernize" their output.[6] By contrast, *Last House* employs a mash-up of folk rock and country bluegrass as part of an original, non-diegetic score. In fact, when measured against a handful of dispersed instrumental cues and a few dissonant synthesizer effects, generic folk style tunes such as "Wait for the Rain" (aka "The Road Leads to Nowhere") and "Now You're All Alone" stand out as the film's principal music.[7] This relatively eccentric horror score is characteristic of Craven's innovative approach to the horror film in particular; but it also stands as a distinguishing film-musical hallmark within American horror cinema and is instantly recognizable to fans and filmmakers alike.[8]

Craven's use of music in *Last House* is perhaps all the more remarkable for the way the cues maintain conspicuous "audibility" throughout the film—that is, they largely proceed in a manner that is clearly noticeable and, oftentimes, glaringly detached from the dramatic action.[9] More than a mere stylistic flourish, the audibility of these songs performs two unique functions with respect to cinematic representation. First, because the folk rock cues are situated prominently in the audio-visual foreground, they maintain a kind of discursive/moral authority within the overall process of narration.[10] Structurally presiding over the events represented on the image track, the lyrics command attention and are endowed with the unusual capacity to comment on the action from a peripheral space, seemingly "outside" the story world. Like the voice-over in classical Hollywood cinema, the music "speaks from a position of superior knowledge:"[11] It is able to foresee events before they happen and articulate a cautionary moral wisdom that ultimately eludes each of the characters as they become ensnared in a harrowing cycle of murderous revenge.

Second, the obtrusive character of the music functions on a pragmatic level to unsettle standard modes of filmic reception. Unlike the traditional horror score, which typically aims to punctuate moments of fright with a few calculated shock effects, the barefaced audibility of the *Last House* cues—especially prominent during some of the film's more gruesome scenes[12]—serves to make us aware of our own voyeuristic involvement.

Forgoing the standardized musical devices (e.g. drones and ostinati, stingers, pitch raises, tone clusters) usually employed to generate (and release) tension in horror films, *Last House* abstains from the conventional practice of creating a "distinctive and enveloping 'sound architecture' or ambience" in which to immerse the audience.[13] Instead, the music complicates spectator identification by subverting the established codes that typically align audience sympathies and steer emotional engagement. The music's detached quality promotes a distancing, or alienating effect (comparable perhaps to Brecht's "epic" theater),[14] which disrupts and renders difficult the reception (and voyeuristic appeal) of screen violence. As a result, *Last House* denies audiences any comfortable or "easy" audio-viewing position from which to consume scenes of traumatic carnage and brutality.

It's Only a Movie . . .

Initially billed (albeit somewhat disingenuously) as a "retelling of Ingmar Bergman's Academy Award Winner *The Virgin Springs* (1960) in 1972 terms," *Last House* officially opened to a (presumably unsuspecting) suburban middle-class audience in Wethersfield, Connecticut on August 23, 1972.[15] The release inspired immediate public protest, prompting a dismayed contingent of audience members to storm out of the screening, where, without delay, a sizeable group organized and signed a petition in the parking lot as part of an effort to coerce the theater manager to discontinue the movie.[16] Later, a scathing editorial appeared in the local *Hartford Courant*, deploring the "horrible, sick film" for its "lingering gore, sadism and fetishism." Echoing these remarks, the *Boston Herald-Traveler* deemed *Last House* "an illustration of loathsomeness." And the *Pittsburg Press* called it "a cheap-jack of a movie with no discernible merit—but considerable tastelessness."[17] Eventually, the hoopla prompted an "open letter" response from Hallmark Releasing Corporation, the film's distributor, espousing the movie's "morally redeeming" quality and its "important social message" as regards the film's more "extreme" subject matter. In a sly bit of "classic exploitation movie hucksterism,"[18] a revised version of the Hallmark letter would later appear as a disclaimer at the top of one of the film's banner ads, along with the admonition: "To avoid fainting, keep repeating, it's only a movie . . . only a movie. . ."

Indeed, the film's undeniable shock value owes much to its unrelenting depictions of brutal violence and "lingering gore," just as the continued hostility directed towards the film might be traced back to its formal and stylistic "tastelessness." A number of scholars have suggested as much, pointing to the film's refusal to sanitize violence through classical realist standards as a way of explaining, at least partially, the tremendous public outcry and vehement calls for censorship surrounding the film's release. Adam Lowenstein, for example, singles out the film's "gritty, unadorned newsreel style" as part of an overall formal and thematic attempt to "demythologize abstracted Hollywood-style violence."[19] Accentuating "the continuity between depictions of brutality and the ordinariness of everyday life," the film's pseudo-documentary visual aesthetic effectively breaks with mainstream media representations of social violence, and thus carries the potential to "penetrate viewer defenses that tend to anesthetize historical trauma."[20]

Lowenstein's comments echo Craven's own description of *Last House* as a deliberate attempt to "show things the way they really are" by subverting the dominant cinematic codes for representing screen violence. Craven acknowledges a deeper political commitment behind the film's documentary look and feel, one aimed at exposing the grim realities and national traumas associated with the Vietnam War:

> *Last House* was very much a product of its era. It was a time when all the rules were thrown out the window, when everybody was trying to break the hold of censorship. The Vietnam War was going on, and the most powerful footage that we saw was in the actual documentary films of the war. There was a great amount of feeling that, "The worst of it is being censored, so let's try to get our hands on what's *really* going on over there."[21]

Especially significant here is the way Craven's overriding desire to cut through the false appearances of US military propaganda and mainstream news coverage[22] is persistently articulated in terms of breaking with Hollywood narrative style:

> In *Last House*, we set out to show violence the way we thought it really was, and to show the dark underbelly of the Hollywood genre film. We consciously took all the B movie conventions and stood them on their heads . . . so that just when you thought the shot would cut away, it didn't. Someone gets stabbed, but then they back up and start crawling . . . *Last House* did not play by the rules that had been established for handling violence, where the people who did violence were always bad, and if a good guy did it to the bad guy, it was very clean and quick . . . That was the sort of attitude that America had gone into Vietnam with . . . that *they* were the bad guys and we'd go in like *Gunsmoke*, face 'em down, and bang, they'd be dead. The fact of the matter was that the war involved horrendous killings piled upon killings.[23]

The film's refusal to treat violence in a clear-cut manner—according to the ideological binaries of good and evil, right and wrong, innocent and culpable—is perhaps most evident in the juxtaposition of the opening and final sequences. The opening sequence presents audiences with a prosaic representation of domestic bliss, complete with chirpy sitcom music and a quaint living room scene involving the Collingwood family and their daughter, Mari, on the morning of her seventeenth birthday. As father John Collingwood reads the newspaper, mother Estelle asks her husband, "What's new in the outside world?" John breezily responds, "Same old stuff, murder and mayhem. What's for dinner tonight?" Conversely, the film's final sequence returns us to the Collingwood home, but under quite different circumstances. Having just brutally raped and murdered young Mari and her friend Phyllis, the Stillo gang (Krug, Weasel, Junior, and Sadie) unwittingly seek asylum with Mari's parents at their residence, where they will eventually receive their grisly comeuppance. Culminating with the lavishly gruesome revenge murders of each Stillo gang member, and the concomitant breakdown of the picturesque Collingwood family facade, the film's looping narrative arc offers us a renewed take on the otherwise "normal" character of the Collingwood home. Refracting the latter through the sordid lens of the "outside world," the final act brings the "murder and mayhem" full circle, drawing a correlation between "outside" and "inside," monstrous and normal, vulnerable and secure.[24]

The Baddies' Theme

The film's "refusal to play by the rules that had been established for handling violence" also extends to the music, which plays a key role in subverting the conventional narrative formulas and ideological binaries that typically align audience sympathies. Deviating sharply from the stylistic codes that underpin most horror film scores, the music in *Last House* goes a long way in generating the kind of shock and distress otherwise attributed solely to the film's visual aspects. For one, the music largely foregoes the kind of modernist avant-garde techniques that have come to characterize modern horror scoring practice.[25] Instead, *Last House* relies predominantly on a host of popular music styles that often sound at odds with the more disturbing images shown on the screen. The incongruity is especially striking when considering the soft acoustic guitar melodies and compact vocal harmonies that suffuse original folk rock songs such as "Wait For the Rain" and "Now You're All Alone." These songs appear reluctant to support or "collaborate" with the visuals and resist the traditional functions of heightening a dramatic mood or atmosphere, or expressing through musical parallel the perceived psychological states of a particular character or group of characters. Rather, the music cues appear to be, at times, formally independent of the images, positioned at the forefront of the film's aural *mise-en-bande*, where they frequently call attention to themselves in order to comment on the narrative action.

Composer David Hess—who also made his acting debut playing the lead villain Krug Stillo—deliberately approached *Last House* with the intention of challenging conventional Hollywood scoring techniques. A former student at New York's Julliard School of Music, Hess worked for a number of years as a professional songwriter and folk rock singer prior to *Last House*.[26] Teaming up with fellow New York area folk rock artist Steve Chapin to arrange and produce the soundtrack for the film, Hess wrote the bulk of the score on set during film production in close collaboration with Craven and producer Sean Cunningham.[27] While claiming this provided him with an exceptional degree of insight into the production process, Hess also admits to drawing inspiration less from the characters and events depicted in the movie and more from his close involvement with cast and crew:

> I feel it's important to be on the set as a composer, because when you're there and you see what's happening . . . you write for the people you're involved with, as opposed to writing for the characters you see on a screen.[28]

Accordingly, Hess's score for *Last House* regularly contradicts the traditional notion that music should serve a subordinate role with respect to the emotional climate and dramatic dictates of the narrative. Rather, the music frequently appears to challenge, or even contradict, the perceived "meaning" of on-screen narrative events, thereby supporting Hess's more general assertion that "music in movies should be a counterpoint to whatever is going on up on the screen."[29]

One might consider here the upbeat, happy-go-lucky "Baddies' Theme" that accompanies Krug and Co. during their escape to the countryside.[30] The entire scene contains little (intelligible) dialogue and is sparse in sound effects; it plays out more like a music video. Having kidnapped Mari and Phyllis, the Stillos attempt a getaway with the two girls bound and gagged in the trunk of their car. As they hightail it out of town, a clunky bit of chase music—the "Baddies' Theme"—materializes over the soundtrack. The music features a range of peculiar instruments (banjo, piano, kazoo), which all sound jarringly out of place. The whimsical melody appears at once inappropriately cheerful and oblivious to the unfortunate circumstances that plague the two hapless girls. For his part, Hess claims "the contrast was absolutely intentional," and that the offbeat tenor of the "Baddies" song remains "consistent with the movie" insofar as "there are so many things about the film that are aberrant."[31]

Yet, we might concretize Hess's statement about the "aberrant" aspects of the "Baddies' Theme" by setting it against the larger backdrop of pop culture and social history. The use of bluegrass-style banjo music in a 1970s low-budget horror film, for example, will inevitably bring with it a host of cultural meanings, values, and associations that cannot be easily mapped onto the stylistic and ideological norms of the horror genre.[32] Karen Linn's intricate cultural history of banjo music is quite helpful in this regard.[33] In her book, *That Half-Barbaric Twang: The Banjo in American Popular Culture*, Linn traces the instrument's cultural genealogy in the US, from its emergence in African American folk spirituals, as well as its popularization by black minstrel performers during the mid-nineteenth century, to its contemporary status as a signifier of Southern white rural culture. Commenting in particular on the familiar pop culture image of the banjo as an authentic "Appalachian folk artifact,"[34] Linn draws a connection between the instrument's Appalachian pedigree and its association with a uniquely "antimodern," populist value system.[35] Indeed, this association remains a staple of American popular culture and, in fact, is a recurrent feature in a number of screen representations depicting "hillbilly" culture appearing at or around the same time as *Last House* (the iconic "dueling banjos" sequence at the beginning of John Boorman's *Deliverance* [1972] being perhaps the most indelible example).[36] The prominence of banjo music in films such as Arthur Penn's 1967 *Bonnie and Clyde* ("Foggy Mountain Breakdown"), for instance, effectively shores up the conception of the banjo as an "antimodern machine," playing off the instrument's nostalgic, mythological connotations—its connection to "Appalachian otherness"[37]—as a means of criticizing the encroachment of big business on modern American society.

In this context, the "Baddies' Theme" in *Last House* might be read as a direct reference to the bluegrass-style chase cues made famous by Penn's film a few years prior.[38] However, where the latter draws a special connection between the "down-home" character of the music and the populist attitudes of the film's titular outlaw heroes, *Last House* deploys this style of music somewhat ironically (if a bit lightheartedly), confusing matters of heroism and violence by lending its irredeemable "baddies" their own upbeat, tuneful theme song. The glib lyrics are especially noteworthy in this regard for the way they reinforce a sense of comedic absurdity, seeming to poke fun at the whole situation: "Weasel and Junior, Sadie and Krug/Out for the day with the Collingwood brood/Out for the day, for some fresh air and sun/Let's have some fun with those two lovely children and off 'em as soon as we're done." Given the cavalier nature of the music, it seems plausible to interpret the "Baddies' Theme" as an expression of the more or less whimsical attitude of the Stillos themselves.

However, as Linn suggests, bluegrass/banjo music persists as a signifier of cultural otherness, and in this sense the "Baddies' Theme" can also be understood as an exaggerated (if slightly perverse) variation of the typical horror scoring practice of "othering" through musical sound. Such is the function of "dueling banjos" in Boorman's film, which, as Lowenstein points out, shares a number of thematic parallels with *Last House*. Both films, for example, utilize a rape-revenge plot structure to engage issues of cultural conflict and class difference, and both rely on an ideological binary structure that hinges on oppositions of center/margin, city/country, and civilized/savage. Lowenstein notes how *Deliverance* ambivalently mobilizes these ideological binary structures by rendering "Appalachian otherness" at once "idyllic" ("dueling banjos") and "horrific" ("squeal like a pig"), only to eventually and unequivocally demonize the local *country* "savages" against the more "civilized" *city* businessmen.[39] The end result is a straightforward, maligning treatment of "Appalachian otherness" that does nothing to redeem an economically dispossessed community of "mountain men," while making it virtually impossible to identify with their alien "redneck" culture. By contrast, *Last House* complicates this process of identification (or anti-identification) through its self-knowing, incongruous deployment of bluegrass/banjo music. During the escape sequence, as the gang takes flight *from* the city and *to* the country, the conventional city-country dyad is called into question (or at least temporarily suspended); here it is the ostensible "baddies" that are endowed with the privileged capacity to move in between and across otherwise impenetrable geographic/narrative boundaries. Hence, it is the Stillos that appear to defy "convenient categorization as either 'country' or 'city' forces."[40] Nevertheless, their attempt to flee the city and get "out of the state" signals a shift in the ideological terrain—a movement from a state of civility and law and order to a realm of anarchic chaos. The breakdown is at once announced and parodied with the onset of the shambling *country* bluegrass music cues.

As Carol J. Clover has suggested, the city/country dyad, which lies at the center of countless horror film narratives, is never innocent; rather, it is an ideological construction that addresses, indirectly, more thorny questions of class affluence and economic guilt:

> To be in the country . . . is not only to confront the poverty that one may have colluded in creating and maintaining; it is to confront poverty without the protection of the judicial system and its coercive apparatus—to face the victims of one's class comforts without recourse to the police. It is no surprise that the site of city/country horror is always just inches beyond the grasp of the law's long arm . . . "out there where no one can hear you scream."[41]

In *Last House*, this conflict is aggravatingly flaunted by the comic presence of an incompetent local sheriff and his equally inept deputy sidekick. The hapless duo repeatedly proves woefully inadequate to the task of tracking down the kidnappers; if anything, they function more on the level of sideshow clowns than as would-be narrative heroes.[42] Appropriately enough, their bungling attempts are more than once accompanied by a clumsy instrumental rendition of the "Baddies' Theme." Furthermore, these brief comic asides are set in sharp narrative contrast to the harrowing scenes depicting Mari's torture and rape at the hands of the Stillos. The juxtaposition directly illustrates the ideological conflict described by Clover, while the gawky music cues, first heard during the Stillos' getaway, underscore the ineptitude of the local (backwoods) law enforcement. In other words, the music aurally links the criminals and the cops, and in doing so makes explicit the underlying connection between an ineffective "coercive apparatus" and a seedier underclass element that might otherwise be kept comfortably at (law's) arm's length.

Additionally, through this crisscrossing of law and order, the "Baddies' Theme" functions to expose (and perhaps even undermine) the fundamental contradiction that underwrites the city/country, civilized/savage, center/margin dichotomy. Because it encodes ideological associations of deviancy and otherness, the music indeed signifies a "threat." But the threat embodied by these "aberrant" music cues is less that of other cultures per se (à la "Appalachian otherness" in *Deliverance*), and more that of an immanent, class-specific danger—a peculiar condition of instability, disorder, and "statelessness" lurking just beyond the bounds of (sub)urban, middle-class comfort.[43] Put differently, while the music signals the kind of topsy-turvy world described by Clover, the film concretizes our degenerate slide into the "wilderness" by tracking the characters as they cross this quasi-mythic threshold to a place where civilization's rules (and class-based appurtenances) no longer apply. In *Last House*, the dialectical contradictions of bourgeois culture return with a vengeance, as it is no longer "out there," on the edge of middle-class luxury "where no one can hear you scream." On the contrary, the nightmare now literally plays out in one's own backyard.

Now You're All Alone

Just as the "Baddies' Theme" taps "urbanoia" anxieties in order to flout the insular, class-based dynamics of horror spectatorship, it also works to unseat traditional, voyeuristic engagements with screen violence. Drawing a sharp (if ironic) contrast with the "unadorned newsreel style" of the images, the music effectively heightens (rather than diminishes) our sense of being both textually and morally decentered. In its outward detachment, the "Baddies' Theme" typifies Hess's contrapuntal approach to film scoring by refusing to resolutely demonize the Stillos through a conventional arrangement of "monstrous" music cues, thus operating in a way that confounds processes of audience (anti)identification. Again, Craven makes the point that the "aberrant" qualities of the soundtrack directly correspond with a certain blasé attitude toward the atrocities in Vietnam:

With that particular song ["Baddies' Theme"], I guess we wanted to create a bizarre juxtaposition between the carnival raucousness of the movie and the profoundly horrific and sad side of it . . . The contrast between that song and the characters was sort of like showing an image of a village getting napalmed and then saying, "Fuck 'em if they can't take a joke" . . . and that type of humor was very specific to the era of the early '70s, and, I think, terribly cynical.[44]

More than merely reiterate the allegorical connection to the historical traumas of Vietnam, however, Craven's remark implicitly raises the question of voyeuristically consuming violence at a comfortable distance. Because the music takes a highly ironic stance with respect to images of violence and brutality, it poses a challenge to ideas about the film's unique claim to realism, including Craven's own assertion that *Last House* simply "shows violence the way it really is." Instead, songs such as the "Baddies' Theme" highlight our own involvement as spectators, exposing and amplifying the contradiction between the profoundly horrific nature of rape and murder and the conventional "rules for handling," or mediating, such traumatic events. Consequently, *Last House* creates a space for audiences to become self-aware of their own complicity, as well as the "terribly cynical" attitudes that underpin the routine consumption of spectacularized violence.

Perhaps the most upsetting audio-visual incongruities occur during the protracted torture scenes in the woods, where the sedate and charming sounds of Hess's folk ballad "Now You're All Alone" regularly saturate the soundtrack. Sounding woefully out of sync with the graphic images on screen, the music roundly denies audiences the opportunity for any kind of (unproblematic) emotional identification by refusing to steer us in a unilateral way toward a sympathetic affinity with any one particular character. Rather, the music seems to do quite the opposite, instantiating what Michel Chion might call an "anempathetic" relationship to the situation depicted.[45] While most horror film scores dutifully adhere (through rhythm, tone, phrasing, timbre) to the perceived feelings of the characters—most often the emotional state of a victim caught in tumultuous throes of fright, shock, anxiety, or pain—the cues in *Last House* mainly deviate from the cinematic-cultural codes typically relied upon for (musically) representing cinematic horror. Successfully carving out an affective space for us to inhabit as spectators, traditional horror music does more than simply register the emotional climate of a particular scene; it also encourages our identification with the appropriately conveyed—that is to say, horrified—emotional response, so that audiences are left with the resounding impression of being able to feel exactly what the characters are feeling. Where conventional horror film music is especially remarkable, then, is in its ability to elicit a direct, or "empathetic," emotional response in the spectator. Conversely, anempathetic music refuses such a response, functioning instead to "exhibit a conspicuous indifference to the situation" at hand.[46]

Building off Chion, Stan Link has outlined the features of anempathetic music cues with respect to cinematic representations of psychopathology. Link contrasts the highly affective strategies of "traditional musical horror," wherein spectators become emotionally wedded to the position of the victim through techniques of musical expressionism, with the more eccentric approach characterized by "musical anempathy."[47] Here, instead of being afforded the impression of an emotional bond with on-screen victims, for example, musical anempathy disallows spectators the ability "to know" and experience their suffering through affective identification. Because it "disagrees with what we take to be either the victim's reaction or the spectator's 'appropriate' empathy with the victim's plight,"[48] musical anempathy closes off the possibility for emotional "intimacy," for sharing the "emotional perspective" of the victim—a path of identification commonly afforded by traditional horror scoring. Moreover, the music's apparent refusal to directly express emotional trauma through sonic parallel "engenders a distancing that may become expressively particular."[49] The effect is one of "emotional confusion," a kind of cine-musical disorientation that carries the potential to trigger awareness within the spectator of film music's overall capacity for affective manipulation.

While Mari and Phyllis are repeatedly tormented, Hess's chorus-like commentary refuses to arrest viewer emotions with the events on the screen. The result is music that "highlights our expectations by thwarting or negating them."[50] By upending a deeply ingrained and culturally over-determined process of hearing horror films, the cues effectively highlight the representational processes involved in discursively constructing screen violence. At the same time, they continue to have a deep impact on spectatorship. Despite their utter refusal to steer our emotional involvement, the music cues do not necessarily fall short of "moving" audiences; rather, they obstinately deny moving us in the "right" way—channeling our sympathies toward the "right" character, or the "right" feeling, or the "right" emotional/moral sense.[51] In other words, Hess's music forecloses the possibility for any kind of unproblematic or unilateral viewer identification. Denying audiences the "music-affective"[52] standpoint of the characters, the song cues merely reiterate the tragic nature of the events from a detached, anempathetic position of mild concern. As Mari and Phyllis are forced to strip naked and "make it with each other," Hess's soft-spoken lyrics ("Now you're all alone/Feeling the world close in on you/And you're looking for someone to hold your hand, someone who will understand . . . Now you're all alone") gingerly coax us through the torment, articulating a kind of cynical regret that reflects dually the position of the characters *and* the position of the spectator. Both Wood[53] and Lowenstein[54] have argued that the scene immediately following Mari's rape effectively conveys a brief, sympathetic moment of remorse and self-regret on the part of the Stillos. Realizing the true horror of their actions, the characters stand over Mari's naked body, exchanging glances and appearing, at least temporarily, alienated and despondent ("Now You're All Alone"). According to Craven, the scene was intended as an especially poignant moment of rupture within the film:

> The real essence of the picture was that moment when the characters went so far that they horrified themselves . . . where they became revulsed and couldn't wait to try to clean up. It was kind of the telling point of the whole story, when everything switched . . . the bad guys became penitent and almost unsure of themselves, while the parents later became completely ruthless.[55]

In this sense, the anempathetic cues provided by Hess's score might be said to correspond with the alienated position of the Stillos, while also maintaining the kind of "clear divisions" between audience, victim, and villain described by Link.[56] Like the Stillos, all we can do at this point is look on haplessly. Bereft of any kind of music-affective contact, our emotional involvement is momentarily suspended and we are forced to assume a rather discomfiting position of isolated, anempathetic confinement.

Accordingly, what is most unsettling about the music in these scenes is the way it refuses to "suture" the audio-visual gap underlying (horror) film spectatorship. Whereas most traditional horror films invite us to become immersed within the diegetic reality of on-screen monsters and their victims, the music in *Last House* does the opposite; it foregrounds the impossibility of total enclosure and instead highlights the fundamental split that, in effect, distances the spectator and the screen image. As Link suggests:

> Perhaps anempathy's most disturbing subversion . . . lies less in ironizing graphic violence than in undermining or mocking the magical thinking that finds redemptive powers in a spectator's sympathy. Without a partner in suffering—without intimacy—the prey is left truly alone.[57]

Likewise, we might say that musical anempathy in *Last House* tarries at the border of the screen world (the "real" site of violence), making apparent the remote character of cinematic reception and forcing audiences to endure the experience of screen violence without the cathartic illusion of musical-emotional intimacy. In effect, the music conditions a self-reflexive mode of horror spectatorship, which roundly denies viewers both the experience of empathic absorption and the corresponding opportunity to disown screen violence as something perfunctorily experienced by audiences and characters alike. Rather, screen violence is made indigestible by conspicuously doing away with the cultural-musical codes typically deployed to aurally represent horrific, traumatic events. Consequently, any attempt we might make as spectators to fall back on the "magical thinking" of immediate emotional identification is confounded by the soundtrack, which mercilessly strips away our customary aural security blankets. In the end, we are left with nothing more than to repeat the hollow mantra, "it's only a movie . . . only a movie."

Notes

1 David A. Szulkin, Wes Craven's "Last House on the Left": The Making of a Cult Classic (Guildford: FAB Press, 2000), 16. Hands down, the most informative work to date on Last House is Szulkin's book, to which this essay owes a great deal.
2 Szulkin, Wes Craven's "Last House on the Left," 15.
3 Adam Lowenstein, Shocking Representation: Historical Trauma, National Cinema, and the Modern Horror Film (New York: Columbia University Press, 2005), 7.
4 See, for example: Robin Wood, Hollywood From Vietnam to Reagan . . . And Beyond (New York: Columbia University Press, 2003), 63–119; Tony Williams, Hearths of Darkness: The Family in the American Horror Film (London: Fairleigh Dickinson University Press, 1996), 137–41; Adam Lowenstein, "Only a Movie: Specters of Vietnam in Wes Craven's Last House on the Left," in Lowenstein, Shocking Representation, 111–43.
5 One might also include here Ennio Morricone's early work for Dario Argento in L'Uccello dalle piume di cristallo (aka The Bird with the Crystal Plumage, 1970) and Il Gatto a nove code (aka The Cat o' Nine Tails, 1971).
6 K. J. Donnelly, The Spectre of Sound: Music in Film and Television (London: BFI Publishing, 2005), 101.
7 Szulkin's book contains original transcripts of both the "Baddies' Theme" and "Wait for the Rain" as well as a copy of the original music cue sheet for the film, which served as my primary source for all song/cue titles.
8 Although scholars typically pay no more than passing reference to the Last House soundtrack, fans and filmmakers have proven to be more astute in their assessment of the music's efficacy as horror film music. Take, for example, Eli Roth's redeployment of "The Road Leads to Nowhere" in the opening minutes of his 2002 film Cabin Fever, or David DeFalco's blatant Last House rip-off, Chaos (2005). In both cases, music lifted from Hess's original score is recycled as both audio homage and narrative film music.
9 Claudia Gorbman cites "inaudibility"—or the imperative to minimize any potentially disruptive elements in the overall subordination of film music to the emotional and dramatic dictates of the narrative—as one of the definitive principles of Hollywood film scoring practice. See Claudia Gorbman, Unheard Melodies (Bloomington, IN: Indiana University Press, 1987).
10 James Buhler and David Neumeyer have suggested elsewhere that the "disembodied" character of non-diegetic film music carries an inherently transcendent "moral force." See "Film Music and Narrative: A Moral Dilemma," Journal of the American Musicological Society 47, 2 (Summer 1994): 377–81.

11 Kaja Silverman has demonstrated the discursive authority granted to the (typically male) voice-over in classical Hollywood cinema: the voice-over "seems separated from the fiction by an absolute partition;" it becomes "a voice on high . . . a voice which speaks from a position of superior knowledge, and which superimposes itself 'on top' of the diegesis." See Kaja Silverman, *The Acoustic Mirror: The Female Voice in Psychoanalysis and Cinema* (Bloomington, IN: Indiana University Press, 1988), 48.

12 Alongside the more prominent folk rock songs, occasional synthesizer effects and experimental cues accompany the torture sequences. During the scene where Phyllis escapes her captors and is chased through the woods, for example, composers David Hess and Steve Chapin relied on percussion instruments—beating xylophone mallets on a leather chair—to simulate a heartbeat sound (Szulkin, *Wes Craven's "Last House on the Left,"* 122–3).

13 Donnelly, *The Spectre of Sound*, 93.

14 Dana Polan, "A Brechtian Cinema? Towards a Politics of Self-Reflexive Film," in *Movies and Methods: Volume II*, edited by Bill Nichols (Berkeley, CA: University of California Press, 1985), 661–72.

15 Lowenstein, *Shocking Representation*, 139.

16 Both Lowenstein (*Shocking Representation*, 139) and Szulkin (*Wes Craven's "Last House on the Left"*, 134–5) explain the curious choice of suburban Wethersfield, Connecticut by pointing to the corporate ties linking the film's distributor (Hallmark Corporation) and Paris Cinema movie theater where the film was initially screened. One might also infer the shrewd marketing tactics motivating the debut of a low-budget, exploitation horror film to a crowd of unwary middle-class viewers—an explosive recipe guaranteed to incite controversy and uproar (if not a jolt of free publicity).

17 Szulkin, *Wes Craven's "Last House on the Left,"* 136–9.

18 Ibid., 135.

19 Lowenstein, *Shocking Representation*, 118, 120.

20 Ibid., 118, 120.

21 Szulkin, *Wes Craven's "Last House on the Left,"* 15.

22 Referencing Daniel C. Halin, Lowenstein counters the historically revisionist notion that mainstream TV news coverage provided an extraordinarily graphic and "uncensored" account of the war:

> Even in the later years of the war, "the Nixon administration retained a good deal of power to 'manage' the news" and "journalists continued to be patriots in the sense that they portrayed the Americans as the 'good guys' in Vietnam." As a result, "the public came to see the war as a 'mistake' or 'tragedy,' rather than the crime the more radical opposition believed it to be.' Television's contribution toward containing public disillusionment with the war can be attributed partly to . . . the relative lack of aired footage depicting actual combat or casualties, "despite the emphasis on military action," and the "almost perfectly one-dimensional image of the North Vietnamese and Vietcong as cruel, ruthless, and fanatical." (Lowenstein, *Shocking Representation*, 129).

23 Szulkin, *Wes Craven's "Last House on the Left,"* 15.

24 The film's refusal to isolate violence as an extraordinary event, situating it instead against the humdrum backdrop of quotidian existence, has prompted a number of critics to interpret *Last House* for its radical sociopolitical meanings. Most notable here is Robin Wood, who argues that *Last House* stands as one among a cluster of 1970s American horror films to incisively

link issues of violence to the patriarchal bourgeois family in a way that highlights the ambiguous relation between perceived normality and dreadful monstrosity (Wood, *Hollywood From Vietnam to Reagan*, 108–15).

25 Although modernist-derived horror scoring techniques appear as early as the 1930s, they do not become a staple feature of horror cinema until the 1950s, when they are frequently used to signify the "alien" quality of a wide swath of fantastic monsters that appear across a host of low-budget, B-grade sci-fi/horror movies. From there, the horror-modernist association continues well into the 1970s and 1980s, where it acquires an implicit seal of approval in the scores for a host of more prestigious, mainstream Hollywood horror movies, including *The Exorcist* (William Friedkin, 1973), *The Omen* (Richard Donner, 1976), and *The Shining* (Stanley Kubrick, 1980).

26 Szulkin, *Wes Craven's "Last House on the Left,"* 118.

27 Ibid., 119–21.

28 Ibid., 119.

29 Ibid., 121.

30 The "Baddies' Theme" also accompanies the film's end credit montage sequence.

31 Szulkin, *Wes Craven's "Last House on the Left,"* 121.

32 I credit Neil Lerner for pushing me to consider this relationship in closer detail, particularly as regards the cultural history of the banjo in the US.

33 Karen Linn, *That Half-Barbaric Twang: The Banjo in American Popular Culture* (Urbana, IL: University of Illinois Press, 1994).

34 Ibid., 117.

35 These "antimodern values" include: a "distrust of luxury and consumer desires . . . [a suspicion of] the evils of the industrial society, the virtue of a spartan simple life, [and] the desire for an egalitarian social structure" (Linn, *That Half-Barbaric Twang*, 123). Linn goes on to point out that such "antimodernist sentiments," first articulated to Appalachian life in the late nineteenth century as part of a larger conservative critique of industrial society, would later be embraced and celebrated by various "admirers of Appalachian otherness" in the late twentieth century, including those in the folk revivalist movement of the 1950s and 1960s (123–4).

36 One might also include here such "small screen" examples as *The Andy Griffith Show*, *The Beverly Hillbillies*, and *Hee Haw*.

37 Linn, *That Half-Barbaric Twang*, 123.

38 Szulkin, *Wes Craven's "Last House on the Left,"* 120.

39 Lowenstein, *Shocking Representation*, 133.

40 Ibid., 133.

41 Carol J. Clover, *Men, Women, and Chainsaws: Gender in the Modern Horror Film* (Princeton, NJ: Princeton University Press, 1992), 132.

42 For example, one scene follows their ham-fisted attempts to hitch a ride from a chicken farmer after their cruiser has run out of gas, making for an odd moment of cheap slapstick as the sheriff and deputy are thrown from the top of the farmer's pick-up.

43 Clover describes the figurative city-country encounter, which distinguishes what she calls the "urbanoia" (or "city revenge") film, in precisely these terms:

> The collision between country and city is also a collision between a state mentality (in which citizens can submit their grievances to the executive function) and statelessness (in which citizens rely on vigilantism) . . . What the city limits mark, in horror, is the boundary between state and no-state. (Clover, *Men, Women, and Chainsaws*, 132–3).

44 Szulkin, *Wes Craven's "Last House on the Left,"* 120
45 Michel Chion, *Audio-Vision: Sound On Screen,* translated by Claudia Gorbman (New York: Columbia University Press, 1994), 9.
46 Ibid., 8.
47 Stan Link, "Sympathy with the Devil? Music of the Psycho Post-*Psycho,*" *Screen* 45, 1 (Spring 2004).
48 Ibid., 20.
49 Ibid., 7.
50 Ibid., 7.
51 As Kay Dickinson points out, the traditional rules of horror scoring embody the "appropriate" strategies not only for musically representing cinematic horror but also for charting an "appropriate" viewer response. Accordingly, they reinforce a shared cultural common sense for what constitutes "both moral and musical right and wrong." See her essay, "Troubling Synthesis: The Horrific Sights and Incompatible Sounds of Video Nasties," in *Sleaze Artists: Cinema at the Margins of Taste Style and Politics,* edited by Jeffrey Sconce (Durham, NC: Duke University Press, 2007), 176.
52 Link, "Sympathy with the Devil?," 3.
53 Wood, *Hollywood From Vietnam to Reagan,* 112–13.
54 Lowenstein, *Shocking Representation,* 120–1.
55 Szulkin, *Wes Craven's "Last House on the Left,"* 81.
56 Link, "Sympathy with the Devil?," 7.
57 Ibid., 20.

Chapter 7

Ramblin' Men and Piano Men

Crises of Music and Masculinity in *The Exorcist*

Claire Sisco King

New York Times film critic Vincent Canby's accusation that *The Exorcist* (William Friedkin, 1973) created a "new low for grotesque special effects" has been echoed by most critical responses to the film, with many crediting (or blaming) it for inaugurating a new breed of gross-out horror.[1] In contrast to these perceptions of the film, Friedkin was reportedly "determined not to make a horror film."[2] Instead, he describes the film as trafficking in realism, explaining, "it's a realistic story about inexplicable things, and it's all going to take place in cold light, with ordinary people, on ordinary streets."[3]

Friedkin cites his desire to make the film realistically and in "documentary fashion" as motivating the film's minimal use of music.[4] With no complete film score, the unconventional soundtrack for *The Exorcist* consists primarily of sound effects and the occasional use of previously composed pieces, including most famously Mike Oldfield's "Tubular Bells."[5] Instead of music that was "transforming" or designed to "lead" audiences, Friedkin sought "music that would operate as textures," which were "almost imperceptible, sometimes not even heard" and in direct contrast to those spectacular visual effects to which Canby so vehemently objected.[6]

Most discussions of the music in *The Exorcist* focus on the aesthetic implications of Friedkin's unconventional approach to sound and emphasis on silence. For instance, David Bordwell considers the film's music in relation to artistic merit and generic reputation, arguing that *The Exorcist* "elevated itself" by making use of a "disquieting music track" and lent "greater respectability" to the horror genre by deploying "striking special effects" in conjunction with "a score culled from experimental music."[7] Likewise, *Film Score Monthly* editors Jeff Bond and Lukas Kendall observe, "The disconnected nature of the avant garde pieces Friedkin eventually used . . . kept audiences off-guard and convinced that they were watching less a hoary Hollywood construct than a chilling glimpse at something that could actually happen."[8]

Considerations of Friedkin's musical stylistics also detail the production difficulties the director faced, and perhaps facilitated—namely, battles with musicians invited to work on the project, including Bernard Herrmann and Lalo Schifrin.[9] What remains to be discussed are the cultural and ideological implications of music within *The Exorcist*. This essay aims to address this lacuna, taking seriously Anahid Kassabian's contention that film music "should be subjected to various semiotic and cultural studies methods," including cultural and ideological criticism.[10]

Although music in *The Exorcist* is rare, its use frequently speaks volumes about the film's ideological preoccupations. Music within the film reveals traces of historically specific anxieties about the state of American masculinity, which the film constructs as in crisis. Discomfiture about the vulnerability of masculinity's master narratives, which the narrative struggles to disavow through reliance on the logic of sacrificial heroism, becomes visible (or, more precisely, audible) in the film's musical moments. Specifically, music might be understood as giving voice to cultural anxieties that *The Exorcist*, in large part, labors to silence.

Behind the Music

Once released, *The Exorcist* was unequivocally successful. The top grossing film of the year, it became Warner Bros.'s most profitable film at the time and garnered ten Oscar nominations and two wins. Nonetheless, histories of the film describe the production process as anything but triumphant, with problems ranging from battles between Friedkin and author William Peter Blatty to what has been described as the film's "curse" based on a number of accidents and deaths affecting the cast and crew.[11] Also central among these problems were Friedkin's crusades to create or find music for the film.

Reportedly, Friedkin initially sought a soundtrack with no music, only "demonic sounds" to be recorded by sound technician Ken Nordine.[12] When this initial plan foundered, Friedkin approached Bernard Herrmann. Friedkin's collaborations with Herrmann are typically described as heated, if not hostile, leading him, instead, to commission a score from Latin-influenced jazz musician Lalo Schifrin.[13] Having composed a variety of scores for successful films—including *Cool Hand Luke* (Stuart Rosenberg, 1967) and *Dirty Harry* (Don Siegel, 1971)—and the popular television series *Mission: Impossible* (1966–73), Schifrin was a "more popular choice with the studio [Warner Bros.] than the mercurial Herrmann."[14] But, most histories construct this collaboration as no less fraught than Friedkin's earlier dealings with Herrmann.

Friedkin claims to have asked Schifrin for a score that did not "sound like music" but was "more tonal and moody . . . Nothing you can put your finger on. Almost monolithic and sterile."[15] However, the partial score Friedkin received from Schifrin did not meet his expectations, leading the director to throw a reel of Schifrin's recordings out a studio window,[16] and this famous end to Schifrin's score oddly mirrors the end of *The Exorcist*'s protagonist, Father Karras, who fatally propels himself out of a second-story window. As Friedkin explained to *Film Score Monthly*, "I never planned to put music in any of the big moments. And Lalo only wanted the big moments."[17] As a result, Schifrin's score was rejected, remaining in the possession of Warner Bros. for years until released as a limited-edition CD alongside the "Twenty-Fifth Anniversary Edition" DVD of *The Exorcist* in 1998.

In turn, Friedkin used an assortment of sources for music and sound in the film, maintaining his minimalist approach and focus on silence. Jack Nitzsche created some musical transitions and bridges, resulting in approximately 193 seconds of music. For instance, the opening sequence features a compilation of sound effects recorded by Nitzsche, "Crystal Glass and Voices," and music composed by Krzysztof Penderecki.[18] Friedkin also instructed dubbing mixer Buzz Knudson not to add any "modulation on the tracks," asking instead for "dead silence" that would stress "contrast" and be in "direct contradiction" with the film's visuals.[19]

Additionally, Friedkin employed David Borden, minimalist composer and founder of the Mother Mallard's Portable Masterpiece Company, to compose two pieces for the film, "Study No. 1" and "Study No. 2," and used several previously recorded pieces, including "Tubular Bells" and the popular Allman Brothers' song, "Ramblin' Man," written by Richard Betts.[20] As Knudson explains in interviews about *The Exorcist*, "The sound of that film was basically the weird, musical noise effects that Jack Nietsche [sic] was making in his studio up in San Francisco, and what we picked up down at the local record store."[21]

The choice to reject Schifrin's score before mixing was complete and to abandon a composed score for a compiled one was, not surprisingly, controversial. As Bond explains, *The Exorcist* often elicits strong reactions from "film music buffs," marking Schifrin's rejected score as something of a "legendary" fetish object akin to Alex North's famously discarded score for *2001: A Space Odyssey* (Stanley Kubrick, 1968). But, interestingly, many musical histories of *The Exorcist*, while acknowledging Schifrin's mistreatment and the quality of his (partial) score, take great pains to defend Friedkin's decisions.

These justifications typically rest on assumptions about both the quality of the finished film and the preeminent status of the director as artist. For example, after chronicling Friedkin's mistreatment of Schifrin, George Park supports the director's choice, arguing that *The Exorcist* offers "one of the most striking and intelligent uses of sound in any motion picture," going on to receive an Academy Award for Best Sound in Film. Fearing Schifrin's score may have detracted from the film's nuanced sound and arresting affectivity, Park declares that the composed music would have "buried" the "complex sound effects that had been labored over for months" and concludes that "as good as Schifrin's score is, it is hard to disagree with the director's creative vision."[22]

Similarly, Bond and Kendall locate the effectiveness of *The Exorcist* in Friedkin's use of sound. They argue, "Lalo Schifrin's amazing score, while technically brilliant, would have still mired the film in the conventional expectations of the horror genre that Friedkin's documentary-style approach was designed to avoid."[23] Citing their experience of reporting on a "half-dozen high-profile rejected scores every year" in *Film Score Monthly*, Bond and Kendall frame *The Exorcist* as an important object lesson about the paramount authority of the director:

> [O]nce in a blue moon there is a movie so unique and so well made that it justifies the artistic decisions of the filmmakers, even when they come at the disservice of an esteemed composer who was improperly instructed. When this happens, we should put aside our outrage and recognize the achievement of the film.[24]

As if to sanctify the end product of Friedkin's creative efforts and graciously ennoble Schifrin in the process, Bond and Kendall title their article, "The Ultimate Sacrifice," casting Schifrin's score as a cherished object ritually offered up toward the greater good, or salvation, of the film. This narrative of creative crisis, the rhetorical consecration of Friedkin as artist, and the emphasis on the sacrality of the sacrificial gesture are significant to this analysis because of the uncanny similarities they bear to assumptions operating within *The Exorcist* itself.

Like the extratextual stories about the production process, the diegesis of *The Exorcist* centers on the crises of men, their struggles for identity, and the redemptive power of sacrifice. Hence, Mark Kermode's description of the troubled production history of *The Exorcist* as creating "a movie at war with itself" and a "divided entity" also applies to the film's internal struggles with the traumas of history and its characters' anxious efforts to articulate what it means to be a man.[25]

Traumatic Traces

The Exorcist tells the story of a world possessed by demonic forces and of Regan MacNeill, an adolescent girl in need of an exorcism. It also features a world populated by troubled men, including priests suffering from crises of faith, a film director crumbling under the weight of addiction, and a lonely police detective struggling to do his job. In particular, as Carol J. Clover notes, "behind the female 'cover'" of Regan's suffering lies "the story of a man in crisis": Father Damien Karras, a trained psychiatrist and one of the Jesuit priests involved in Regan's exorcism.[26] While the camera lavishes much attention on Regan's spectacular transformation from adolescent girl to grotesque monster, "Regan's story is finally significant only insofar as it affects the lives of others, above all the tormented spiritual life of Karras."[27]

Much of the film's violence centers on the "psyche of the exorcist himself," as indicated by the titular focus on the priest, not the possessed young girl.[28] The Exorcist depicts Karras as warring with himself—torn between his devotion to his biological family and his church family, between his training as a physician and a priest, and between his feelings of vulnerability and his impulse to act heroically. These conflicts reach fever pitch when Karras loses his mother and witnesses Regan's tragedy, traumatic experiences that will compel him toward his sacrificial death.

This narrative of masculine crisis can be understood as responding to the historical traumas of the Vietnam era, a period of what Adam Lowenstein calls "extraordinary national crisis" in which the "definition of 'America' is subjected to such fiercely opposed forces that the nation often verges on tearing itself in half."[29] As Marita Sturken has suggested, the cultural conflicts of the Vietnam era were often framed in relationship to prevailing fictions about masculinity, with the nation itself depicted as emasculated and impotent.[30] As such, The Exorcist's intensely divided male protagonist may be understood to stand in for the conflicted nation and to register disruptions to hegemonic gendered norms. If, as Sturken argues, the "Vietnam veteran has become the emblem of the American male's crisis of masculinity," Father Karras represents a cinematic variation on this theme, anticipating and giving voice to what was an emerging construction of "irretrievably damaged" American masculinity.[31]

As synecdoche for the wounded culture, Karras gets coded as suffering from trauma, an experience that, at the time of the film's release, was gaining attention based on accumulating evidence of veterans' combat neuroses—soon to be called "post-traumatic stress disorder."[32] As Dominick LaCapra explains, trauma "disarticulates the self and creates holes in existence," wrenching the survivor from the social and shattering his/her narrative of self.[33] What is more, as Cathy Caruth explains, traumatized subjects are often "possessed by an image or event" that repeatedly interrupts memory and consciousness; often, the "literal return of the event" intrudes "against the will of the one it inhabits," manifesting as nightmares, flashbacks, hallucinations, and repetition compulsions.[34]

It is not insignificant that Karras's story of traumatic loss takes place under the cover of a story of possession. While Regan is literally possessed—her body and mind literally occupied and inhabited by demons—Karras is also consumed and taken hostage by loss, self-doubt, and guilt. Like the trauma survivor, Karras appears symptomatic and can no longer articulate a coherent story of who he is as a son, a Father, and a man. For instance, Karras suffers nightmares and hallucinations of his dead mother. Additionally, his dialogue frequently conveys his struggles with the responsibilities and roles dictated by patriarchal culture; and the music that plays behind (or on top of) Karras echoes this nightmare of masculinity in crisis.

In the end, *The Exorcist* uses the trope of sacrifice to disavow ruptures with Karras's subjectivity by suturing together his conflicting identity formations. As a psychiatrist and a priest, Karras is compelled to cure the suffering he encounters, and the narrative frames Karras's self-sacrificial death as not only healing Regan (physically, mentally, and spiritually) but also atoning for and expiating his traumas and, by extension, those of the nation. Nevertheless, as I argue below, these narrative attempts at closure cannot fully contain, or silence, the traumas given voice by the film's music. I now turn to the moments in which Karras's traumas become most visible—and audible.

The Exorcist introduces Karras in a charged context: on the Georgetown University campus during the production of a film, *Crash Course*. Regan's mother, Chris, stars as a professor and is shooting a protest scene. Students waving anti-military posters and threatening to destroy a campus building, question the sacrificial logic of war, asking, "Hasn't there been enough killing?" Although this sequence references Vietnam only obliquely (as in Chris's later description of *Crash Course* as "the Walt Disney version of the Ho Chi Minh story"), links to the anti-war movement are obvious, especially given what would have been recent memory about violence at Kent State in 1970, which was memorialized by John Filo's iconic and Pulitzer Prize-winning photograph.[35] As such, this scene invites readings of *The Exorcist* in relation to the historical context of wartime violence and dissent.

As Chris unsuccessfully seeks guidance about the scene from her director, a reaction shot reveals Karras and other onlookers watching the film shoot. This context is significant because it introduces Karras as marked by the traumas of war and shaped by the unsettlement of American national identity. He witnesses painful revolt and the questioning of authority, and the dismantling of traditional institutions that unfolds before Karras, albeit fictionally, replays the destabilization of his own identity and institutional position.

Interestingly, the staging of protesters on campus steps foreshadows Karras's final position in the film: broken and bloodied at the bottom of a staircase. These moments of conflict and of violence bookend the film, framing the narrative as one struggling with the logic of "ultimate sacrifice" that undergirds both the politics of war and the film itself. While the protesters question the sacrificial economy and the value of war—as one asserts, "I've seen enough killing in my lifetime. There's no need for it"—Karras ultimately maintains the importance of sacrifice, trading his life for Regan's and seeking redemption in the process.

This protest scene also warrants attention for Karras's positioning as a bystander. Not an active participant in the scene (indeed, he is not an *actor*), Karras is a passive onlooker on the margins of the film shoot, unable to participate in its actions or speak within its borders. This position of impotence and marginalization allegorizes Karras's social and cultural disenfranchisement and echoes constructions of the nation as wounded and emasculated. This positioning also restages that of the Vietnam veteran who, in the midst of the anti-war movement, was largely marginalized by insufficient governmental support and public objection to the war.[36]

Immediately following this scene comes one of the rare uses of dramatic scoring and Karras's second appearance. As Chris walks home from the movie set, Mike Oldfield's "Tubular Bells" begins to play, for the first of only two times in the film. Passing a cathedral, Chris hears a male voice, at first off-screen. He laments, "There's not a day in my life that I don't feel like a fraud." As Chris walks on, two men become visible in the background of the frame, Karras and another priest. Chris stops to hear their conversation, and the unnamed priest continues, "I mean, priests, doctors, lawyers. I've talked to them all." Karras counsels, "I don't know anyone who hasn't felt like that." Gradually, the sound of an airplane becomes audible, replacing Oldfield's music and silencing Karras. This sequence constructs the film's male characters as post-traumatic subjects and is significant on two levels.

First, the musical logic of "Tubular Bells" aesthetically enacts the traumatic crisis of subjectivity experienced by the young priest within this scene and by Karras throughout the narrative. An example of minimalism, "Tubular Bells" is built around repetition and the insistent cycling of a small number of notes. It is the music of stasis and fragmentation, which disavows interest in progress or moving on. As Tom Johnson explains, minimalism "includes pieces that move in endless circles" and "take a very long time to move gradually from one kind of music to another kind."[37] This sensibility relates to what Robert Fink defines as a "culture of repetition."[38] Fink positions the "extremely high level of repetitive structuring" in music as a kind of response to the "painfully excessive, alienating, and (thus) sublime" conditions of life in late modern, capitalist societies and the fear that humans may be "repeating ourselves" to death;[39] thus, although he does not deploy the language of trauma, Fink does locate a particularly traumatic sensibility within minimalist music.

Specifically, ostinato functions, not unlike a still photograph, to embody the "phenomenological structure of trauma," in which "one simultaneously feels stopped in time while constantly repeating the actions within that isolated moment."[40] While "Tubular Bells" does eventually change through a gradual additive process, its struggle against the continuity of time recalls the paralysis engendered by traumatic memory and positions its listener within a relatively fixed musical moment. While the forward-moving and linear narrative of *The Exorcist* may suggest the moving-on process that Freud calls "mourning," Oldfield's "Tubular Bells" enacts a melancholic response, acting out and compulsively repeating itself. Although the music begins as Chris walks, her journey is cut short, the priests' conversation literally stopping her in her tracks. This scene enacts the difficulty of "moving on" in the face of trauma, and we, as audience members, are likewise halted—tethered to this painful scene of crisis and confession.

Second, the placement of "Tubular Bells" alongside this moment of psychological crisis positions the music to speak for the film's troubled characters. The dramatic scoring echoes the anxious conversation of the priests, encouraging spectators to witness their suffering, as Chris does. What is more, "Tubular Bells" gives voice to the traumas suffered not only by the characters within the scene but also by the larger cultural context. Emerging on the soundtrack immediately before we see the two priests, "Tubular Bells" gets linked to Karras and his patient but *not exclusively*; rather, this music embodies the anxious melancholy that *The Exorcist* suggests is not peculiar to these men but constitutes the entire culture. Their moment of crisis becomes not singular but emblematic, not private but collective.

At the end of this scene, however, occurs a dramatic transformation in the sound mix: the roar of an airplane supplants Karras's dialogue and Oldfield's music after fewer than 45 seconds of audibility. On one hand, the aural modulation further enacts Karras's marginalization, leaving him literally silenced. Although his lips move, he has become, in effect, voiceless. If Karras's professional authority depends on his role as a counselor, the silencing of this therapeutic context denies Karras agency and registers his disenfranchisement. The aural saturation produced by the sound of the plane also refuses any recuperative gesture that might quiet the audience's worries about the uneasy priest. Although the troubled priest presumably gets to hear Karras's guidance, the film denies audience members such counsel. The scene, thus, ends on a helpless and despondent note, the characters (and spectators) overrun by the world around them.

Fully understanding the implications of this scene requires returning briefly to the one prior. We first see Karras in close-up following a conversation between Chris and her director, Burke Dennings.[41] When Chris questions the motivation behind the student protest scene ("Well, why are they tearing the building down?"), Dennings cannot answer and dodges her question with one of his own ("Shall we summon the writer?"). He can offer no guidance, or direction. With the failure of Burke's counsel, Chris enters her scene with no sense of why she and her costars are there. Inserting Karras into this instance of communicative breakdown suggests links between this moment of failed counsel and the one that Chris, only moments later, witnesses between Karras and his peer/patient. Accordingly, this link raises the troubling possibility that this Father may share Dennings' inability to direct his flock and implies the potential collapse of patriarchal authority.

On the other hand, this transformation in the sound mix acts as a literal and figurative act of displacement, a defensive gesture (not unlike psychic displacement) that covers over what might become a troubling confession: that Karras, too, feels like a "fraud." If "Tubular Bells" gives voice to a crisis of subjectivity, which Karras might himself repeat, the film cuts short and disavows this confession through the change in the sound mix. As if anxious about what might be revealed, like the nervous priest that speaks secretly to Karras, the film silences both the diegetic and non-diegetic confessions, thus denying (or, repressing) the traumatic disclosures Karras might (and eventually will) make about his own crisis of faith.

It is telling that a forward-moving plane, an iconic symbol of modernist progress, displaces Oldfield's traumatic music and Karras' dialogue. Quite forcefully (and loudly), this aural displacement cuts short a potentially disturbing moment of acting out and insists that the narrative move on. Quite literally, this moment of transformation in the sound mix ends the scene and advances the narrative. However, the text cannot completely repress Karras's traumas, and it is not long before his anxieties return to the surface of the text.

The next musical moment also coincides with Karras's on-screen presence. Traveling to New York to visit his ailing mother, Karras encounters a homeless man who asks, "Father, could you help an old altar boy? I'm a Catholic." Karras does not respond and only walks away, thus far largely silent throughout the film and failing, once again, to remedy the suffering of another. This experience sets the stage for Karras's tragic relationship with his mother who lives alone in Hell's Kitchen, comforted only by the constant sounds of the radio and the rare visit from her son.

The apartment surrounds Karras with his personal archive—evidence of his life before the priesthood, including pictures, trophies, and other mementos. Significantly, chief among these relics are pictures of Karras as a boxer, emphasizing physical prowess and brute force and reminding audiences that he traded a "hard," violent, and traditionally masculine profession for one that, arguably, requires him to be "soft," nurturing, and even feminine. Further, traces of Karras's former potency bring his current impotence into sharp relief, and these past signifiers of physical aggression allegorize the psychic violence Karras suffers in his present wars with himself.

Standing at his figurative memorial, Karras removes his collar, stripping himself of his mark of distinction and casting off the signifier of his position of authority. His interactions with his mother also disrobe him of his priestly authority. While he is typically called Damien or Father Karras, his mother infantilizes him, hailing him as "Dimmy." Like his discarded collar, Karras's nickname extracts him from the public sphere, signifying tensions between his family/personal/secular life and his professional/public/ religious life. It is also worth noting that "Dimmy" can be read as an aural pun, positioning Karras as incomplete, partial, only "half" a man.

Throughout this scene, a radio plays in the background. But the source music is always just out of grasp, as the radio itself is out of tune. Voices, music, and static overlap in confusing and chaotic cacophony. Like the conflicts waging within Karras, the radio's sounds struggle with one another, fighting to become audible. In this light, the radio that is almost but not quite intelligible mirrors Karras's inability to articulate his suffering. When his mother repeatedly asks what worries him, Karras cannot explain and, therefore, denies his disquietude.

The radio also signifies Karras's troubled role as a son. A close-up on the radio punctuates his conversation with his mother, in which Karras vacillates between his positions as dependent child (eating food she has prepared) and caregiver (tending to her wounded leg). Recalling his absence and her isolation, it is the radio that remains when Karras leaves. Although Karras tries to persuade her to move to a nursing home— imploring, "I could take you someplace where you'd be safe. You wouldn't be alone. There would be people around. You know, you wouldn't be sitting here listening to a radio"—she refuses to leave her home, choosing the comfort of her out-of-tune radio over the solace that her out-of-touch son might provide.

Karras, thus, remains torn: trapped between his desire to help and his inability to act, between his role as son and his role as Father, between his (potent) past and his (impotent) present. As he leaves, Karras places money on the dresser and tunes the radio. The constant, fuzzy background clatter becomes instantly audible and clear. As much as the Greek music of his mother's homeland signals Karras's attempts to provide his mother with company and absolve his filial guilt, it also signifies the failure of these attempts. Like his neglect of the homeless man on the subway, Karras forsakes his mother, falling short as both a son and a Father. The music on the radio, hence, echoes Karras's feelings of inadequacy and his inability to live up to the patriarchal injunctions that assert he should lead, protect, and rule his family. And, as the music comes into better "focus," so, too, does Karras's inability to live up to his patrimonial responsibilities.

The next prominent use of music, Richard Betts's "Ramblin' Man," frames another confessional scene, opening with the prayer-like refrain, "Lord, I was born a ramblin' man." Playing on a jukebox in a bar, the song repeats Karras's expression of anxiety and self-doubt to an advisor, Father Tom. Karras begins by admitting his guilt for having abandoned his mother, explaining, "It's my mother, Tom. She's alone. I never should have left her." Karras then admits that his grievances also derive from a prevailing crisis of subjectivity afflicting his male ministerial peers.

Describing the plights of his colleagues as "more than just psychiatry," Karras declares, "Some of their problems come down to faith, their vocation, the meaning of their lives." And, quickly, he counts himself among this troubled population, admitting, "I can't cut it anymore. I need out. I'm unfit. I think I've lost my faith."

Recalling the properly tuned radio, Karras's personal crises and his troubling revelation become, at once, intelligible; the doubts and conflicts that he (and perhaps the film text) had attempted to repress return loudly, not unlike Regan's tormented screams and cries for help that will follow. In this scene, as Kermode says, the "subtext is as loud as the jukebox," or, more precisely, the jukebox gives voice to the subtext.[42] Once again, music not only echoes this anxious confession but also suggests the pervasiveness of such disquietude. Rather than articulating a fear unique to Karras (or to his priestly peers), Friedkin's diegetic use of the Allman Brothers' music introduces the "immediate threat of history," positioning Karras to stand in for the larger culture's struggles with damaged public narratives about masculinity and patriarchal authority.[43] After all, this jukebox tune is popular, contemporaneous music that plays publicly in a crowded bar—its sentiments and anxieties speaking to (and perhaps for) a mass audience.

A Billboard "Top 100" song of 1973, "Ramblin' Man" tells the story of a man who is unwilling, or unable, to fulfill patriarchal and heteronormative expectations about his role within a traditional family construct. Prone to roam aimlessly with no purposeful destination, the narrator speaks to a lover as he picks up and moves on. Confessing professional shortcomings and his inability (or refusal) to commit, he says, "Tryin' to make a livin' and doin' the best I can/And when it's time for leavin', I hope you'll understand." Like Karras, this narrator neglects his patriarchal directives by abandoning those in his care and expresses ambivalence about his adequacies and the damage he leaves in his wake.

While Karras's narrative emphasizes a maternal relationship, the shortcomings of the song's narrator derive from those of his father. Another failed patriarch, his father "was a gambler down in Georgia" that "wound up on the wrong end of a gun." This lineage of wounded families is noteworthy for two primary reasons. First, "Ramblin' Man" ties together the film narrative with a chain of paternal disappointments. In the previous scene, Regan and her mother discuss her absent father, who is estranged from Chris and never appears on-screen. Cutting directly from this scene to Karras's confession, with "Ramblin' Man" as a connecting device, *The Exorcist* positions patriarchal failure as a persistent and pervasive problem, insinuating that the distress of the nation is being replayed within the nuclear family.

As Vivian Sobchack argues in her discussion of horror films in the 1970s, "the nuclear family has found itself in nuclear crisis."[44] Owing to such disruptions as the Vietnam War, the critiques of white male privilege by the feminist and Civil Rights movements, and new legislation affecting both reproductive and marital politics, these crises register profoundly in horror films. Unseating the heterosexual family and "bourgeois patriarchy" as spaces protected from "social upheavals," such films position the family as the "site" and "sign" of historical traumas.[45] In *The Exorcist*, then, imperfect fathers (or Fathers) become a repeated refrain the film returns to time and again, and although the wounds of these fathers are not as spectacular as those the devil will inflict on Regan, the legacy of the failed patriarch, within the logic of the film, is devastating.

Second, "Ramblin' Man" directly links its narrator's compulsions to his own traumatic history, coding the narrator's patriarchal failures and incessant need to ramble as mimetic consequences of his father's absence. He may be continually "moving on" but in doing so he is also "acting out" and replaying the scene of his father's loss. The narrator, like the trauma survivor, feels compelled to return to his etiological scene and reenact his own traumatogenic abandonment. To this end, it is also worth noting that "Ramblin' Man" itself becomes an act of repetition, remaking a similarly maudlin country song of the same name by a "father" of country music, Hank Williams, Sr. (and the language and thematics of this song would again be repeated the following year by country musician and "outlaw" figure Waylon Jennings in his song "I'm a Ramblin' Man").

Like "Tubular Bells," Betts's "Ramblin' Man" embodies the disarticulation of the post-traumatic subject. There is a paradox at the heart of this song. At one level, this song recounts the privileges and pleasures of mobility. Its narrator is free to ramble, free to roam—his life so utterly constituted by movement that he was "born in the backseat of a Greyhound Bus/Rolling down highway forty-one." Yet this movement goes nowhere and endlessly cycles back on itself. Though its tone may appear lackadaisical, if not careless, about the painful implications of the narrator's ramblin', the tendency toward minimalist repetition also mimes the experiences of loss and melancholy central to trauma.

Musically, the song's repetition compulsion gets enacted in the use of ostinato, linking this song to Oldfield's piece. In particular, Betts's guitar solo at the end of the song cycles through the same three or four notes insistently, almost as if the music itself is incapable of moving forward. While melodic repetition in popular songs is not uncommon, this particular take on repetition seems exaggerated, comprising almost forty-five seconds of the song's final measures. This refusal to move forward echoes the lyric's story of a pathological tendency to repeat the past. Beginning with a warning ("When it's time for leaving"), the narrator alerts his lover to his absence as the inevitable conclusion of their relationship. He can predict his departure because it is a move he has made before. The song opens *and* closes with the refrain ("I was born a ramblin' man") because, although its narrator is always moving, he is going nowhere, and lyrically, the song ends exactly where it begins.

Shortly after Karras's rambling admission of his doubts, *The Exorcist* cuts back to the MacNeill house, where the disturbances to Regan's mind and body suddenly escalate. At one level, this narrative progression assigns a causal relationship between Karras's crisis of subjectivity and Regan's possession, as if airing his metaphorical demons enabled the literal ones that would soon strike. Yet the film's structure also reveals discomfort with and attempts to disavow the dangerous implications of Karras's crisis of masculinity. By turning directly to Regan's suffering, which is fetishized in her grotesque and spectacular physical transformation, the film diverts attention from Karras's breakdown. The violent lacerations of her body— the source of the controversy about the film's gross-out effects—become, as Clover says, the "cover" for Karras's figurative disintegration. Though the film has exposed Karras's psychic wounds, it quickly obscures them by putting Regan's bodily scars forcefully on display.[46]

To Be Continued

In contrast to Karras's grave, even tortured, demeanor stands his friend Father Dyer. Characterized as a trickster, Dyer, like Regan, deflects attention from Karras's collapsing sense of self. While Karras appears mired by self-doubt and dissatisfaction, Dyer is hopeful and playful. His irreverence toward social positioning seems, at least initially, to offer a productive, rather than traumatic, response to the turbulent cultural context. To wit, the musical depiction of traumatic patriarchal failure offered by "Ramblin' Man" gets replayed and reworked by Dyer's charismatic rendition of Ben Ryan's 1926 song, "Down on Thoity Thoid and Thoid" ("Down on 33rd and 3rd").

Through its use of dialect, or "New Yorkese," Ryan's song gives voice to the largely disenfranchised working-class population of New York City's Eastside. This song registers the anxieties that accompany economic hardship but uses irreverent humor to temper and deny the traumas of poverty, singing of "guys [that] don't wear collars and ties" and their resistance to "[debt] collectors when they come to call." Although these characters signify their marginalization—like Father Karras—through the rejection of the "collar," they seem to do so unreservedly. "Down on Thoity Thoid and Thoid" explicitly calls to task what Sobchack names "bourgeois patriarchy," not out of fear but willful resistance, an impious position Dyer himself adopts.

While attending an event at the MacNeill home, Dyer plays the piano and leads partygoers in a singalong of Ryan's song. Sitting at the piano, surrounded by revelers, Dyer defines himself as a "frustrated musician and performer" and exuberantly confesses, "My idea of heaven is a solid white night club with me as a headliner for all eternity, and they love me." Initially, Dyer's description of his fantasy and "frustrated" dreams of musical celebrity marks one of several moments in which this priest playfully rejects his social position. Earlier in the night, Dyer flirtatiously asked a NASA astronaut to take him along on his next mission, and later he makes, presumably facetious, admissions that he steals for pleasure and read fortunes to make money. Taken together, these fantasies articulate Dyer's desire for freedom and mobility, marking him as a transgressive figure with distaste for social directives. Rather than expressing anxiety about shifting cultural norms and historical traumas, Dyer appears to embrace social fluidity and change. Like Ryan's musical heroes, Dyer mischievously resists the norms dictating the lives of his largely solemn and disciplined ministerial peers. He is a trickster at odds with the institutional, social, and cultural norms that govern his life. As such, Dyer's resistant "positionality" with respect to "the normal, the legitimate, the dominant" makes it possible to read him as queer, and this possibility is reinforced by textual traces of his non-heteronormative masculinity.[47]

Specifically, the particular connotations of Dyer's musical fantasy suggest resistance to heteronormative imperatives central to hegemonic masculinity. Reading almost like a scene from *Boys in the Band*, which Friedkin had directed only three years prior, Dyer's musical performance summons the specter of queer sexuality. Calling himself a "frustrated" performer, this closeted musician recalls the experiences of gay men similarly expected to temper, or even contain, their desires. But, as he excitedly describes his version of heaven, his arms thrown boisterously in the air, Dyer, at least temporarily, rejects these restrictions and "comes out" on the piano in what one review calls a "gayer-than-gay proclamation."[48]

Becoming a headliner on an imaginative stage, Dyer performs "camp stereotypes of gay masculinity," revealing that the Father might be a queen and furthering the metonymic links that Philip Brett identifies between musicality and homosexuality.[49] While the stereotypic, if not hyperbolic, nature of this performance might be problematic, Dyer's subject positioning does offer a counter to the heteronormative constructs that underwrite the narrative. By adopting a position as a performer and an object of visual consumption, Dyer also occupies a position typically reserved for feminine subjects and aligns himself more with Regan's movie star mother than with Karras. Hence, Dyer seems to anticipate Peter Lehman's assertion that "[g]ay men have become today's women," in a pairing that "appears to be a cinematic match made in heaven."[50] And, as such, Dyer suggests the possibility for fluid and mobile understandings of gendered identity, subversively embracing gender trouble.

However, as much as Dyer's performance may expose and embrace potential ruptures in hegemonic, heteronormative assertions of masculinity, *The Exorcist* also attempts to cover over and silence this disruption. Rather than celebrating Dyer's transgressive behavior, the film appears anxious about his queer positionality, reproducing what Philip Brett describes as overlapping fears about homosexuality and music as agents of "moral ambiguity always in danger of bestowing deviant status upon [their] practitioners."[51] To wit, Dyer's confessional singalong gets interrupted when Regan enters the room and urinates on the floor, telling the astronaut, "You're going to die up there." Hence, Ryan's song celebrating the disruptive and largely marginalized "guys" that "don't wear collars and ties" gets displaced by Regan's spectacle, and Dyer's fantasies of mobility and freedom are halted by references to the gravity of death. Once again, evidence of troubled and/or transgressive masculinity gets disavowed by signs of female monstrosity, averting spectators' eyes from signs of Dyer's contraventions and fixating them on Regan's.[52] But the film's final and most spectacular efforts at disavowal take shape through Karras's self-sacrificial demise, which endeavors to reaffirm conventional understandings of hegemonic masculinity.

In one of the film's final scenes, Karras realizes Regan's exorcism is failing and uses his body as her salvation. He compels the demon to leave Reagan's body and take possession of his own, commanding, "Take me." After the devil inhabits Karras, his visage transforms—his skin pale and greenish, his eyes a glowing yellow. But, seconds before throwing himself from the window, Karras's demonized features temporarily take their original form. A close-up on Father Karras's human face confirms that his death is willed, not accident or murder, and, therefore, marks his death as sacrificial. Reenacting (or, compulsively repeating) a Christological model of sacrifice, Karras offers up his own body for the sake of Regan's, earning redemption for himself in the process and creating a lineage between the Son and the Father.

This scene, at first glance, affirms the masculinist logic of sacrifice, valorizing violence and exalting male bodies as salvific. In this sense, Karras's death seems to counter the protests offered by students in *Crash Course*, asserting the value of giving up one's life for a cause. In addition to resolving the conflicts of the narrative—freeing Regan from her possession and ending the devil's reign of terror—Karras's sacrifice also seems to recuperate his identity. Indeed, the once-passive bystander becomes an active agent and fulfills his obligations to save. This scene also seems to counter Dyer's impious attitude, celebrating Karras's adherence to normative expectations about his salvific authority. Consequently, Karras's story appears to achieve coherence and closure: his purpose clearly enunciated, his traumas cured. Karras's death, however, is as traumatic as it is recuperative. Hence, Karras' s final scene, ultimately, implies the impossibility of moving past traumatic loss.

As he struggles with the demon—his face a mutable and injured surface that signals the fragility of his subjectivity—Karras embodies the alienating and disruptive effects of trauma. He, quite literally, becomes alien to himself. Oscillating between priestly self and demonic other, Karras makes trauma visible as a "vertiginously relational scene in which shock, violence, and a scene of death or its threat, undoes the psychic architecture of inside and out, undoing at the same time a coherent subject."[53] Though his human appearance returns briefly, Karras remains possessed, inhabited, fragmented. And, this rupture of inside and out becomes literal as Karras's broken body remains splayed on the concrete, his blood spilling out onto the street.

Although Karras may have saved Reagan, *The Exorcist* further exposes, perhaps unwittingly, the failure of his "ultimate sacrifice" to contain trauma by positioning Father Dyer as Karras's traumatic heir. Creating another lineage of broken families, it is Dyer that witnesses Karras's loss and finds his dying body at the bottom of the stairs. In another moment of failed counsel, it is Dyer that unsuccessfully offers Karras his last rites and final confession—to which Karras can only remain mute. And, after Regan recovers and the MacNeills leave Georgetown, in the original ending of the film, it is Dyer that is left standing, alone and marginalized, on the street outside their home.

The MacNeill women are able to move away and perhaps move on— Regan, we learn, has no memory of her possession. But Dyer remains trapped and possessed by traumatic memory. In the final shots of the film, he walks down the sidewalk and returns to the scene of Karras's death, his earlier exuberance and joy now gone, before the camera fades to black. Dyer stands at the top of the steps, and a point-of-view shot down the staircase invites spectators to share in his pain and traumatic memory.

Dyer rambles and, like the trauma survivor, returns to the violent scene that is the source of his own trauma. Interestingly, then, the third installment in *The Exorcist* trilogy, *Legion: The Exorcist III*, tells the story of Dyer's fifteen-year long grief over Karras's death, the rather melancholic rituals with which he honors his dead friend, and his violent death at the hands of the devil.[54] This sequel also repeats, in flashbacks through Dyer's point of view, the scene of Karras's death. Thus, Dyer becomes the figure through which the story of the traumatized male subject gets repeated, once again. No longer an irreverent or queer trickster, Dyer becomes a wounded subject inhabited by his own traumatic past. In contrast, however, the revised version of the film, released in 2000 as *The Exorcist: The Version You've Never Seen*, modifies this ending— rendering it more hopeful by the addition of a prologue in which Dyer strikes up a friendship with the police officer investigating Burke Dennings's and Karras's deaths. Removed from the historical context of trauma, this revision might be understood as a belated act of displacement attempting to disavow more completely the traumatic ruptures so evident within the original film.

What also gets repeated within the final scene of the original, Vietnam-era film is Oldfield's "Tubular Bells." As Dyer walks, "Tubular Bells" replays the traumatic crisis of subjectivity voiced throughout the film, betraying the closure that the narrative works to achieve. This act of musical repetition suggests that the characters of *The Exorcist* (and its male protagonists in particular) have not moved forward but remain trapped, revealing the threats of history persist and remain unresolved. The "ultimate sacrifice" has not been successful, and the question lingers, "Hasn't there been enough killing?"

The final shots of *The Exorcist* remove spectators from its elaborate special effects matrix and the grotesque horrors of Regan's possession, leaving them in what Friedkin describes as "ordinary streets" in "cold light." But, as the dramatic scoring suggests, these are streets stained with blood and mapped by traumatic history. Thus, music in *The Exorcist* works simultaneously with and against the narrative, struggling and giving voice to cultural anxieties and the injuries of history; within a film that strives to assert its own wholeness and coherence, this music becomes like a wound, lacerating the text and revealing indelible traces of trauma.

Notes

1   Vincent Canby, "Blatty's 'The Exorcist' Comes to the Screen," review of *The Exorcist*, *New York Times*, December 27, 1973. On *The Exorcist* as reinventing horror, see David Cook, *Lost Illusions: American Cinema in the Shadow of Watergate and Vietnam, 1970–1979* (New York: Simon and Schuster, 1990), 226.
2   Chris Chase, "Everyone's Reading It, Billy's Filming It," *New York Times*, August 27, 1972: D9.
3   Chase, "Everyone's Reading It," D9.
4   George Park, "The Devil's Music: The Filming of 'The Exorcist,'" *Film Score Monthly* 4.2 (February 1999): 29.
5   *The Exorcist*, DVD, directed by William Friedkin (1973; Burbank, CA: Warner Home Video, 1997)
6   Park, "The Devil's Music," 25. This approach to music mirrors was adopted by Stanley Kubrick in such films as *2001: A Space Odyssey* (1968) and *The Shining* (1980), both of which are roughly historical and generic contemporaries of *The Exorcist*.
7   David Bordwell, *The Way Hollywood Tells It: Story and Style in Modern Movies*, (Berkeley, CA: University of California Press, 2006), 52–3.
8   Jeff Bond and Lukas Kendall, "The Ultimate Sacrifice," *Film Score Monthly* 4.2 (February 1999): 2.
9   Park, "The Devil's Music," 25. This information about the production history of *The Exorcist* is also corroborated in Bob McCabe, *The Exorcist: Out of the Shadows* (New York: Omnibus Press, 1999); and Mark Kermode, *The Exorcist* (London: British Film Institute, 1997).

10 Anahid Kassabian, *Hearing Film: Tracking Identifications in Contemporary Hollywood Film Music* (New York: Routledge, 2001), 36.
11 McCabe, *The Exorcist*, 81–4.
12 Park, "The Devil's Music," 24.
13 Park, "The Devil's Music," 25; McCabe, *The Exorcist*, 116–17.
14 Park, "The Devil's Music," 25.
15 McCabe, *The Exorcist*, 117.
16 Ibid., 118.
17 Park, "The Devil's Music," 25.
18 Nitzsche reportedly worked with Ron Nagle to create these effects by rubbing together pieces of crystal stemware (Kermode, *The Exorcist*, 121).
19 Park, "The Devil's Music," 28–9.
20 Borden's pieces are listed in the film's credit sequence but do not appear on the official soundtrack released by Warner Bros. Records, Inc., *Music Excerpts from William Peter Blatty's The Exorcist*, 1974, B000QV55C6.
21 Dan Daley, "The Exorcist Returns: Buzz Knudson's Sounds of Silence," *The Mix* 22.7 (July 1998): 64.
22 Park, "The Devil's Music," 29.
23 Bond and Kendall, "The Ultimate Sacrifice," 2.
24 Ibid., 2.
25 Kermode, *The Exorcist*, 10.
26 Carol J. Clover, *Men, Women and Chainsaws: Gender in the Modern Horror Film* (Princeton, NJ: Princeton University Press, 1992), 65.
27 Ibid., 87.
28 Ibid., 87.
29 Adam Lowenstein, *Shocking Representation: Historical Trauma, National Cinema, and the Modern Horror Film* (New York: Columbia University Press, 2005), 111.
30 Marita Sturken, *Tangled Memories: The Vietnam War, the AIDS Epidemic, and the Politics of Remembering* (Berkeley, CA: University of California Press, 1997), 123.
31 Ibid., 70.
32 The phrase "post-traumatic stress disorder" (PTSD) was coined in the mid-1970s and introduced into the Diagnostic and Statistical Manual of Mental Disorders (DSM-IV) in 1980. On increasing public awareness of trauma in the Vietnam era, see Judith Herman, *Trauma and Recovery: The Aftermath of Violence—From Domestic Abuse to Political Terror* (New York: Basic Books, 1997), 9.
33 Dominick LaCapra, *Writing History, Writing Trauma* (Baltimore, MD: Johns Hopkins University Press, 2001), 41.
34 Cathy Caruth, *Trauma: Explorations in Memory* (Baltimore, MD: Johns Hopkins University Press, 2001), 5; emphasis added.
35 Lowenstein notes a similar evocation of this photograph and the traumatic history it is said to represent in *Last House on the Left* (Wes Craven, 1972), a contemporary of *The Exorcist* that also graphically depicts violence against young women (Lowenstein, *Shocking Representation*, 115).
36 Sturken, *Tangled Memories*, 45.
37 Tom Johnson, *The Voice of New Music: A Collection of Articles Originally Published in The Village Voice* (Eindhoven: Apollohuis, 1991), 5.
38 Robert Fink, *Repeating Ourselves: American Minimal Music as Cultural Practice* (Berkeley, CA: University of California Press, 2005), 4.
39 Ibid., 4.

40 Robert Hariman and John Louis Lucaites, *No Caption Needed: Iconic Photographs, Public Culture, and Liberal Democracy* (Chicago, IL: University of Chicago Press, 2007), 182.

41 Dennings is another male character marked by traumatic history, as indicated by his frequent references to the horrors of the Holocaust and the atrocities of Nazi Germany.

42 Kermode, *The Exorcist*, 35.

43 Kassabian, *Hearing Film*, 3.

44 Vivian Sobchack, "Bringing it All Back Home: Family Economy and Generic Exchange," in *Dread of Difference: Gender and the Horror Film*, edited by Barry Keith Grant (Austin, TX: University of Texas Press, 1996), 146.

45 Ibid., 146.

46 Like Clover, Rhona Berenstein argues that female horror frequently obscures masculine transgressions. See Rhona Berenstein, *Attack of the Leading Ladies: Gender, Sexuality, and Spectatorship in Classic Horror Cinema* (New York: Columbia University Press, 1996), 9; hereafter cited in text.

47 Michael Warner, *The Trouble with Normal: Sex, Politics, and the Ethics of Queer Life.* (Cambridge, MA: Harvard University Press, 2000), 62.

48 Jason Shamai, "Cruising for a Bruising," *San Francisco Bay Guardian Online*, at www.sfbg.com/entry.php?entry_id=4412&catid=85.

49 Peter Lehman, "The Saviors and the Saved: Masculine Redemption in Contemporary Films," in *Masculinity: Bodies, Movies, Culture* (New York: Routledge, 2001). Philip Brett, "Musicality, Essentialism, and the Closet," in *Queering the Pitch: The New Gay and Lesbian Musicology*, edited by Philip Brett, Elizabeth Wood, and Gary C. Thomas (New York: Routledge, 2006).

50 Lehman, "The Saviors and the Saved," 47.

51 Brett, "Musicality, Essentialism, and the Closet," 11.

52 Berenstein, *Attack of the Leading Ladies*, 9.

53 Jackie Orr, *Panic Diaries: A Genealogy of Panic Disorder*, (Durham, NC: Duke University Press, 2006), 21.

54 *Legion: The Exorcist III*, DVD, directed by William Peter Blatty (1990; Burbank, CA: Warner Home Video, 1999).

Chapter 8

Rehearing *The Shining*

Musical Undercurrents in the Overlook Hotel

David J. Code

Like *The Exorcist* and *Rosemary's Baby* of a few years before, and in keeping with a central lineage of horror films extending back through *Psycho* to the earliest contributions to the genre, Stanley Kubrick's cult 1980 film *The Shining* is notable for a score that makes abundant use of radically dissonant, sonorously extreme modernist musical languages. In fact, with this film's renowned selection of pre-existing compositions by Béla Bartók, György Ligeti, and Krzysztof Penderecki, it is tempting to say that this central musical convention of the horror genre reaches a kind of apogee, as measured in terms of pervasiveness and prominence. As Kevin Donnelly suggests in the most significant published study of the score, the importance of this whole array of avant-garde music to the overall experience of *The Shining* demands a change in the usual descriptions of film's multi-media interactions. In this case, he rightly implies, any reference to "background music" falls so obviously short of the music's presence and power, scene by harrowing scene, that we are forced to think, instead, in the exactly opposite terms of "foreground music."[1]

Donnelly usefully counterbalances this emphasis on the score's exceptional qualities when he later notes that one of Kubrick's prominent musical choices, the medieval chant *Dies Irae* ("Day of Wrath," from the Requiem Mass), also features in numerous other horror films, from *Garden of Evil* (1954) to *The Return of Dracula* (1958), from *Poltergeist* (1982) to *The Nightmare Before Christmas* (1993).[2] Indeed, the portentous synthesizer adaptation of the chant by Wendy Carlos and Rachel Elkind that underscores the film's initial, stunning helicopter shots of the Colorado Rockies must be recognized as one of the most blatant imaginable instances of music's power to act as independent generic signature. Even with the sound turned off many viewers, forewarned by countless reproductions of Jack Nicholson's "Here's Johnny!" moment, may sense something vaguely disconcerting about the camera's long, slow swoop down the lake, over the trees, and into the mountains to follow the car that (we soon learn) is carrying Jack Torrance up to his job interview at the Overlook Hotel. But in truth, there is little visual information in the whole, sunlit title scene to perturb the clichéd "natural sublime" of an expensively produced car commercial. It is only the music, which accumulates low pedal tones and manic shrieks around the grimly repetitive tread of the chant tune, that clearly tells us what kind of film we are watching, and signals the crescendo of horrors lying ahead.

The question remains, however, as to whether this initial, almost self-caricaturally blatant affective underscoring sets the stage for a film whose later, far more extensive samplings from three different avant-garde composers all serve their attendant visual imagery with the same forceful directness. Donnelly, in considering the relationship between the modernist compositions that predominate in the score and the British interwar dancehall songs heard in one hallucinatory episode, develops sophisticated Adornian reflections about the implications of this dichotomy between popular and art music for an understanding of the "evil" embodied in the hotel.[3] But any finer distinction within his two broad musical categories is lost when, after frankly admitting that he discovered Bartók through Kubrick, he goes on to invoke the similar "vertiginous" effects projected by the *Music for Strings* and the Penderecki excerpts alike.[4] Such generalized hearing has so far been widespread. Beyond the many film critics who refer indiscriminately to the panoply of "shrieks and wails" that render the soundtrack iconic of its genre, even as influential a film music scholar as Claudia Gorbman readily opts for equally broad-brushed characterization when, in the course of a discussion of the complex bond between "story world and soundtrack" in the "Kubrick universe," she opines that the "thoroughly non-ironic" use of Ligeti's 1953 *Musica ricercata* for piano in *Eyes Wide Shut* "resembles the director's uses of Ligeti in *2001* and *The Shining* for purely visceral effect."[5]

Gorbman's invocation of the "Kubrick universe" should inspire more considered reflection about the precise deployment, and potential semiotic richness, of all the modernist musical snippets—including the three from Ligeti's *Lontano*—that interweave across the whole sound structure of *The Shining*. After all, Gorbman's nod to *2001*—a reminder of another film genre that consistently draws on up-to-date musical languages to serve its otherworldly encounters—brings into view behind *The Shining* a film whose polysemous selection of nineteenth- and twentieth-century art music has gained it pivotal status in many histories of film music. As Royal S. Brown once suggested, even in view of the long precedent for such composite film scores, the new complexity with which pre-existing music becomes woven into the later products of the "Kubrick universe" (from *2001* through *A Clockwork Orange* (1971), *Barry Lyndon* (1975), *The Shining*, and beyond) can be seen as one mark of a shift away from "classical" scoring conventions towards a "postmodern" film-music aesthetic in which the music, in some significant sense, "stands as an image in its own right."[6]

This essay offers a rehearing of the distinct, Bartókian, Ligetian and Pendereckian musical images deployed across *The Shining* in order to suggest, through close analysis, how the whole score might be understood as a partially independent contribution to a more characteristically Kubrickian version of cinematic horror than is captured by any reference to "visceral" or "vertiginous" effects alone. To this end, I search beneath the most viscerally compelling sounds for traces of the same reflexive multimedia sensibility previously exemplified (for one notorious example) in *A Clockwork Orange*, whose shockingly vivid confrontation with the unstable ideological implications of Beethoven's *Ninth Symphony* remains one of the most disconcerting of all interrogations of the powers of music in film.[7] To be sure, it is much harder to unearth such subtexts from the late twentieth-century soundscapes in *The Shining* than it is from the semiotically overloaded strains of the Ninth—or even (for another famous instance) the "Blue Danube" waltz that accompanies the dance of spaceships in *2001*.[8] But an attempt to rehear the specific contribution of each avant-garde musical "image" to this finely formed multimedia interaction promises not only a deeper understanding of what has often been seen as Kubrick's "parodic" or "ironic" postmodern take on the horror film but also to open, beneath the terrors experienced by the Torrance family in the Overlook Hotel, subtextual echoes of deeper, cultural-historical horrors whose implications resonate far beyond those maze-like halls.[9]

A Polysemous Overture and a Bartókian Maze

Any search for fresh hearing might well begin by considering whether the blatant "horror film" title music itself bears any of the polysemous richness often noted in the most famous of all Kubrick's musical cues, the fanfare from Richard Strauss's *Also Sprach Zarathustra* now indelibly associated with *2001*.[10] At the first layer of implication (roughly equivalent to the Nietzschean subtexts that enter Kubrick's science fiction epic with Strauss's tone poem) it is easy to see the *Dies Irae* as a particularly apt musical "overture" for a film whose structure, as delineated by title cards, focuses on a single "Day of Wrath" ("WEDNESDAY") during which the axe-wielding Jack—like the judging God in the chant—murderously tries to "correct" his wife and son. At a more esoteric level (along the lines of the "Boëthian" resonance between the harmonic series of the *2001* fanfare and the visual "music of the spheres" it accompanies, which informs David Patterson's entire analysis) the chant also brings with it distant echoes of music history. A product of the first notated traditions of European church music, so-called Gregorian chant, the *Dies Irae* launches Kubrick's most up-to-date appropriation of avant-garde sounds with a reminder of the deepest bedrock of the Western literate musical tradition. But at the same time, Carlos's synthesizer sonorously echoes a famous prior adaptation of the same chant in the last movement of Berlioz's *Symphonie Fantastique*. Beyond the obvious link to that movement's supernatural subject—the "Dream of a Witches' Sabbath"—there seems some potential relevance in this invocation of a symphony based on the tortured hallucinations of an arch-Romantic artist. *The Shining*, after all, is Kubrick's only film to take an artist as protagonist: it is the struggles of the writer Jack Torrance with the pressures of post-Romantic literary creativity that send him over the edge of madness in the Overlook Hotel.

If preliminary musings about the musical "overture" thus raise into view a suggestive subtextual tangle of texts and traditions, notations and adaptations, literacy and thwarted creativity, any attempt to pursue such prefatory hints into the film encounters a daunting problem of formal complexity. In a rough overview, the three excerpts from Bartók's 1936 *Music for Strings, Percussion and Celesta* and the three from Ligeti's 1967 *Lontano* all appear, interwoven, within what we might call (borrowing again from music analysis) the "Introduction" and "Exposition," during which Jack gains his job as winter caretaker in the hotel, brings his wife Wendy and son Danny with him into the Rockies, and then, as snowy isolation settles over his literary struggles, descends into murderous insanity. The excerpts from several Penderecki works (1961–75), a few of which appear early on, ultimately come to dominate the whole latter portion of the film, with the exception of the one interlude of hallucinatory dancehall music.

To borrow an image from the film, this interwoven tangle of excerpts presents the analyst with something of a musical maze. In pursuit of subtextual understanding, I will put aside the parenthetical sequence of popular songs (which seem chosen for the clear thematic hints in their titles: "Home"; "It's All Forgotten Now") and thread the more puzzling maze of art music by considering the three composers in historical order. First, I will simply highlight what I see as some largely unnoticed congruencies between music and imagery. Clearly, at this stage the exercise falls short of the dialectical ideal of film-music criticism widely upheld at least since Eisler and Adorno. But it is worth adopting, for interpretive ends, Nicholas Cook's apposite framing of this dialectic from the poietic perspective: "attempts to force media into close superficial alignment (for instance, by cutting film to music) have the paradoxical effect of emphasizing the difference between the two media."[11] In other words, by excavating precise resonances between sound and image from several of the many passages in *The Shining* that are cut to pre-existing music it becomes possible to illuminate those points of disparity between media that prove most suggestive of deeper, continuous undercurrents.

Table 8.1 presents an overview of *The Shining*'s three excerpts from the third movement of Bartók's *Music for Strings, Percussion and Celesta*. The same few passages of music, up to the first fortissimo arrival at bar 45, are repeated three times at slightly greater length; the whole series proceeds as an incremental expansion backwards to the beginning of the movement. Looking to the film, we find that its first appearance (00:38:10 in the Warner Home Videos DVD) establishes a clear relationship between the Bartók and the hedge maze in the hotel yard—one of the most significant additions Kubrick and his screenwriter Diane Johnson made to the Stephen King novel on which *The Shining* is based.[12] By carefully showing us a map of the maze before zooming in to follow Wendy and Danny into its corridors, furthermore, Kubrick pointedly ties this musical infusion to the beginning of a studied visual game with levels of representational iconicity.[13] It is only at the second stage of the game, further into the same Bartók segment, that a strikingly precise parallel between maze imagery and modern musical syntax comes into view. As the sinuous violin and celesta melody winds to its end, a dissolve brings us back inside the hotel to show Jack looking over a model of the maze. The model is no sooner shown in its higher-order, three-dimensional iconicity than it flattens onto the screen, seeming briefly like another two-dimensional map, which is immediately identified (to our confusion) as the actual maze Wendy and Danny are exploring.

As I have shown with the stills in Figure 8.1, the flattened model maps a different maze than the one shown before. Not only is it massively more extensive than the one in the earlier map, but it also displays a new, manically detailed symmetry across both horizontal and vertical axes. (This is most clear from the large X shape spanning the four quadrants). On this point, it is possible to discern an esoteric parallel between the chosen music and the imagery with which it is associated. *Music for Strings* exemplifies as richly as any other work by Bartók his characteristic organizational principles based on the "axes of symmetry" derived from equal division of the octave into two tritones, and four minor thirds.

This esoteric parallel between image and music at the level of organizing syntax is more than merely "superficial." A glance to the score of the work would find that the first music we hear—the violin trills—sets the stage by framing the main tritone axis (A–D-sharp) of the whole multi-movement work, before the high, eerie tune for violin and celesta begins its trajectory oriented, metrically and melodically, around a different minor-thirds rotation (A-sharp–Fx–E–C-sharp). No doubt the distinctive orchestration contributes significantly to the vertiginous effect Donnelly noted. But I would argue that it is precisely the non-hierarchical, symmetrical alternative to the compelling teleology of diatonic syntax that makes the melody seem so apt an accompaniment to the looping

Table 8.1 Summary chart of the three excerpts from Bartók's *Music for Strings, Percussion and Celesta* in *The Shining*

Bartók, *Music for Strings, Percussion and Celesta*, mvt. III	SCENE 1 [00:38:10] Jack in lounge; Wendy and Danny "escape"	SCENE 2 [00:41:15] Danny on bigwheel: the hallways of the hotel	SCENE 3 [00:52:35] the family apartment
m.1 xylophone and timpani glissando			door opens, D enters
m.6 improvisatory string melody, punctuated by xylophone rattle NB contrapuntal dialogue abrupt crescendo to end			D tiptoes in; sees J on bed "come here"; embrace "how's it going?" "... Dad?"
m.17 xylophone rattle; fragment from mvt. I (Fugue) for strings		D bigwheel, room to room	D: "you feel bad?" J: "tired" D: "why not sleep?"
m.20 high trills (whole-tone chord) ... leads to:	D + into maze [note map of maze]	[into hallways: Steadicam follows ...]	J: "too much to do"
m.22 string glissandi and trills, sinuous melody in celesta and violin I [NB "axes of symmetry"]	within the maze; Steadicam loops and glides DISSOLVE to Jack	passes and turns to notice "room 237" approaches ... tries door ...	D: "Dad?" J, the hotel: "I love it ... wish to stay for ever" D: "hurt mom+me?"
m.31 piano punctuation xylophone rattle and timpani glissando, return of mvt. I fragment	Synchronized: tennis ball J over to model maze [compare map]	finds door is locked CUT to ghostly twins (synchronized); D leaves	[J's reaction] cut: "did mother say" "no" / "sure?" / "yes"
m.34 otherwordly sweeps for celesta and piano and harp; string counterpoint crescendo to ...	view of W&D in real maze CUT back into maze	CUT to Jack at typewriter [see his face, not text] Wendy enters "hi hon"	J: "I love you Danny ... I would never do anything to hurt you"
m.45 chord and cymbal crash	Title: TUESDAY	TEARS OUT PAPER	Title: WEDNESDAY

Figure 8.1 The two-dimensional map and three-dimensional model of the hedge maze

trajectory of Kubrick's Steadicam within the maze. In addition to this symmetrical order within the pitch syntax of the entire excerpt, finally, note also that the music that begins with Jack's overview of the model affirms another, more clearly audible kind of syntactical symmetry in the expanding inversional dialogue between string groups that leads to the climactic cymbal crash at bar 45.

With this esoteric resonance between visual and aural symmetries in view, it is possible to pass summarily over the second Bartók excerpt (00:41:15), noting only that it adds one more ingredient to the representational games by marking a clear metaphorical relationship (at the same, three-dimensional level) between the maze and the hotel hall-ways Danny explores on his bigwheel.[14] (Once again, the geometrically patterned carpet also keeps a two-dimensional equivalent in view.) Perhaps more significantly, I suggest, this same segment establishes the precedent of backwards expansion that is to be fulfilled in the third segment where it extends to embrace the beginning of the movement.

The third and last Bartók segment, which accompanies an encounter between Jack and Danny in the family apartment, begins with a palin-dromic xylophone rattle that sets the stage for an extensive, improvisatory, loosely contrapuntal string dialogue (00:52:35). As this scene unfolds, the background wind noise contributes significantly to the overall sound-scape; representational games continue in the mirror reflection that doubles Jack as he beckons to Danny; the symbolic resonances of the maze carry over, implicitly, to color his invocations of insomnia and work pressures. But the most important point concerns the formal weight this whole structure imparts to the exceptional appearance of the highly expressive string writing that begins at bar 6. Again, close analysis would find that the successive, seemingly improvisatory string entries are consistently oriented around the axes of symmetry that define the work's underlying syntactical principles. But it is best to recognize the whole passage as one of those heavily charged moments of equipoise, in Bartók's music, between the urge to a modernist, systematic pitch language and the attachment to the humane traditions of Romantic lyricism that have been borne, archetypically, by expressive, melodic string writing.[15]

   In the attempt to interpret the implications of this formally charged moment, it helps to refer to a page from the working sketches for *The Shining* fortuitously reproduced on page 447 of *The Stanley Kubrick Archives* (an anthology of stills and creative materials for all Kubrick's films).[16] Taken from the director's 1977 "Brown Notebook," this sketch begins with a scribbled question in Kubrick's handwriting: "How do we show Jack's affection for Danny? It should be seen at least once." The director then scrawls a little diagram: four rectangles followed by two arrows in mirror relationship—that is, in rough transcription, something like this:

   No doubt there are various ways to interpret this tantalizing poietic trace. In view of the meticulous precision with which the film is cut to the Bartók excerpts, I see it as a preliminary shorthand for the formal ambitions enacted across the whole repetitive series, whose incremental backwards expansion might be said to come as close as is possible, in a temporal art form, to placing the exceptional moment of lyricism between those two facing arrows. Extrapolating from this glimpse of temporal symmetry, we could say that my summary chart crudely maps the highest order of maze in play here: a four-dimensional, temporal maze that embraces all other levels of representation precisely in order to fix this film's single affectionate scene between father and son at its heart.

   But it is at this point, I find, that sonorous and imagistic worlds also encounter an essential incongruity. The simultaneous visual symmetries of the flattened maze model are only fictively congruent with the temporal symmetry I am reading from Kubrick's arrows: to put it bluntly, Bartók's lyricism can only take its place at the heart of the notional four-dimensional maze once the string dialogues have been lost to the unidirectionality of lived time. The point may seem arcane, but I think it holds significant implications for a reconsideration of the status of lyrical expression within the "Kubrick universe"—a film world that has often been described as deliberately and coldly anti-lyrical. Through the formal craft of this particular sequence in *The Shining*, the possibility for archetypical musical lyricism to underpin (indeed, in a sense, to secure) something like genuine affection between filmed characters, is both singled out with profound formal weight—and, at the same time, acknowledged as irretrievably lost.

   The immediate implications for the relationship between Jack and Danny might seem relatively obvious. In a classic instance of what has occasionally been termed anempathetic underscoring, by the end of the scene Jack's profession of love for his son has been thoroughly undermined by the eerie harp, piano, and celesta swirls that crescendo to the close of the Bartók excerpt.[17] But in a longer view, it could be said that this finely formed game with musical and visual symmetries effectively isolates, in a pre-war musical language not yet too far removed from traditional pitch syntax, a subtextual concern with the fate of lyricism in modernity that can conceivably be pursued further into the more radical, postwar reaches of the score.

To that end, it is worth noting that my arcane point about incommensurable symmetries has been made before, in one of Michel Chion's influential discussions of the effect of early film sound on the temporal qualities of the cinematic image. As he put it most succinctly: "aural phenomena are much more characteristically vectorized in time, with an irreversible beginning, middle, and end, than are visual phenomena." To reinforce his point, Chion invokes a notional scene of a woman reading on a porch, suggesting that without sound we could view it backwards with little trouble. But once the same scene is given a soundtrack—say, diegetic wind chimes—the same reversal becomes much more problematic, because of the "little indices of vectorized real time" in each of the thousands of finite sound events.[18] No doubt Chion overstates his distinction by choosing an example from the perishingly small set of real-life scenes that could, in fact, read unproblematically in reverse. But the notion of vectorization, as adapted beyond Chion's initial meaning, proves a key opening into the deeper reaches of *The Shining*'s musical and imagistic maze. The question has already implicitly come into view with the recognition that Bartók's rotational symmetries create a less vectorized harmonic language than diatonic tonality. But this is a conceptual translation of a term Chion introduced with more narrowly sonorous implications that provide a useful point to begin the next stage of inquiry into the score.

Ligeti's Orchestral Telepathy

Table 8.2 summarizes the film's threefold use of Ligeti's *Lontano*. In this case all excerpts begin at the same point some way into the piece, and the repetitions do not show the same systematic expansion as the Bartók series. To continue along the lines of inquiry just opened, a hearing of this sequence might start by noting that the moment chosen to begin each excerpt belongs to that special category of musical event that *can* conceivably be described as sonorously "non-vectorized." In other words, the yawning pedal tone between violin harmonics and tuba that enters like a vertical spatial embodiment of Ligeti's title—*Lontano* means "from a distance"—also hovers temporally without strong implications of pastness

Table 8.2 Summary chart of the three excerpts from Ligeti's *Lontano* in *The Shining*

Ligeti, *Lontano* (from b. 41, rehearsal figure F)	SCENE 1 [00:21:20] Danny in games room	SCENE 2 [00:27:20] Danny "shines" with Halloran in storeroom	SCENE 3 [00:46:10] W+D outside; J "shines"?
a) initial "sonorous chasm" (violin harmonic + tuba)	Danny throws darts; oblivious [pan back, across] D turns . . . [zoom]	D, W and H enter store room: oblivious [cut] Danny aware [cut] and [zm] to H	W and D running in snow [cut] Jack inside staring . . . [zoom] to
b) abrupt crescendo "like a sudden eruption" (NB horn)	. . . [cut] to two girls [cut] back to D	. . . "how'dya like some ice cream Doc?" [cut] to D	hint of smile, maximum close-up title "SATURDAY"
c) entry of tpt, followed by tbns and tuba	[cut] back to girls girls look at each other and leave	[cut] back to H [[FADE]]	. . . exterior: snow [cut] Jack typing
d) sudden "down to earth" scoring; tritone for all strings	[cut] back to Danny [cut] U+J+W: apartment		[cut] Wendy tries telephone . . .
e) characteristic "micropolyphony" begins			. . . telephone broken, W through hall to radio [FADE]

or futurity. Perhaps this is one way to understand its initial use to signal a ghostly vision from the past that appears to Danny in the games room soon after the family's arrival in the hotel (00:21:20).

Still, while an interpretation of this initial sonorous chasm as a kind of non-vectorized temporal gateway might enrich our sense of its congruence with the telepathic "shining" across time that gives the film its title, such a reduced hearing—to borrow the term *musique concrète* composer Pierre Schaeffer gave to his ideal of an unmediated hearing of material sound qualities alone—underplays the ways in which the same sound, and all the timbral events of this short segment, remain palpably in touch with the traditions of lyrical expression.[19] Conversely, Ligeti's own discussion of *Lontano* in a 1968 interview offers strong grounds to hear the high violin keening in this excerpt as a tremulous afterglow of the same Romantic ideal of communicative immediacy fleetingly resurrected in Bartók's string dialogues. Indeed, noting that beyond its spatial implications his title also aimed to capture some sense of historical distance from the late-Romantic sound world he believed to persist, as an "aura" of hints and allusions in the piece, Ligeti proceeded to scatter his responses to his interviewer with variants of a visual image that fits this discussion almost too perfectly to be purely coincidental—for example, when he claims that the ambivalent attitude to tradition in *Lontano* "den[ies] tradition by creating something new, and yet at the same time allow[s] tradition to *shine through* indirectly through allusions."[20]

Given the well-attested thoroughness of Kubrick's researches into the music for his films, we might well imagine a conscious decision behind this apt use of a piece Ligeti himself described in terms of its "shining." But there is no need to pin down authorial intention (whether to Kubrick or to his sound designer Gordon Stainforth or to some admixture of the two) in order to pursue the subtextual implications of the *Lontano* excerpts into the film. In its second instance (00:27:20), *Lontano* again accompanies an explicit "shining" within the story world—between Danny and the hotel cook, Dick Hallorann, in the kitchen store-room—which can be understood, on the whole, as a further reinforcement of this allusive power of music to speak across time, space, and history. Up to this point, the *Lontano* sequence can be said to identify the time-honored seductions of affective underscoring as a kind of "telepathy"—a word whose etymological meaning (from the Greek "*tele-pathos*") is not actually "mind-reading," as conventionally understood, but rather the transmission of *feeling* [*pathos*] over distance.

But the third instance of *Lontano* again proves exceptional. This sequence is not best described as another case of notional congruency between music and imagery breaking down in the face of essential disparity. Rather, the potential for *Lontano* to speak across time and space seems pointedly called into question by its last formal placement (00:46:10). The yawning registral chasm now enters beneath a short scene of Danny and Wendy playing in the snow. Then a cut brings us before Jack, staring out from the Colorado Lounge. It may be possible, at first, to associate his gaze with his family outside the window, but as the camera slowly zooms in it seems more and more like he is rapt in inscrutable inner visions. Unlike the previous two scenes with *Lontano* underscoring, this one lacks the careful edits that stake out the distance traversed by the keening violins within the film's story world (between Danny and the girls; then Danny and the cook). This time, it is just us and Jack. And this time, exceptionally, the *Lontano* excerpt extends across the film's structural apparatus (the title card "SATURDAY") to underscore Wendy's discovery that the telephone lines linking the hotel to the outside world are down due to the storm.

Many critics have found the naked confrontation with the staring Jack visually problematic. As Mario Falsetto put it in his book *Stanley Kubrick: A Narrative and Stylistic Analysis*, "Jack's interior life remains closed. The close view does not bring the audience any closer to understanding."[21]

Figure 8.2 Jack's "blocked" moment of "shining" and two visual offshoots

In other words, the sense in the previous scenes of resurrected communicative powers in the faint traces of tradition that shine through Ligeti's *Lontano* is ultimately deflected through a last, unconsummated instance of musical telepathy. (It seems telling that only this third excerpt is extended to include a brief passage of Ligeti's signature micropolyphonic texture—the most freighted trace of tradition in his syntax—as accompaniment for an encounter with a faulty traditional communicative device, the *tele-phone*.) For a preliminary sense of the embracing formal significance of the questions raised by this moment, it helps to look ahead and note that the film closes with two distinct visual echoes of that telepathically blocked portrait of Jack—one, an image of his corpse in the snow; the other, a photograph of him at a festive ball many years earlier (see Figure 8.2). For some understanding of the contribution Kubrick's last modernist composer makes to the tangled paths that lead to this double visual conclusion, it is necessary to plunge once more into the musical maze.

Penderecki's Tangles and Scrawls

The third composer in the score is the hardest to grapple with critically, because of the sheer number of pieces by Penderecki used in the film and the exceptional editorial freedom with which they are spliced and overlaid.[22] Perhaps there is a broad point to be made about this very distinction between modernist soundscapes that seem (even when excerpted) to enforce their own temporal integrity and those more readily treated as repositories of visceral effects. Indeed this last layer of the film's avant-garde score seems generally to operate most simply, as a crude reinforcement of gesture and a blatant infusion of horror affect (as distinct from the intimate emotional suture tenuously revived through Bartók and Ligeti). But at one or two moments, it is possible to discern subtler implications, which carry the questions already raised to a deeper level of multimedia parallel.

In one memorable scene, for example, Penderecki's *The Awakening of Jacob* (1975) is used to underscore Jack's hallucinatory encounter in one of the hotel bathrooms with what he thinks is a nubile young woman

(01:11:45). After gaping desirously as she emerges naked from the bath, then embracing her and beginning to kiss her, he is horrified to see in the mirror that her body is actually that of a decaying corpse. At this point, filmic continuity shatters into a bizarrely incoherent series of images, during which Jack backs from the room in disgust as the camera lurches from the pursuing, cackling crone to her putrefying corpse still rising, zombie-like, from the bath—all to a soundtrack that overlays the Penderecki with a heartbeat and cackling laughter. Although these clichéd horror sound effects just about overwhelm any narrowly musical hearing, a search for subtexts in the scene might begin by taking conscious notice of the exceptional nature of its editing. There have been many previous examples of montage in *The Shining*, but up to this point all have been in some sense parenthetical to the momentary narrative unfolding. This is the first time that the local plot vector—the linear temporal experience of a character—breaks into incoherence: there is no way to make narrative sense of that strangely recursive repositioning of the corpse in the bath, even as the same ghoulish figure totters after Jack into the bedroom.

This momentary lapse into temporal incoherence can be said to carry a faint resonance with the particular choice of Penderecki underscoring for this moment. *The Awakening of Jacob* is largely written in relatively conventional notation. Copious glissandi impart pervasive local indeterminacies, but the broad succession of sound events is controlled through several initial passages. Precisely at the moment when the film loses its grip on unitary time, the score briefly shifts to a slightly freer relationship between notated gesture and sonorous succession, as indicated by the parentheses (which indicate some degree of improvisational rendition) at rehearsal figure 7, in every line of the score excerpt shown in Figure 8.3.

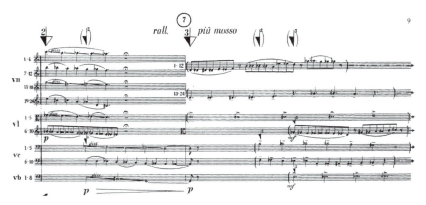

Figure 8.3 Excerpt from Penderecki, *The Awakening of Jacob* ... showing shift to notational parentheses at Rehearsal Figure 7

Could it be that the affinities previously sensed between music and imagery here extend yet deeper, beneath the symmetries of Bartókian pitch syntax and the traces of tradition in Ligetian soundscapes, to touch the even more esoteric relationship between sound and its secret notational substrate? Perhaps this first example, which presents Penderecki as only one layer in the *mise-en-bande*, offers frail support for such a proposition. It is possible, I think, to indicate a second, stronger instance in support of the same parallel—but this one, by contrast, could be said to pose the opposite problem of seeming too crude a congruency, devoid of dialectical nuance.

In this pivotal scene, Wendy, coming in search of Jack, discovers to her horror that he has been typing, day after day, the same stupid phrase: "All work and no play makes Jack a dull boy" (01:41:20). An immediate hearing of the scene might simply note how radically the alien smears and spatterings of this new string palette efface any vestige of traditional lyrical expression. But if it is difficult to locate this music precisely as a subjective emanation—it seems equally associable with Jack's disordered subjectivity and Wendy's horror on finding evidence of that disorder—deeper questions come into view once we consider precisely what has happened to Jack's written language. It is not just that his words become garbled, but the minute vectorization of each typographical character and the higher-order temporal coherence of each grammatical chain both become subsumed within a cruder, embracing graphic design—which, as Wendy shuffles through the manuscript in dismay, throws up random visual rhymes with the similarly patterned, clichéd visual primitivism of the hotel's mock-Indian décor. (Figure 8.4 isolates one exemplary, fleeting parallel between the triangular pattern that comes into view on one page and the colored triangles that appear on the ceiling beams in several shots from below.)

Figure 8.4 One representative visual rhyme between Jack's typographical designs and the mock-primitivism of the hotel décor

A glance to Figure 8.5, a brief score excerpt from the passage from Penderecki's *Polymorphia* that sounds through this scene, should be enough to adumbrate this subtextual connection. In rough parallel to Jack's denatured, crudely patterned typography, Penderecki's graphic scrawls here relinquish all vestige of conventional musical notation as they settle into random successions of jagged peaks and troughs. Apparently, Penderecki derived this notation from electroencephalographs of the brain activity of listeners to his *Threnody for the Victims of Hiroshima*—a fact with some obvious relevance to this first full exposure of Jack's derangement.[23] But with a view to embracing critical concerns, I am more struck by the simpler parallel between visual and sonorous worlds, which hinges on a vivid transition from the notational to the graphic. While it might seem meretricious to note that Penderecki's scrawls represent a "non-vectorized" musical writing, that observation can actually deepen the cross-media parallel yet further if it serves to remind us of the degree to which the traditional musical notation here relinquished— whose conventions of stemming and beaming make up the first lesson for all students of musical rudiments—was rigorously vectorized, and thus closer to an alphabetic than a pictographic or hieroglyphic language.

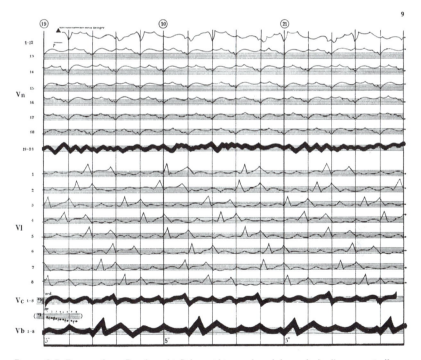

Figure 8.5 Excerpt from Penderecki, *Polymorphia*, as played through the "manuscript" scene
© 1963 By Moeck Verlag, Celle, Germany. Worldwide rights assigned 2006 to Schott Music GmbH & Co. KG, Mainz—Germany. All Rights Reserved. Used by permission of European American Music Distributors LLC.

Conclusion: Music and the Subtexts of Kubrickian Horror

A search for musical subtexts beneath the compellingly powerful modernist sounds in *The Shining* unearths a suggestive, three-stage, interrelated confrontation with both the expressive powers and the vectoral properties of music. The Bartók sequence frames a question about lyrical expression most deliberately, through a finely structured confrontation with the limits of a parallel between symmetries in visual imagery and musical syntax. In the Ligeti sequence, the same sort of question can be said to migrate from the level of syntactical order into the very material of orchestral sound, as a temporal pivot and a tradition-saturated medium of expressive telepathy. Pursued to the third stage, at certain key moments in the most visceral, Pendereckian layer of modernism in *The Shining* it is possible to discern an even more esoteric formulation of the same kind of question—one that touches the bedrock multimedia identity of all music in the literate, notated tradition that developed from the repertories of the medieval church. Perhaps it is here, looking back, that we can see the subtlest outgrowth of that blatant musical "overture"—the *Dies Irae* chant that had been carried forward, via musical writing, from its thirteenth-century origins into Berlioz's "Dream of a Witches' Sabbath" and then into countless horror films before Carlos revised it for Kubrick.

But looking ahead, the question remains as to how such a reading of deep musical subtexts helps us interpret the puzzle of the two concluding portraits of Jack (as foreshadowed in the thwarted telepathy of the third Ligeti excerpt). Clearly, interpretation of the film's closing image of a tuxedoed Jack smiling from a photograph of a 1921 ball, underscored by Al Bowlly's suave 1934 rendition of "Midnight, the Stars, and You" with Ray Noble and his orchestra, requires more careful consideration of the popular music strand of this score than has been possible in this one-sided discussion of its art music. But if this final image must also be seen to confuse the film's vectors of narrative and history beyond any coherent resolution, it is the other, immediately previous portrait of Jack—his frozen face in the maze, underscored by a last blast of Penderecki—that most starkly rounds off both the horror plot and the progression through three stages of musical modernism.

It is tempting, in pondering this ghastly penultimate image, to widen the lens again and consider precedents in the "Kubrick universe" as a guide to interpretation. In *2001*, by associating Ligeti's music with the mystical monolith—and, more broadly, with the mysteries of deep space and post-human intelligences—Kubrick effectively used the twentieth-century's most influential post-Wagnerian medium to herald such avant-garde sounds as the music of the future. Against this background, the suspicion arises that the much different generic framing of his next exploration of modernist scoring implies a markedly changed perspective, a dozen years later, on the promises of avant-garde music—as if the degradation of the literate tradition symbolized by the parallel between Penderecki's scrawls and Jack's deranged typography now is seen to promise only a frozen, dead-end future like Jack's fate in the maze.

But a glance back to the events that precede the penultimate portrait discovers grounds for a more complex, dialectical conclusion about the film's subtextual tracing of a horrifying breakdown in ancient expressive traditions. As a more immediate background to the closing pursuit, consider the earlier scene in which Danny, accompanied by Penderecki, mouths the word "REDRUM" in the voice of his alter-ego Tony as he writes this word on the bathroom door. Wendy awakens to read "MURDER" in the mirror just as Jack starts to chop his way in with an axe (see Figure 8.6). The reversible word is arguably the least significant aspect of this scene: Wendy has no need to *read* anything to know there is something amiss. Much more significant is the way the scene underlines the fact that Danny is no writer. Even with the help of Tony, he is still able to treat "E" and "R" as reversible graphic signs—he has not yet succumbed to the symbolic order of literacy.[24] Compare the boy's instinctive mastery of a more primitive vectorized sign system later on, at the dénouement of the film. As he flees his axe-wielding father into the hedge maze, he notices that his footprints are leaving a clear trail in the snow—and takes the inspired risk of walking *backwards* far enough to jump aside and hide. The trick works: in his enthrallment to literacy Jack is unable to read the simpler semiotic message of footprints leading nowhere, so he plunges on to his death.

With this crafty bit of trickery, a new allegorical interpretation comes into view for the terrifying Oedipal conflict always noted as one engine of this film's horror plot. Jack, the failed writer, becomes the frustrated—and ultimately deranged—representative of a generation unable to cope with the erosion of the cultural prestige invested in printed texts beneath the onslaught of more seductively immediate, post-literate communicative

Figure 8.6 Danny's "writing," featuring reversible R and E

practices. On the other hand, Danny's pre-literate game with his footsteps identifies him as the herald of a new generation more at home with such modes of communication due to life-long immersion in the graphic messages of mass-mediated image culture. (Note that the first time we see Danny in the film he is watching cartoons on TV, alongside Wendy reading a book.)[25] No doubt a considerable interpretive stretch is required to read Penderecki's graphic scores—a marginal phenomenon in any wide view of musical culture—as a symbol of a historical shift defined in such terms. But countless precedents in the Kubrick universe justify an attempt to rehear the "shrieks and wails" that spring from those scrawls in *The Shining* as the expression, in part, of existential terrors originating far beyond the confines of the Overlook Hotel. A close analysis can only ever support such a rehearing by highlighting one of infinite paths through the filmic maze. But it might also serve to inspire other, different interpretations of the ways in which modernist music helps to project, through the generic frame of the horror film, even more frightening nightmares than those about vampires, zombies, or ghouls.

Notes

1 See K. J. Donnelly, "The Anti-Matter of Film Music: *The Shining*," in *The Spectre of Sound: Music in Film and Television* (London: BFI, 2005), 36–54. See also Leonard Lionnet, "Point Counter Point: Interactions Between Pre-Existing Music and Narrative Structure in Stanley Kubrick's 'The Shining'" (D.MA dissertation, CUNY, 2003).
2 Donnelly, "The Anti-Matter of Film Music," 47–8.
3 Ibid., 52.
4 Ibid., 43–4.
5 Claudia Gorbman, "Kubrick's Music," in *Changing Tunes: The Use of Pre-existing Music in Film*, edited by Phil Powrie and Robynn Stilwell (Aldershot: Ashgate, 2006), 4–18, at 12. Of the film scholars, Geoffrey Cocks says most about the music: see his *The Wolf at the Door: Stanley Kubrick, History, and the Holocaust* (New York: Peter Lang, 2004).
6 Royal S. Brown, *Overtones and Undertones: Reading Film Music* (Berkeley, CA: University of California Press, 1994), 240.
7 See for example Katherine McQuiston, "Value, Violence, and Music Recognized: A *Clockwork Orange* as Musicology," in *Stanley Kubrick: Essays on His Films and Legacy*, edited by Gary D. Rhodes (Jefferson, NC: McFarland, 2008), 105–22.
8 See David Patterson, "Music, Structure and Metaphor in Stanley Kubrick's *2001: A Space Odyssey*," *American Music* 22, 3 (Fall 2004), 444–74; Michel Chion, *Kubrick's Cinema Odyssey*, translated by Claudia Gorbman (London: BFI, 2001), especially 90–103; and Katherine McQuiston, "Recognizing Music in the Films of Stanley Kubrick" (PhD dissertation, Columbia University, 2005), 166–228.
9 See for example Fredric Jameson, "Historicism in *The Shining*," in his *Signatures of the Visible* (New York: Routledge, 1990), 82–98; Tony Pipolo, "The Modernist and the Misanthrope: The Cinema of Stanley Kubrick," *Cineaste* 27, 2 (Spring 2002), 4–15; James Morrison, "The Old Masters: Kubrick,

Polanski and the Late Style in Modern Cinema," *Raritan* 21, 2 (Fall 2001), 29–47.

10 See for example Robynn J. Stilwell, "Music in Films: A Critical Review of the Literature, 1980–1996," *The Journal of Film Music* 1, 1 (2001), 19–61, at 47.

11 See Nicholas Cook, *Analyzing Musical Multimedia* (Oxford: Oxford University Press, 1998), 124.

12 The novel features topiary animals who come to life and attack. On Johnson's collaboration with Kubrick, see her "Writing *The Shining*," in *Depth of Field: Stanley Kubrick, Film, and the Uses of History*, edited by Geoffrey Cocks, James Diedrick, and Glenn Perusek (Madison, WI: University of Wisconsin Press, 2006), 55–61. My analysis was developed from the shorter British version of the film (DVD by Warner Home Video UK, 2001); timings for the US version (DVD by Warner Home Video, 1999) are taken from Lionnet's dissertation.

13 "Iconicity" refers to the closeness with which any sign system resembles the worldly features it indicates or represents. See Brown, *Overtones and Undertones*, 18.

14 Note also the sonorous "rhymes" between Danny's rattling axles and Bartók's xylophone. For a summary of some arguments for attention to the *mise-en-bande* as a whole, see James Buhler, "Analytical and Interpretive Approaches to Film Music (II): Analysing Interactions of Music and Film," in *Film Music: Critical Approaches*, edited by Kevin Donnelly (Edinburgh: Edinburgh University Press, 2001), 39–61.

15 It is worth recalling Richard Taruskin's description of this passage as redolent of "a figure in a landscape" in *The Oxford History of Western Music*, vol. 4 (Oxford: Oxford University Press, 2004), 394. Taruskin emphasizes the rhythms that link the melodies to Magyar speech; the point is reinforced by the warmth of the string writing within this timbral context.

16 Alison Castle (ed.) *The Stanley Kubrick Archives* (Köln: Taschen, 2008), 447.

17 See Michel Chion, *Audio-Vision: Sound on Screen*, edited and translated by Claudia Gorbman (New York: Columbia University Press, 1994), 8–9. Clearly the binary distinction between "empathetic" and "anempathetic" somewhat oversimplifies.

18 Ibid., 17–20.

19 Ibid., from 25 onwards.

20 Emphasis added. See Ligeti's interview with Josef Häusler before the première of *Lontano*, translated by Sarah E. Soulsby in *György Ligeti in Conversation* (London: Eulenberg, 1983), 83–110, at 104–5.

21 Mario Falsetto, *Stanley Kubrick: A Narrative and Stylistic Analysis* (Westport, CT: Greenwood Press, 1994), 135. See also Jason Sperb, *The Kubrick Façade: Faces and Voices in the Films of Stanley Kubrick* (Lanham, MD: Scarecrow Press, 2006).

22 See the pages from Gordon Stainforth's dubbing charts reproduced on the website devoted to the music of the film at www.drummerman.net/shining/charts.html.

23 See Ray Robinson and Allen Winold, A *Study of the Penderecki St. Luke Passion* (Celle: Moeck Verlag, 1983), 14–15.

24 The REDRUM/MURDER device was present in King's novel, but the graphic game with the letters is new to the filmic realization.

25 For thoughts on the transition from an epoch of "linear writing" to one of "technical images" see Vilém Flusser, *Towards a Philosophy of Photography*, translated by Anthony Mathews (London: Reaktion Books, 2000).

Chapter 9

Hearing Deep Seated Fears
John Carpenter's *The Fog* (1980)

K. J. Donnelly

When my mother was young her household was plagued by a poltergeist. I have always been intrigued by the story, not least hearing about how the phenomenon was nothing like "special effect" ghosts in films, but had a sonic presence rather than a visual presence. Indeed, paranormal happenings seemingly often involve noise, particularly of the infrasonic and ultrasonic variety. My mother's poltergeist activity exhibited an early warning on each occasion through the family dog becoming frenzied in clear reaction to sounds outside the range of human hearing, before the onset of a spate of audible banging and scraping sounds. Sounds can be disturbing, and one might argue that films often have scarier and more disturbing sounds and music than their visuals.

There is something primal about affecting sounds. Acoustic ecologist R. Murray Schafer has speculated and experimented concerning ambient sounds that are internalized unconsciously. He has been concerned about mains hum, also known as power line hum:

> in countries operating on an alternating current of 60 cycles, it is this sound which now provides the resonant frequency, for it will be heard (together with its harmonics) in the operation of all electrical devices from lights and amplifiers to generators. Where C is tuned to 256 cycles, this resonant frequency is B natural. In ear training exercises I have discovered that students find B natural much the easiest pitch to retain and recall spontaneously. Also during meditation exercises, after which the whole body has been relaxed and students are asked to sing the tone of "primary unity"—the tone which seems to arise naturally from the center of their being—B natural is more frequent than any other. I have also experimented with this in Europe where the resonant electrical frequency of 50 cycles is approximately G sharp. At the Stuttgart Music High School I led a group of students in a series of relaxation exercises and then asked them to hum the tone of "primary unity." They centered on G sharp.[1]

On the standard, equally tempered scale, 60 Hz is slightly flatter than B natural and is in fact pretty much half way between A-sharp and B (two octaves below middle C).

Droning tones dominate John Carpenter's electronic music for *The Fog* (1980). Qualitatively, they are an analogue of mains hum, delivering a sound that embodies the electric essence of the synthesizer as instrument. There is something primal about the film's music. While perhaps *The Fog's* music *should* have centered on a (slightly flat) B natural drone, its opening music centers on A natural. (It is in the key of A minor, which is easier to play on keyboards, in essence consisting of white keys only.) Some of the later drones in the film, however, center on B and a slightly flatter pitch. While we should remember that analog recordings on tape often raise or lower pitch through changing the speed of the tape, we should not discount a direct connection between these sounds and the frequency of mains electricity, particularly as electronic music embodies an essence of electricity and non-organic music making. Philip Brophy discusses Carpenter's music for *Escape from New York* (1981):

> Played by synthesizer banks triggered by sequencers, the pulse is exceedingly inhuman. . . . it is the product of electrical energy— always stated and presented as such and never allowed to "become music". . . . [T]he synthesizer's innate capacity for "inhumanness" is exploited to conduct (literally) energy and channel it through the score.[2]

This account alights on the character of analog synthesizer music as an emanation from technology and particularly electricity, a characteristic of Carpenter's music in the 1970s and 1980s that is evident across his films.

A fairly straightforward horror genre film, *The Fog* concerns a mysterious eponymous fog that descends upon a coastal town, containing the revenge-seeking ghosts of those who were robbed and killed to enable the foundation of the town. The film's director, John Carpenter, usually creates his own incidental music, utilizing primarily 1970s keyboard synthesizers. On the face of it, his music bears more resemblance to his popular contemporaries Jean-Michel Jarre or Vangelis than electronic experimentalists such as Vladimir Ussachevsky or Pierre Henry. Carpenter's film scores tend toward the basic and highly repetitive with clear textures, carrying an influence from minimalism, which is also evident in that the listener can hear and follow the developmental processes. The music regularly consists of a couple of basic themes, and extended pieces that are based on drones or ostinati, which provide stark tension and tend to grace the moments of climax in Carpenter's films. This procedure is perhaps most clearly illustrated in his breakthrough film, *Halloween* (1978), which established the highly distinctive style of Carpenter's film scores. Being electronic and premised upon spare texture and repetition, the scores initially appear characterized by musical primitivism. Burnand and Mera noted that "The obvious features of Carpenter's scores are obsessive repetition, primitivism and minimalism, and an improvisational approach that works at the most basic level of musical communication."[3] His music, particularly in his earlier films, appears to revel in its "lo-tech" sound and what might be called a "homebrew" status. In other words, this film music emanates from outside the established industry for producing incidental film music, standing in distinct contrast with modes of traditional mainstream film scores. Indeed, Carpenter's music provides a distinct contrast with modes of traditional mainstream film scores. Classical Hollywood film composers "operated within a paradigmatic range of classical norms. The combination of these stylistic parameters yielded a remarkably uniform group style among Hollywood composers that emphasized leitmotifs, theme writing and symphonic orchestrations."[4] Jeff Smith's succinct stylistic summary of classical cinema's incidental music might well be applicable to the overwhelming majority of contemporary film incidental music.[5] Carpenter's score for The Fog does include a number of traditional horror film score elements. Apart from the identifiable, repeated "themes" (leitmotifs), the film contains music for direct atmosphere rendering, intermittent bursts of music ("stingers") to accentuate violent action, pulses that bear some resemblance to heartbeats and repeated loops of musical material (as either ostinati or sustained droning tones).

Carpenter's score contains two repeated musical themes, but their placement appears not important structurally and not particularly interesting from the point of view of analysis. It is hardly surprising that the score's structure and unity is minimal; it revels in its fragmentary and repetitious nature. Rather than being written to fit the film, Carpenter's music arises more a part of the genetic make-up of the film—in its DNA. As the film's director, Carpenter occupies a profoundly different position from most film composers, from where he includes music as an essential component of the overall conception of film as an organic object, and therefore as an integrated part of film sound design. Carpenter's style involves fairly minimalist camerawork and lighting, and although he often uses Steadicam there tend to be few ostentatious visual flourishes, despite shooting all his films in widescreen (anamorphic 2.35:1).[6]

After being dissatisfied with the film once it was finished, Carpenter decided that the film needed redevelopment. Some set pieces were shot and added, and many of the sequences of impact violence were made more explicit with additional gore shots. The added scenes included the prologue and the attack on Stevie Wayne on the roof of the lighthouse.[7] While the film might have sacrificed some of its subtle atmospheric intention for bludgeoning action, it remains a haunting film.[8] It is highly likely that the music and sound effects were also bolstered and expanded, following the common assumption that music can save a failing film. This is evident at times in the superimposed sounds of "stingers on top of stingers" to give a massive sonic shock at precise moments of *The Fog*. For instance, at 16:32 when the first stabbing impact of the film takes place (on the Seagrass) the stinger is treated with electronic echo to enhance its force, while at 1:18:12, when the ghosts threaten Stevie Wayne on the roof of the lighthouse, an electronic stinger is augmented by the sudden and simultaneous onset of an organ chord.

The film's prologue has the character of an entirely separate scene in that it entails a cameo from John Houseman, who narrates a ghost story to a group of children around a campfire. Houseman had been a part of the Mercury Theater with Orson Welles, worked on *Citizen Kane* (1941), and enjoyed a long and distinguished career as a film producer and character actor. In terms of music, this sequence remains isolated in that his voice has accompaniment from a piece of music that does not emerge again in full, only in fragments. The relationship of music and voice has something of the operatic aria about it, with an interplay of dynamics and phrasing taking place between the two. It is preceded by a screen card quoting the conclusion of an Edgar Allen Poe poem ("Is All We See and Seem but a Dream Within a Dream?") which cues regular pulsing notes on the piano along with the subtle appearance of the deep drone that becomes ubiquitous throughout the film. It is accompanied initially by the ticking of a pocket watch that dangles at the right of the frame until the snapping shut of the case alongside a shock stinger. It appears alongside a sequentially descending melody on the piano (in A minor with an A pedal), which appears only intermittently in this pre-credit sequence (see Figure 9.1).

The melody opens the film over the Poe title card and then appears in the opening sequence when the camera alights on Andy among the children listening enrapt, which suggests the possibility that the ensuing film might be read as his fantasy. The opening melody is then subjected to a blockage, where the music remains as the opening three notes and refuses to run to the full twelve notes of the theme apart from on isolated occasions. The structure of the music in this sequence follows

[sustain pedal throughout]

Figure 9.1 Opening ghost story music (transcribed from the film)

an alternation between this melodic line on piano that is based on a descending minor key chord pattern over a synthesizer drone and a section of more sustained piano notes that is more dramatic and less melodic than the previous motif. The other section involves a so-called "drop out," where the existing melodic and harmonic structure dissipates to be replaced by sustained notes on the piano that cohere into sustained chords. The characteristic aspect here is the drop by a minor 6th in the bass, causing an unusual underlying chord change (A minor to C-sharp minor, then C-sharp minor to F minor). These piano chord changes that stress rising pitch function as powerful emphases, adding further drama and tension to Houseman's story. The conclusion of the narration involves a succession of the slow chord changes on the piano in sequence. The mix of timbres has the ethereal synthesizer representing the unknown counterposed with the organic sound of the piano that marks the familiar. These co-ordinate points place us into an "in between" state, emphasizing the spooky music as the sonic equivalent of a ghost story.

During this narrated sequence the music is highly effective and manipulative. The second section of the two alternated sections of musical material punctuates the scary story most dramatically with its sustained tones and pitch ascents, some of which occur between the cadences of Houseman's voice. The first section, in its quiet but insistent droning and repetition, soporifically lulls the audience into a dream state. The falling pitch (by sequence) and repeated melody depicts the entry to a vortex, and invokes fatality, and the inevitability of the story of the demise of Blake and his fellow lepers at the hands of a conspiracy returning to find justice in Antonio Bay. The sequence ends with the closure enabled by the equivalence of sound fading. The camera moves upwards and away in a classic concluding visual cadence, and simultaneously displacing the sound of the electronic drone with a fading-in radio tone. The structure of the music in this pre-credit sequence boosts the sense of inevitability and the importance of time invoked from the outset by the ticking clock. The sequence concludes with music accompanied by another iconic diegetic sound: a tolling bell, which often signifies impending doom.

Carpenter played in a band called the Coup de Villes, which also included the film's editor Tommy Lee Wallace and cinematographer Nick Castle. One of the group's songs appears in Carpenter's comedy *Big Trouble in Little China* (1986), and they even made a pop promo to accompany the single release. One of their songs graces the soundtrack of *The Fog*. Disc jockey Stevie Wayne introduces it (although he fails to give it a title) and dedicates it to the crew of the Seagrass, shortly before they are attacked by the ghostly ship.[9] Indeed, the film has a prominent unifying device in the town radio station ("KAB Antonio Bay"), which Andy's mother Stevie Wayne operates alone, playing a constant run of records. A sonic and conceptual opposition between the records played on the radio, and the film's electronic incidental music structure the film's soundtrack.[10] Michel Chion points to the importance of the radio station certain sections of *The Fog*, where it remains constant and ubiquitous, traversing the diegetic locations of the film. He notes that the compassionate disembodied voice of Wayne unifies and saves those under threat despite her isolation.[11] Her voice marks certainly a significant aspect of narrative development, interspersed with a selection of banal recordings, verging on muzak.[12] However, the music on the radio also serves a notable function, one that makes for a complex relationship with *The Fog*'s incidental score. The diegetic (but off-screen) and non-diegetic music forms a matrix of sorts. A notable opposition exists between the two musical formats, each with different functions, qualities, and affects. However, the associations reverse, where the music on the radio, originally conceived as emotional or sentimental, finds its function converted to that of emotionless music. As part of this process, the film's electronic underscore, which uses sounds that traditionally have not been accorded sentimental status, becomes the chief sonic emotional element.

Radio records	Electronics
Diegetic	Non-diegetic
Mostly jazz recordings	Functional incidental music
Cheap sentiment	Emotionless
Background noise	Affecting sound

The broad schematic division of the two different musical discourses in *The Fog* not only illustrates their radically different characters but also differentiates their functions and effects within the film. The radio's music embodies the human: organic, weak, and fallible in contrast with the synthetic sonic embodiment of the supernatural, killing machines, which appear to be highly efficient (perhaps like the machines of the synthesizers). Furthermore, the pieces of music on the radio are compromised, existing in the film as fragments without their fullness.[13] While musical underscores traditionally have been thought of as simply "background" or "wallpaper," *The Fog* includes music on the radio as precisely the sort of banal background music that might have been related to film music of the most undistinguished kind. Indeed, Claudia Gorbman noted the similarities between film incidental music and muzak.[14] While the radio music is associated with sentiment, its use in the film is without sentiment: precisely as an absence of emotion. Conversely, the synthesizer music of the underscore, a type of music that is normally associated with the mechanical and unemotional, works in the film to make direct emotional effects.

The processes that govern the use of these two musical discourses in *The Fog* are dominated by superimposition and displacement, where the electronics override records (and vice versa). These are not traditional "musical" developments. Indeed, David Burnand and Miguel Mera point to there being little musical development in Carpenter's music.[15] Instead, one might argue, these procedures emanate from the recording process, an aspect at the heart of film scoring even if it is rarely acknowledged by film music composers or scholars. While broadly speaking Burnand and Mera are correct, Carpenter's music forms a complex dialogue with diegetic music and diegetic sound effects. Indeed, diegetic music can take on a dramatic significance in the occasional absence of underscore. The sequence of weather man Dan being killed by the ghosts at the weather station has no incidental music but instead the anempathetic music from the radio station.[16] The anodyne character of the music functions particularly effectively in this situation, and in the aftermath of the attack continues without inspiring pity.

The records played on the radio throughout the film include swing, cool jazz, jazz-funk, Dixieland jazz, and other pieces, all of which take on something of the generic in their character. It all comes across as emotionless, soporific music, what might be deemed "sound filler" or aural wallpaper. Of course, this is precisely the sort of pejorative description that has been leveled at incidental music in film over the years. I find it impossible to regard the music as distinct pieces, which, I would argue, is precisely the intention of the film: to create a bland and soporific musical backdrop that illustrates a characterless continuum, an easy listening "much of a muchness." One might say that it is precisely "not music." Now, of course, electronic music was often also dismissed as "not music" in the 1970s and earlier. There was a persistent assumption that playing synthesizers required no musical ability.[17] It is easy to make an assumption that Carpenter's music is unsophisticated "one-finger" synthesizer playing, but this would be erroneous. During the 1970s, and even more strikingly during the 1980s, keyboard synthesizers became more accessible: both becoming easier to play and program, as well as becoming dramatically cheaper and more available. The proliferation of synthpop in the late 1970s, such as Gary Numan, The Normal, The Human League, Soft Cell and Depeche Mode is testament to the paramount importance of technological and production developments of the time. The limitations of musicians are often very evident in this sort of music, although they are not important.[18] For instance, The Human League's top-selling *Dare* (1981) album was completed with keyboard synthesizers played by people with no training on keyboards. However, the nature of the instruments themselves—which often allowed only one note to be played at a time— precluded the sort of keyboard playing that a trained organist or pianist might perform. The nature of the hardware allied often with untrained and naive musicians led to a "path of least resistance" approach to synthesizers at this point, and their "presets" of voices dominated over more sophisticated programming of sounds. Yet the instruments nevertheless tended to showcase sound qualities that arguably dominated melodic and harmonic concerns. While the technology to a lesser or greater degree decided how it was used, as evidenced by the propensity for clear and distinctive timbres and tones, this should not be mistaken for widespread simplicity or blanket lack of musical knowledge or ability.

Carpenter's official website fails to note which synthesizers were used for *The Fog's* soundtrack.[19] However, due to the distinctiveness of the sound, it is most likely that they were Moog synthesizers (see Figure 9.2) rather than the Prophet 5 and ARP synthesizers he used later. Carpenter tends to use regular collaborators on his film soundtracks. Alan Howarth began collaborating with Carpenter on *Escape from New York* (1981), which uses ARP synthesizers, and has a qualitatively different sound from Carpenter's earlier films.[20] For *The Fog*, Dan Wyman was credited as "orchestrator" (as he was on *Halloween* in 1978) and for "electronic realization."[21] The use of Moog synthesizers characterizes this earlier period; the difference is not insignificant. A perusal of progressive rock or

Figure 9.2 A Moog modular synthesizer

electronic "space music" records of the 1970s should illustrate the significance of different synthesizer hardware, which musicians listed precisely as if each brand of synthesizer was a wholly different instrument. Their sounds and "feel" as instruments are often profoundly different, despite following a similar basic physiology and sonic logic.

The likely synthesizer was not the Mini Moog but a Moog Series 3. The former was a mass-produced instrument with a simplified programming capability in comparison with the earlier Series 3. This, along with Carpenter's aid from specialist synthesizer players, illustrates that the music is far more than "one finger" simplicity. Upon closer inspection, Carpenter's score for The Fog betrays far more sophistication than might be noted upon a shallow engagement. Musical themes are less important than manipulating sound qualities and textures. Indeed, it is interested in exploiting the capabilities of synthesizers rather simply than pumping away at single notes as a basic accompaniment to the image.

The process of analog synthesis takes place wholly electronically and has its foundation in the manipulation of an electronic speaker often with a keyboard controller (or pre-programmed "sequencer"). The process involves at least one oscillator that provides a basic waveform that often will then be modified by modulating the signal with another signal, and cleaned up and adapted by filtering out overtones. In 1970s synthesizers these operations are all voltage controlled. This procedure is usually known as subtractive synthesis and leads to highly distinctive timbres.[22] I would like to suggest a high degree of technological determinism in the music of The Fog. The current orthodoxy in the humanities persists in human-centered approaches at the expense of all else. Such hyper-humanism finds it difficult to see processes that evacuate human activity as having much validity. It is not terribly fashionable to point to the foundations in human physiology of music (or indeed other culture). Primary sounds include the rhythmic pumping of blood in our veins and the slower rhythm of our breathing, while we are permanently attached to the high pitched whine of our nervous system. Furthermore, perhaps such sustained sounds might be related to tinnitus, a physical disorder of the ear that gives an impulse of resonance and focuses on often painful noise.[23]

The drones that grace The Fog clearly equate with foghorns on a symbolic-representational level. That is the logic of their foundation as music for the film. However, and more importantly, there is an equivalence between the fog in the film and the drones in the incidental music. This is beyond mere representation. It has something of the character of diegetic sound effects rather than non-diegetic music. The equivalence means that the appearance of the drone without the appearance of the fog still indicates that the fog is present.[24] This Pavlovian response is highly reminiscent of John Williams's iconic musical theme for the shark in

Jaws (1975). Such direct connections between sonic activity and diegetic action provide the music with the function of being a non-diegetic sound effect, where the conventional function of diegetic sound has been systematically and powerfully adopted by an aspect of the musical score.

In Rod Giblett's discussion of the symbolism of wetlands in literature and wider culture, he notes the "taxonomic anomaly of wetland: mud as mixing earth and water, fog as a mixture of air and water. Water is thus a kind of promiscuous substance that gets around, even sleeps around, too much with earth and air . . ."[25] This characterization suggests something of the mythic resonance that the fog brings with it to the film. Mist and fog are thus an encroachment on air by water, and water commonly signifies the boundary of consciousness (or unconsciousness).[26] Perhaps the musical equivalent would be white noise, a complex of all pitches that sounds like a river or a detuned radio. This sonic "primal soup" might be conceived as a sonic equivalent of the unconscious, from which sounds can emerge. In *The Fog*, the film's stingers (blasts of sound for dramatic shock effect) consist of actual blasts of synthesized white noise, an absolute rarity in the horror genre. There is also an extended passage of music that accompanies the onset of the siege of the church, which consists of a regular pulse of white noise blasts, which have something of the character of explosions or smashed glass. Apart from this, the repetitive pulses are predominantly deep in pitch. According to R. Murray Schafer, "In stressing low-frequency sound popular music seeks blend and diffusion rather than clarity and focus, which had been the aim of previous music . . ."[27] The drones in *The Fog* certainly make something of a sonic continuum for large sections of the film, varying in volume and intensity and at times even remaining on the verge of audibility.

Sustained droning might be conceived as closely related to sonic repetition; indeed, traditional musicology has conceived of the two as closely related in that they use a minimal amount of different musical material (i.e. pitches, durations, and articulations) and might often be notated with the repeat symbol. Such music has often been approached as musically simplistic and not terribly interesting. However, repetition has its own psychology as well as its own aesthetics. In the context of film, particularly horror films, repetitive music functions to induce instant tension as well as having a cumulative effect of disquiet or extreme anxiety. While the techniques of minimalism have been well established in art music since the 1960s, this is not the same as repetitive approaches in film music. Here, musical processes are never fully autonomous and work with the rest of the film almost as if they were an integral part of the composition. *The Fog*'s final confrontation, the siege at the church and immediately beforehand, illustrate vividly the psychology of repetition, where there is a cumulative effect rather than any specific value in the musical material itself that is being repeated.[28]

The Fog's music is highly distinctive in its approach to repetition, drone, and sonority. It is premised upon playing with resonances and sound intensities, largely through the use of varied volume and frequency filter controls. While this is a regular process in the non-diegetic music, at times it is also apparent in some of the diegetic music played by DJ Stevie Wayne at the KAB Antonio Bay radio station. Here, from time to time, the songs and musical pieces are treated to sound as if the radio is drifting in and out of tuning, giving a phasing effect and losing higher and lower overtones—in effect becoming as filtered as some of the droning underscore.

The use of fade-ins, as well as raising and lowering volume, supplies a strong intimation of movement in the droning music. Such a clear suggestion of movement, specifically a coming towards the film spectator, conjures a profound threat. It is perhaps surprising that there has been so little written about the sense of movement evident in some music. Robert Morgan noted the sense of distance, and the essential divisions and movement, between musical surface and background.[29] In *The Philosophy and Aesthetics of Music*, Edward Lippman notes that we perceive high pitch as close by, and that our impression of proximity or distance comes through elements such as high and low pitch, as well as the degree of surface detail and busyness of the music.[30] It is a mistake to assume that a sense of sonic movement is absent in films before the advent of stereo sound or spatialized sound design. While *The Fog* benefits from stereo sound, rather than relying upon the illusion of spatial placement afforded by different volumes in separate stereo channels, often the general sense of drone volume bringing the sound forwards or backwards in the mix indicates the fog's spatial proximity.

An illustrative moment of the music's processes takes place on the Seagrass trawler when the ghostly sailing ship comes up alongside and attackers come out of the accompanying fog. The fog's appearance is doubled by the appearance of a deep pulsing drone note (at 17:14), soon joined by a higher sustained pitch, which has something of the character of a jet airplane engine sound. This two-note drone chord is then joined by a distorted pitch in between (which makes one of the most dissonant intervals to one of the existing notes—the tritone). The last tone tunes in (at 17:49), and then the intensity of the music lulls, making for a drop-out that leaves the quiet initial single note drone. The development in dynamics matches the on-screen activity, where there is a short period of repose before further action. The initial musical configuration returns with a white noise stinger, which embodies violence in sonic terms. The initial chord then returns with pulsing 4/4 deep notes and some white noise ambience. The middle-pitched tone (which is high) begins a process of beating due to its harmonics conflicting with those of the other tones.

It then tunes dramatically to a unison note (as the ghost ship pulls aside the Seagrass), which halts the beating, and then all fades.

The complexity of this piece of synthesizer music demonstrates that it is far from the simple act of a keyboard note being depressed and held down continuously. Upon closer inspection, the sounds are premised upon variations within the same note and with concerns central for density and textural quality of sound. Indeed, the manipulation of the drones with volume and filtering controls (regulating the degree of low and high-pitched harmonics) makes a startling parallel to the basic functioning of analog synthesis. One of the best illustrations of this takes place at the film's denouement, specifically where the group of people takes shelter in the church from the ghostly assailants contained in the fog. At one point, the music drops out to almost nothing, through a process of filtering out the existing sounds (precisely like synthesizers filtering out defining overtones) and then returns, as before, very dramatically.[31] This is a process of withholding, which suggests that the droning music has less become absent and returned than been consistent and only been obscured from being heard. Such a strategy of withholding is remarkably similar to the general process of subtractive synthesis, where filters remove overtones from complex waveforms to allow for simpler and less "noisy" tones. (Furthermore, there is also a processual similarity with the sort of withholding strategies evident in horror film narratives.) Perhaps the most obvious similarity is to the so-called "drop-out" sections in popular songs, where most of the instruments stop playing for a short period. This technique proliferates on electronic dance records, where the "drop-out" provides a moment of respite but also an anticipation, ready for the onset of the music in full effect.

The mixture of manipulating overtones and playing around with tuning (moving pitches upwards and downwards) leads to what is known as beating, where the extremely close proximity of pitches vibrate against one another and make for interference between their vibrations. This is significant, as such micro-tunings (an effect of going out of tune) form a fundamental dis-harmony and appear only occasionally in horror films as a device, a disturbing effect. It should also be borne in mind that the use of this technique in the form that it appears in *The Fog* might well emanate more from the particular characteristics of the synthesizers. Notoriously difficult to keep in tune, analog Moog synthesizers had a habit of allowing pitch to slip, particularly once the solid state electronic components became hot. Thus, there is the possibility of approaching some of the aesthetics of the music from the point of view of hardware capabilities.

The Fog's utilization of a sonic continuum that embraces and moves between drone and pulse does not derive in any way from the tradition of incidental film music, but emanates from the basics of acoustics, furnishing a *primal* sonic character to the film. This process is far closer to sound design than it is to traditional "music."[32] This can further be underlined with reference to the opening "sound symphony" section of unexplained events providing a succession of distinct diegetic sounds, which takes place shortly after *The Fog*'s prologue delivered by John Houseman at the fireside and marks an extended and extremely leisurely title sequence. The following section of the film depicts a number of mysterious incidents transpiring in the town of Antonio Bay, including bottles falling and smashing and untouched diesel pumps spilling their fuel on the ground. This involves an extended part of the film without dialogue or music but premised upon the succession of showcased sounds that is a clear *homage* to the start of Sergio Leone's *Once Upon a Time in the West* (1968), where the succession of sounds build tension and convey the boredom of the cowboy assassins waiting at the railroad station for their target. Both cases are clear examples of the modernist notion of composing with disparate sounds. It is this logic, more than any tradition of film scoring, that is the principal determinant upon Carpenter's music for *The Fog*. Mera and Burnand note a blurring of the distinction between music and sound effects in Carpenter's later film *Escape from New York*.[33] *The Fog*, a year earlier, evinces a similar sonic blurring, with music encroaching upon the traditional domain of diegetic sound for the purposes of terror.

One might ask, "When is music not music?" The answer might be: "When it is film sound design." Of course, this could account for all music in films. Horror films, which tend to retain a visceral focus on brute effect and gaining a reaction from the audience, illustrate the modes of film music particularly well, as music's role in film is often of a sensual rather than necessarily of a communicative nature.

In part a story of the sea's perennial mystery, *The Fog* also concerns a return of repressed past events. The repeated piano note that inaugurates the opening theme suggests and then doubles a clock ticking, thereby implying an inevitability, or the workings of fate.[34] The fog represents an uncertain state, predating the solidity of the current world. The radio station plays a good amount of antiquated material, with swing and Dixieland jazz prominent. Indeed, it is striking that, apart from the odd piece, KAB seems to play a remarkably old-fashioned roster of music, which manifests an ignored background, much like the origin of the town itself. So, the radio station's concern with a musical past parallels the center of the story, about the return of the past for the purposes of revenge on the ancestors of wrongdoers.

There was a related soundtrack album, which later ran to an expanded CD edition with the addition of an interview with Jamie Lee Curtis, who had played Elizabeth in the film. As befits a scholar of film music,

I procured a bootleg CD of the film's music that included almost all the music from the film and was twice as long as the official release. The difference between the two CDs is instructive. The official release packages the most traditionally musical aspects of the score into a listenable format that, if the listener was unaware of the film, might lead one to believe that the film had a strong set of diverse melodic cues. The bootleg CD, on the other hand, makes no concessions to molding a listening experience and merely holds together the music that graced the film. As a consequence, it is dominated by droning cues and soporific radio music. The former exemplifies the pressure to develop "music" as a marketable resource, while the latter clearly demonstrates the music's function as film sound and its delineation of a psychological continuum in the film rather than any distinctively "musical" character.

Carpenter's *The Fog* was remade in 2005.[35] The remake re-imagined the original in the form of a fairly straightforward mainstream teen horror film. One aspect that helped resituate the new film was the fairly stereotypical contemporary horror film music by Graeme Revell. His score was fully in accord with the tone of the remake and has some fine atmospheric moments, but it remains strikingly distant from Carpenter's music. Significantly, it lacks the relentless drones that embody the fog, and thus loses the fundamental psychology of primal sound that makes Carpenter's film and music so disturbing and so effective. In the original version, music adopts the foreground in the film, constituting a *primary effect* rather than mere incidental background. This is exemplified most clearly in the way that the eponymous fog of the film is sounded by synthesizers, forming as much a *sonic* as a visual threat. Such an affordance stems from the properties of sound itself, as invisible, enveloping, and potentially disturbing.[36] Like my family's poltergeist, disquieting sound can generate a clear and physical embodiment of the threat of the inexplicable in a far more effective manner than mere visuals.

Notes

1 R. Murray Schafer, *Our Sonic Environment and the Soundscape: The Tuning of the World* (Rochester, VT: Destiny, 1994) [first published 1977], 98–9.
2 Philip Brophy, *100 Modern Soundtracks* (London: BFI, 2004), 99.
3 David Burnand and Miguel Mera, "Fast and Cheap? The Film Music of John Carpenter," in *The Cinema of John Carpenter: The Technique of Terror*, edited by Ian Conrich and David Woods (London: Wallflower, 2004), 65.
4 Jeff Smith, *The Sounds of Commerce: Marketing Popular Film Music* (New York: Columbia University Press, 1998), 6.
5 David Bordwell and Janet Staiger argue for a broad persistence of classical cinema into the present era. See David Bordwell and Janet Staiger, "Since 1960: the Persistence of a Mode of Film Practice," in David Bordwell, Janet Staiger, and Kristin Thompson, *The Classical Hollywood Cinema: Film Style and Mode of Production to 1960* (London: Routledge, 1985), 367.

6 The film is full of cameos, in-jokes, and references. Carpenter appears as Bennett, Jamie Lee Curtis's mother, Janet Leigh, plays Mrs. Williams, and characters are named after some of the film's technicians.

7 John Carpenter, sleeve notes to *John Carpenter's The Fog* (new expanded edition, Silva Screen FILMCD 342, 2000).

8 *The Fog* connects directly with the Val Lewton tradition of atmosphere-centered horror films. Edmund G. Bansak, *Fearing the Dark: The Val Lewton Career* (Jefferson, NC: MacFarland, 2003), 521.

9 The piece sounds quite distant from the band's song in *Big Trouble in Little China* (1986), starting out sounding a little like Steely Dan and then ending up sounding more like Spyro Gyra. At this time, the Coup de Villes released an album called *Waiting Out the Eighties*.

10 Indeed, there is a similar mix of diegetic songs and underscore in his later film *Christine* (1983).

11 Michel Chion, *The Voice in Cinema*, edited and translated by Claudia Gorbman (New York: Columbia University Press, 1999), 118–19.

12 The radio station also lacks the characteristic advertisements of US radio stations.

13 The radio's music is premised upon band-pass filters that remove high and low frequencies to produce characteristic lo-fi radio sound (also like a telephone), while the synthesizer music is premised upon the use of a similar frequency filter process.

14 Claudia Gorbman, *Unheard Melodies: Narrative Film Music* (London: BFI, 1987), 56–9.

15 Burnand and Mera, "Fast and Cheap?," 60.

16 According to Michel Chion, anempathetic music redoubles its effect through its indifference to the action (while making apparent the mechanical character of film). Michel Chion, *Audio-Vision: Sound on Screen*, edited and translated by Claudia Gorbman (New York: University of Columbia Press, 1994), 8–9.

17 Indeed, synthesizers regularly were approached as if they were "machines." This is dramatized by Kraftwerk's song "Pocket Calculator." "I'm the operator with my pocket calculator" in the German version is rendered as: "Ich bin der Musikant, mit Taschenrechner in der Hand" ("I'm the musician . . ."). Apart from merely enabling the rhyme, this suggests that in Germany there was less of a sense of synthesizers being "unmusical" and operated by technicians rather than musicians.

18 Robert Walser notes that trained musicians often fail to register strategies for producing music outside the logic of "trained" musicianship. Robert Walser, "Rhyme, Rhythm and Rhetoric in the Music of Public Enemy," *Ethnomusicology*, 39, 2 (Spring/Summer 1995), 198.

19 www.theofficialjohncarpenter.com (accessed 2 May 2008).

20 Howarth worked on special sound effects for the first *Star Trek* films, and also as a sound designer and supervising sound editor on various films.

21 Carpenter and Wyman play the synthesizers although the music credit in the film is to the "Bowling Green Wayne County Chamber Orchestra."

22 They are very good at certain things—indeed, vintage analog synthesizers are highly prized today for bass sounds. This is in stark contrast to the 1970s fear (actually a perennial fear) that analog synthesizers would simply replace the use of other instruments.

23 John Cage wrote about hearing these two primal sounds upon entering an anechoic chamber at Harvard University. John Cage, *Silence: Lectures and Writings* (London: Marion Boyars, 1980), 8.

24 The fog's first appearance cues drone, but this remains in cut-away shots of Stevie Wayne at the lighthouse.

25 Rod Giblett, *Postmodern Wetlands: Culture, History, Ecology* (Edinburgh: Edinburgh University Press, 1996), 14.

26 Another good example of this is the appearance of amphibious Marshmen at the fogbound "Mistfall" in the *Doctor Who* story "Full Circle" (1980) that were also accompanied by repetitive electronic music.

27 Schafer, *Our Sonic Environment*, 117.

28 Incidental music in film regularly follows a clear pattern of tension and release that is less straightforward in minimalist art music. Robert Fink notes a focus by analysts on minimalism as non-dialectical and related to Freud's death instinct, a reaction to the compulsion to repeat. Robert Fink, *Repeating Ourselves: American Minimal Music as Cultural Practice* (Berkeley, CA: University of California Press, 2005), 5.

29 Robert Morgan, "Musical Time/Musical Space," *Critical Inquiry* 8 (1980), 527–38.

30 Edward A. Lippman, *The Philosophy and Aesthetics of Music* (Lincoln, NE: University of Nebraska Press, 1999), 27.

31 Claudia Gorbman notes the "tom tom" rhythm of regular repeated beats with a strong emphasis on the first, which is represents Native Americans and their music in traditional Hollywood film scores. Its clear appearance here might point to the ghosts as a metaphor for those displaced by the manifest destiny of the settlement and creation of the United States. Claudia Gorbman, "Scoring the Indian: Music in the Liberal Western," in *Western Music and Its Others: Difference, Representation and Appropriation in Music*, edited by Georgina Born and David Hesmondhalgh (Berkeley, CA: University of California Press, 2000), 235.

32 In terms of mixing music and sound effects, an argument certainly might be made that horror films have done this many times before almost as a matter of course.

33 Mera and Burnand, "Fast and Cheap?," 61.

34 A similar instance of tension and the implication of a ticking clock in the music is detailed in Neil Lerner, "'Look at that big hand move along': Clocks, Containment, and Music in *High Noon*," *South Atlantic Quarterly* 104, 1 (Winter 2005), 158.

35 Carpenter and Debra Hill were among the film's producers; the film was directed by Rupert Wainwright.

36 See further discussion in K. J. Donnelly, *The Spectre of Sound: Film and Television Music* (London: BFI, 2005), 88–110.

Chapter 10

Music and the Adult Ideal in *A Nightmare on Elm Street*

James Buhler

A Nightmare on Elm Street (1984) appeared after the basic semantics and syntax of the slasher subgenre had already been well established: a psychotic killer stalks a group of teens (or young college kids), killing them off in unexpected, theatrical, and usually gory ways. At least one of the kids, usually a smart plucky female, survives the ordeal, and the last part of the film is typically structured around an elaborate confrontation of the killer and this so-called "final girl." This confrontation leads to the climax where the final girl apparently dispatches the killer in some suitably grisly manner.[1] The end of the film, however, nearly always calls into question the finality of the victory, intimating that the killer has, in fact, somehow survived, thus providing the space for an indefinite number of sequels.

The *Nightmare* series reworked this slasher formula to emphasize the teens' relationship to adult society as a prominent secondary conflict. From the formula, the series retained especially the figure of the final girl and what Gary Heba identifies as the "incoherent" structure, whose most prominent feature is the inconclusive ending. It also configured the formula so that the monster, Freddy, appears fairly explicitly as a perverse reflection of adult society. Freddy survives from film to film because his character preserves, albeit in negative form, the adult ideal that is missing in actual adult society but that is still required by the teens to understand and negotiate the terms of that society. For various reasons outlined below, the terms of this adult ideal are most clearly expressed in the soundtrack, which is decisively shaped by the filmmakers' decision to rely heavily on the synthesizer and what I call the principle of surreal sound synthesis for scoring.

The Final Girl and Incoherence in the Slasher

According to Carol J. Clover's analysis, the figure of the final girl "combine[d] the functions of suffering victim and avenging hero," roles that the traditional horror film usually was careful to separate.[2] Prior to the slasher, the principal heroine in a horror film was usually either killed by the monster or saved by a hero, who was either a father figure or a (future) mate. Syntactically, this resulted in editing into lines of parallel action especially in the climactic sequence, often culminating in the hero rescuing the victim from the grips of the monster at the very last possible moment. A good example occurs in *Dracula* (1931), where Harker saves Mina as van Helsing stakes Dracula at the conclusion of the film. The defeat of the monster coincided with the union of the hero and heroine as well as with the restoration of the order that had been disrupted by the monster.[3] In the characteristic syntax of the slasher, by contrast, the victim is also the hero, and the final girl usually finds that father figures or boyfriends are unconcerned or useless—in any case, ineffectual.[4] The result is that the final girl must defeat (or at least escape) the monster using her own wits and powers. As Clover notes, the character of the final girl alters the terms of the social allegory considerably, as her active presence seems to undermine the role of social authority. "For whatever reason, modern horror seems especially interested in the trials of everyperson, and everyperson is on his or her own in facing the menace, without help from 'authorities.'"[5] Since one of the major thematic oppositions in these films is between the youth (who are under attack) and an older (ineffectual if not indifferent) community, this fusion of victim and hero in the figure of the final girl serves to diminish the importance of the adults. Indeed, the final girl often enough must succeed in spite of the adults (or against the backdrop of their indifference).

A second way that the slasher subgenre differs from the traditional horror film is in its principled refusal of narrative closure; this refusal serves as a primary source of its incoherence. Robin Wood defines the basic narrative of horror film this way: "Normality is threatened by the monster."[6] For Wood, this means that traditional horror is at root a socially and politically conservative genre.[7] Mark Jancovich provides an excellent summary:

> In the case of horror, it is claimed that the pleasure offered by the genre is based on the process of narrative closure in which the horrifying or monstrous is destroyed or contained. The structure of horror narratives are [sic] said to set out from a situation of order, move through a period of disorder caused by the eruptions of the horrifying or monstrous forces, and finally reach a point of closure and completion in which disruptive, monstrous elements are contained or destroyed and the original order is re-established. The audience's pleasure is supposed to be based upon the expectation that the narrative will reach this particular type of conclusion, and eventual fulfillment of this expectation.[8]

For Wood, the narrative closure of horror serves to reassert the norm, and he finds the ideological force and insistence of this closure troubling.

Wood therefore celebrates films that refuse this sort of closure and points to *The Texas Chainsaw Massacre* (1974), in particular, as charting a different path. It ends not with the defeat (and/or containment) of the monster but only with escape.

Heba calls films that lack such closure "incoherent," which he contrasts with the traditional horror's "coherence," especially its adherence to syntactical closure that reinscribes traditional notions of order. Incoherent films, he says, "can be characterized by a lack of definite closure or conflict resolution." Heba adds that:

> while coherent versions of horror depend on humanity being able to control and vanquish external sources of horror, incoherent movies focus on humanity's limited abilities to control the horrors—or worse, on humanity's capacity to create its own horrors that cannot be contained by the coherent master narrative.[9]

Films in the slasher subgenre, even when not part of a series, are inconclusive; their endings attack the closure that makes the coherence of traditional horror film possible.[10]

If we take "incoherence" as extending beyond opening up a space for the sequel, we will find that these films tend to systematically undermine other methods of narrative control; that is, they feature unreliable narration. Incoherence results when unreliable narration is extended from a local technique of suspense, common to horror, into a principle that structures the whole narration: an unreliable narrative no longer has the power to contain its monster. Continued unreliability of the narrative signifies that the threat of the monster has not dissipated. Indeed, a considerable degree of narrative unreliability—or at least lack of narrative control—forms one of the hallmarks of the slasher subgenre, and the audience just as much as the final girl learns to be paranoid: these films horrify by presenting radical short circuits with wanton deaths of innocents on the one hand and a monster who can never quite be contained by the closure of the narrative on the other. This horror scares at least in part because it encourages the imagination to outstrip the narrative containment. We know that bad things can happen, and the narrative has apparently no ability to control them. The narrative seems particularly incapable of controlling the representation of the monster—that is what horrifies us as we leave the theater. And this lack of narrative control seems simply a reflection of the failure of parental authority so characteristic of the final girl pattern.

A Nightmare on Elm Street as Slasher

The original *A Nightmare on Elm Street* and its seven sequels (as of 2009) follow the slasher subgenre strictly in fusing the functions of victim and hero—though *Freddy's Revenge* (1985) centers on a male protagonist (i.e. a final boy), and in all but the first, more than a single individual survives. All but *Freddy's Dead* (1991) and perhaps *Wes Craven's New Nightmare* (1994)—actually a metacinematic take on the series—are "incoherent" in the sense that they end with ambiguity about fate of the monster, Freddy, and so leave space for sequels.

The *Nightmare* series differs from the slasher subgenre in some characteristic ways, primarily having to do with the treatment of Freddy, its monster. First of all, the films lack the characteristic two-part structure of films such as *Halloween* (1978) and *Friday the 13th* (1980), where a prologue reveals some original trauma, while the remainder of the film serves as a repetition, or return of the repressed, of that event.[11] The series does have such an event (or rather a series of events associated with Freddy's history), and its mythology circulates around that origin as a figure of repression, but the presentation of the originary event is handled either through dialogue among characters, such as Nancy's mom's tale of Freddy's death in the first film, or through (dreamed) flashback (as in parts 3 through 6). For the most part, the flashbacks avoid the point-of-view camera work associated with the murderer in the prologue as in the slasher formula (e.g. *Halloween*, *Friday the 13th*). In this way, the *Nightmare* series constructs a different relationship to the source of its repression, and some of the particular distinguishing features of Freddy as monster come from the way in which his return obscures as much as it reveals. Second, perhaps because Freddy does not originally appear as the point of view of the camera, he is not particularly concerned about being seen. Although perfectly willing to play the role of the unseen monster when it suits his purposes, he does not diminish in power nor increase in vulnerability once visible: indeed, he likes to taunt his victims with this fact. (Here, again, *Freddy's Revenge* remains something of an exception, as the film treats Freddy as a monster akin to traditional horror film, especially possession stories, more so than do the other films of the series.) Third, Freddy is relatively loquacious for the killer of the slasher subgenre. In this respect, compare Freddy with the mute Michael Myers of *Halloween* or Jason of *Friday the 13th*. Both of these latter two monsters seem like supernatural killing machines, whereas Freddy, by contrast, seems far more human.

Finally, the "terrible place" of the monster is not a physical location such as the prototypical old dark house (although in later films Nancy's house will become something of a terrible place) but rather as a fantasy space of a nightmare. Freddy appears as a phantom of the dream world, one of whose powers involves the ability to blur the distinction between dream and reality. The films themselves mark a thematic distinction between a waking "real" world governed nominally by social institutions of adults and the "nightmare" world of the dream governed by the rules of Freddy. In this way the films map an external geography onto an internal, psychological one of reality and dream world. But the series does not really psychologize the relation inasmuch as the nightmare is collective. Thus, again and again, the adults approach the nightmare as an individual delusion and each time treating it as such leads to failure (and usually at least one of the kids dies as a result). Only those individuals who recognize the threat as collective and so not treatable at the individual level manage to survive. This division into real world and nightmare makes the teens' relationship to the adult social world a much greater factor in this series than in other slashers—though, as Vera Dika notes, most films in the subgenre explore in some fashion the transition "from a state of childhood innocence to an adult knowledge of evil."[12]

Nightmare, the Adult Ideal, and the Soundtrack

The prologue of the original film shows Freddy assembling his finger knives, his characteristic instruments of torture (Figure 10.1). Along with labored breathing and sound effects associated with the knives, we hear an atmospheric synthesizer pad, modeled to some extent on vocal sounds and string harmonics, interspersed with hits on synthesized drums. This music is interrupted by a more specifically synthesized sound that sweeps from high to low as the film title appears (00:01:05) before settling into an oscillating repeated two-note pattern behind a disembodied scream. The music at this point shifts to a more string-like tone but it is overlaid with a wind sound and some low-level unidentifiable sounds (laughter,

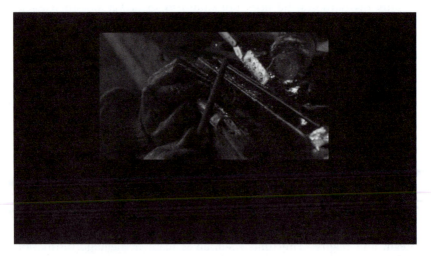

Figure 10.1 Freddy manufactures his finger knives in the dream prologue to *A Nightmare on Elm Street*

Figure 10.2 Transcription of Elm Street Theme in dream prologue to *A Nightmare on Elm Street*

farm animals?) before a prototype of the Nightmare theme (Figure 10.2) appears in bell-like tones (00:01:18). The remainder of the sequence, which is later revealed to be a nightmare of Tina, plays similarly. Beyond the fractured presentation of narrative information, this sequence serves to bind the surreal timbres of the synthesizer to the terrible place of the nightmare in general and to Freddy in particular. From this point onward, the presence of music outside the nightmares tends to signify the potential of Freddy's menace to expand.

Compare the music in the dream prologue of the first film to the extended introduction of the graduation-day sequence near the beginning of *A Nightmare on Elm Street 5: The Dream Child* (1989). Whereas the synthesizer had dominated the earlier sequence, here the famous trio from Edward Elgar's Pomp and Circumstance March, No. 1 plays in a full orchestra version (the music begins at 00:08:03), as we hear, in voice-over, what sounds like a graduation speech: "And as adults we must now prepare for a new life outside this wonderful environment known as Springwood High." The theme of the speech here hardly surprises: it speaks to initiation and rite of passage, to the experience of coming into adulthood. Nothing could be more common or appropriate to the occasion of graduation day. The same could be said for the Pomp and Circumstance March, which is remarkable only because it is wholly unremarkable and so might almost pass without notice: this is exactly the music that we would expect to accompany a graduation. In that sense, the music here simply fulfills its conventional role in the ritual and projects a conventional musical image of the adult ideal. Yet if the ritual justifies and even mandates the conventional appearance of this music, its placement within the ritual masks its status as a musical legacy of an older social order.

This order descends in the first place from that of British imperialism: Elgar composed the March in 1901. It thus served to mark the passing of the Victorian era and to inaugurate the reign of Edward VII: Elgar redeployed the trio in his 1902 Coronation Ode, where, as "The Land of Hope and Glory," the tune has come to serve as an unofficial English (as opposed to British) national anthem, used regularly, for instance, at the Last Night of the Proms and occasionally for sporting events. The imperialist claim, however, is made clearer in the original context, which plays specifically on the pageantry and spectacle of war. The title of

Elgar's March comes from Shakespeare's *Othello*, which speaks of the "pride, pomp, and circumstance of glorious war." Elgar also inscribed lines from "The March of Glory" by Lord de Tabley as an epigraph for the First March: "Like a proud music that draws men on to die/Madly upon the spears in martial ecstasy,/A measure that sets heaven in all their veins/And iron in their hands." If the full horror of this world view would become evident only in the tragedy of the First World War, the imperialism that supported and even possibly required that world view in order to sustain itself declined in the aftermath of a social order, rigidly demarcated by class, nation, and race, broken by that war. Where in England "The Land of Hope and Glory" might, in the aftermath of the First World War, be a nostalgic reminder of faded imperial glory, in the United States, the tune stripped of its words (if not its ideals—the United States likewise sees itself as a "land of hope and glory") served to mark the ceremonial coming of age at precisely the moment that the country itself was coming of age as an imperial power. Already in 1905, Elgar's trio had been appropriated by Yale as a graduation recessional. By the 1920s, its use for graduation ceremonies in the United States would be ubiquitous. Jump forward sixty years, however, and the imperial designs of the United States had suffered a serious setback in Vietnam and a lesser one in Iran, and the country had also experienced a crisis of confidence in the various social and political institutions that had led to the war and general social unrest. If Ronald Reagan came to the presidency in 1981 with the promise of restoring America's prestige in the world, this call for restoration implied that the social order itself had fallen into disrepair. It is in this context that we should understand the appearance of "Pomp and Circumstance" in *The Dream Child*: while in connection with the graduation ceremony it is a musical representation of the adult ideal, it is also the legacy of a social order that is no longer.

This use of "Pomp and Circumstance" is completely ordinary, and aside from the mention of Springwood High, the speech, too, could appear in any number of films for a brief graduation scene. The latent historicity of Elgar's march, however, may or may not be activated in a particular film. In *The Dream Child*, both the speech and the music begin off-screen. The music enters, in fact, as a sound advance under the sound of the shower, as Alice is preparing for graduation after having woken from a nightmare. The voice-over—it is her boyfriend, Dan— starts with a dissolve to the exterior of the high school, roughly five seconds later. At the end of the line quoted above, a cut to Dan brings a marked change in registers. The graduates are in fact not recognized as adults—even by themselves. Just as Dan's speech tries comic irony in delivering "wonderful environment," so too the rest of the post-graduation scene makes us see that "and as adults" is equally ironic. The film makes this abundantly clear when Dan (Figure 10.3) dons silly glasses and ends

Figure 10.3 "So let's blow this pop stand": Dan's call for graduation regression in
A Nightmare on Elm Street 5: The Dream Child

his speech with an explicit call for regression: "So let's blow this pop stand."

The music disappears in the approving cheers of the crowd. Overbearing parental relationships begin to assert themselves in the post-graduation scene that follows, which completely undermines the terms of the graduation as a coming of age. The parents see themselves as guiding their kids in socially appropriate directions (becoming economically productive members of society), but the graduates see regression as a temptation, not so much because they do not want to grow up as because they want to escape this parental control, which seemingly demands an absolute identity between social and economic being. In any event, both parents and graduates lack an adult ideal that could recognize the gap between these values. The graduation ceremony in fact serves merely to underscore a point of exclusion: the graduates are no longer high schoolers even if it is not at all clear what their new social role will be. At the pool party celebrating their graduation, little of substance has changed. Certainly the music at the party is indistinguishable from music that they would have had at a party prior to graduation. This suggests that the graduates continue to identify with their pre-graduation self rather than any emerging adult self. (None of this is particularly surprising: the continuity of the music just points to the fact that high school graduation has, to a large extent, ceased to function in the United States as initiating subjects into adulthood proper.)[13]

The particular use of Elgar's Pomp and Circumstance March in *The Dream Child* is arguably the only place in the entire series that we hear a musical representation of the adult ideal. The general absence of such musical representation is hardly accidental: whether or not an explicit intention of the filmmakers, this absence nevertheless marks a point of repression in the films. Indeed, at a thematic level, the films, like the slasher genre in general, are obsessed with the adult ideal—or rather its absence, that is, with the breakdown of social institutions and adult authority. This scene is so telling because the presence of the adult ideal here in a highly ritualized context makes us aware of its absence elsewhere in the series. This does not mean that the series lacks in sympathetic adult characters. Obviously, it has them. But these characters—for instance, Nancy and Neil in the third film, Maggie and Doc in the sixth—tend to be positioned at the margins of adult society and are often presented as in conflict with it. They may model an ideal adult (from the teens' perspective at least) but they do not project the adult ideal of society. Nevertheless, the presence of these sympathetic adults can confuse the relationship between ideal adult and adult ideal. The soundtrack, on the contrary, makes the systemic absence of the adult ideal abundantly clear.

Indeed, in terms of the soundtrack, the adult world is basically represented by talk (lecturing as much as dialogue) and noise (ambient sound). This is appropriate inasmuch as adults function as agents and creatures of reality. Sounds of place—the police station, the hospital, the street—are common. Nature sounds—birds during the day, crickets at night—are likewise common; indeed these sounds often pass easily through windows and doors of houses, where they serve as backdrops to conversations, especially when adults speak to the kids. The marked presence of such nature sounds in the home is telling, as it suggests both that the family is a natural state of society and that, more ominously, a state of nature (entropy) has begun to encroach on and determine the social category of the family.

In fact, music does not generally play a substantial part in the representation of adult society. Indeed, aside from the Pomp and Circumstance March, other uses of music in association with adults generally run counter to an adult ideal, and indeed explicitly use music as an explicit sign of regression. One example might be the bar scene in A Nightmare on Elm Street 3: The Dream Warriors (1987) where Nancy's dad, once a proud detective but now reduced to being a security guard, drowns his sorrows to the strains of blues guitar. Here, music represents the opposite of the adult ideal: it underscores the sense that Nancy's dad has become an embodiment of regression; by extension it suggests the inability of the social institution to deal with its failure. Something similar happens with the scene at the Springwood fair in Freddy's Dead: The Final Nightmare (1991), where detuned carousel music serves to underscore the collective psychosis of the town, whose adults and institutions have proven incapable of saving even a single kid. Again, the music here clearly signifies regression, as the adult behavior it accompanies is appropriately juvenile if not infantile. More complicated is the use of big band music at the pool party of A *Nightmare on Elm Street 2: Freddy's Revenge* (1985), but even here Lisa's father is modeling old-fashioned adolescence rather than anything like an adult ideal. In all these cases, including the graduation scene in *The Dream Child*, moreover, the limits of the adult world are those of diegetic representation, which therefore offer no guidance to the social imaginary. Although filled with social actors in such authority roles as doctors, police, teachers, parents, and so forth, the adult world gives no effective representation to which the teens can aspire aside from reality itself. When the nightmare strikes in these films, the diegetic representation of the adult world can only insist on its own reality and priority, but it has no defense against being overwritten by the representational network of the nightmare, and music makes this especially clear. Attention to the soundtrack of these films is exceptionally revealing in this respect: it shows the adult world to be not only impotent but without content; it is indeed impotent because it is without content, that is, without a positive image of the adult ideal.

Freddy and the Adult Ideal

Largely absent from reality in the series, the adult ideal finds negative representation in the nightmare sequences, where Freddy assumes the role of surrogate, obscene parent.[14] Freddy is indeed both defined against social norms—he is a monster—and explicitly presented as a product of the breakdown of the social authority that enforces such norms. "Horror films," Robin Wood claims:

> are our collective nightmares. The conditions under which a dream becomes a nightmare are that the repressed wish is, from the point of view of consciousness, so terrible that it must be repudiated as loathsome, and that it is so strong and powerful as to constitute a serious threat.[15]

This definition fits Freddy inasmuch as his traumatic appearance is both horrific and necessary. According to the back story, Freddy's monstrosity is the manifestation of social failure: when the legal system failed to secure the safety of the town's children from Fred Krueger, a local child molester, a group of vigilante parents burned him to death; he returned, however, in the nightmares of the children of the vigilantes. Freddy in this sense is a figure of social repression, and his return suggests that the failure of the social institution has not been addressed. In taking matters into their own hands and practicing vigilante justice, the parents charted a path of social regression that undermined the foundations of those institutions, and their silence before the children represents an outward sign of this repression. The result is impotence, a product of the short circuit of the institutions that support the social order. It is not by chance that Nancy's dad, a law officer, participated in the original unlawful act against Freddy, and that he at the time of the first film no longer lives with his wife and daughter. Nor is it an accident that he seems essentially irrelevant throughout the film, offering little but useless, backbiting criticism of Nancy and his estranged wife. By participating in the vigilantism—the third film implies that he was a leader of the group—Nancy's dad negated the power of his official position, and the broken relationships of the home reflect the diminished power of his social role. If Nancy's dad has in a sense inadvertently served as the leader of his own social demise, the breakdown of his family stands as a microcosm of the breakdown of society.

In the nightmare sequences, Freddy realizes the implications of the breakdown of social institutions in inverted form. According to Reynold Humphries:

> Freddy is pure drive, the drive for absolute and complete satisfaction of any and every whim imaginable. What he wants he gets, and he gets it by any means at his disposal. Freddy is the epitome of the American way of life: success is yours if you want it badly enough.[16]

In taking matters into their own hands and practicing vigilante justice, the parents regressed to a state prior to the institution, where the institution no longer carried force. As a return of this social repressed, Freddy's monstrosity represents the social nightmare of permanent adolescence. In this respect, Nancy's father's regression serves as the quintessential example and it is significant that his character is offered no redemption.

However we take the nightmare—as an expression of the unconscious, as a return of the repressed—the teens are the ones who must endure it. That is, insofar as Freddy is the condensation of unconscious and psychological forces, these forces have been unleashed on the teens by the failures of adult society. But, strikingly, aside from Nancy's parents, the coach in *Freddy's Revenge*, and Lori's mom in the back story to *Freddy vs. Jason* (2003), the consequences of social failure fall on the kids, who serve as scapegoats in turn and are often institutionalized for the social failure. Few figures of adult authority take the teens' concerns seriously or are willing to recognize the truth—that adult society is the ultimate source of the danger. Commenting on the first film of the series, Humphries notes:

> the scene in the cemetery where Nancy is with both her parents gives us a clue as to what is happening. When she describes Freddy, her parents look anxiously at one another: they know but the children do not. In other words, the parents are keeping the children in the

dark, withholding from them the very information that could help them, not to fight Freddy, but to understand what sort of society they are living in.[17]

Adult society does not recognize that it has made the nightmare world of the teens. The teens themselves frequently do not recognize the danger themselves, and, when they do, they survive only to the extent that they do not put their faith in the adults to protect them.

What we can easily lose in all of this, however, is Freddy's status as a symptom of social disorder and malaise; he cannot be easily dispatched. Indeed, most of the characters of the films, including the survivors, equate Freddy's defeat with his destruction. In this respect, they mimic the original vigilante social violence that created Freddy as monster. Heba astutely notes that in ignoring their parents, fighting Freddy and seeking his destruction, "the young people are only doing what their parents have done, taking matters into their own hands when the traditional authorities do not provide an adequate solution to a problem, and killing Freddy themselves."[18] Predictably, this strategy is not very effective; the young people rarely live to grow up. (*Freddy's Dead: The Final Nightmare* even makes a joke of this, keeping score of the thousands of dead kids in Springwood.) Characters survive one film only to perish in another. Thus if Heba is correct that "the greatest horror and irony for the young people . . . is the realization that their rite of passage has transported them into the world of the adults—the very group they have struggled to resist,"[19] this must come with the caveat that the world of the adults was never all that much different from the world of adolescence to begin with. Though such authority figures as parents, police, teachers, doctors, and so forth populate the adult world, the particular individuals occupying these positions are usually presented as "overbearing and incompetent" and so less than ideal; this situation results in institutions that are inadequate to their social need and whose "lack of responsiveness and resourcefulness makes them as dangerous to the young people as Freddy."[20] Freddy is in this sense both symptom of and antidote to society: he may indeed be dangerous, but he also retains, in a way that broken social institutions apparently cannot, the image of the adult ideal that society would need to function in reality.

Of all the characters in the series, only Alice—the one character to survive to see the end of more than one film (*A Nightmare on Elm Street 4: The Dream Master* (1988) and *The Dream Child*)—seems to appreciate the symptomatic aspect of Freddy, as she does not seek to destroy him. Indeed, when, at the end of *The Dream Child*, Jacob, her son, uses Freddy's powers against Freddy, this act seems to acknowledge that Freddy and his powers have a necessary role to play with respect to the articulation of the adult ideal. Indeed, at this moment of becoming mother, Alice at

Figure 10.4 Family tableau at the end of *A Nightmare on Elm Street: The Dream Child*

last "graduates" to the status of an adult. The politics of maternal essen-tialism and self-sacrifice (especially with respect to Freddy's mother, Amanda) are admittedly heavy-handed in the sequence, but the "incoherent" epilogue with Alice, her dad, and Yvonne undoes some of that ideological work. Yvonne asks Alice, "Is he still keeping you up at night?"—and initially it is ambiguous as to whether "he" refers to Jacob or Freddy. Although Alice quickly deflects the question to Jacob, their cooing over the baby is unsettled by the appearance of the recurring jump rope rhyme (hummed here rather than chanted and associated throughout the series with Freddy) and by Freddy's disembodied laughter, which resounds into the credits. Freddy therefore haunts this tableau of the generations (Figure 10.4), which otherwise portends the restoration of social order; it is unclear whether this haunting represents the predictable return of the menace or an adult recognition that Freddy is the necessary shadow of the appearance of the adult ideal.

Surreal Sound Synthesis and the Adult Ideal

The soundtrack makes apparent Freddy's relationship to the adult ideal as a negative image. If the adult world of reality has no music proper to it other than Elgar's Pomp and Circumstance March, music suffuses the nightmare world of Freddy; it is a world synthesized and thereby rendered surreal. We might take the acoustic instrumentation of Elgar's March to represent something like a missing term—it signifies the adult ideal, the dream of society. The synthesizer, by contrast, represents the negative musical image of this dream—the nightmare. In this respect it is striking that the scores for these films usually deploy the synthesizer in imitation of acoustic instruments—strings, voices, and bells are three common ones. The principle of sound synthesis in these scores, in other words, is surreal: it simulates and counterfeits the real sound of acoustic instruments.[21] The synthetic timbres of the nightmare rework reality.

This principle of surreal sound synthesis is also a musical complement to Freddy's character. Tony Magistrale points out that "Freddy is a shape changer—capable of taking on the form of something abject, erotic, or even switching genders in a constant effort to confuse, trick, and seduce his hapless victims."[22] The synthesizer is similarly able to change its tone, to transform itself into other instruments and sounds. Surreal sound synthesis also extends to the effects, which often have a musical quality to them—the wind blowing, a door creaking, even the scraping of Freddy's finger knives are sufficiently musical that they sometimes pose difficulty in determining whether a particular sound is score or effect. Voices, especially, are often disembodied in the nightmare sequences, and, while not synthesized, they follow the principle of surreal sound synthesis in being processed with reverb and other filters to make them sound unnatural.

These surreal synthetic timbres give these scores an adolescent feel, and it is tempting to interpret the synthetic string tones, for instance, as the teenagers' image of what grown-up music would sound like. If we take the music as representing—as traditional film music theory would have it—feeling, the fact that these are synthesized sounds becomes even more significant: they are not, it seems, what they would be. In short, they are the adolescent's representation of the adult feeling; or better yet, they sound like an adult feeling as felt by an adolescent. The synthesized underscoring of feeling in that sense would mark the adolescent as not yet an adult. Even more, in the nightmare, the teens experience in surreal form what reality, the world given to them by their parents, has repressed. They also learn, if they listen, that reality has no music comparable to the nightmare; as noted, on the soundtrack, society consists of reality as natural process, the natural ambient sounds of the world. Indeed, the music that underscores reality extends from the nightmare: it marks the menace, reflects the expansion of Freddy's power. In the early parts of each film, music usually has a diegetic justification whenever it appears in the waking world. But these distinctions tend to break down over the course of each film. Thus, even by the middle of a film, music often extends into the non-dream sequences, both in terms of commonplace overlaps that unsettle the real world by placing it in proximity to the dream, or by indicating the effect of the dream world in the real world (such as when Nancy, in the first film, mentions to Tina that she had a similar dream). Through music, we sense the expansionary powers of Freddy, his ability to cross boundaries and affect even the real world, which seems no longer safe and indeed as if it is defenseless. This remains the case even though the teens understand that Freddy cannot get them so long as they do not sleep. As with point of view camera angles in the slasher genre, music, even brooding, shocking music, does "not signify the presence of the killer, but the menace of his potential presence."[23] "Fake" attacks, such as when Rod leaps out of the dark and tackles Glen to the accompaniment of a musical stinger, serve to increase Freddy's power in his absence, for they suggest purposeful ambiguity and surprise; and the shock they produce makes music into an unreliable and perverse narrating agent—one, in fact, allied directly with the powers of Freddy.

The opposite case, sounds and music from reality intruding into the nightmare, is rare. Certainly, the nightmare commonly appropriates the sound of reality. Many of the dream sequences begin with ambiguity based on misrecognition: initially, we (and so also the characters) are often unsure whether a particular sequence is nightmare or reality.[24] Music conspicuously drops out, and the remaining ambient sounds of reality initially serve to disguise the presence of the nightmare; when these sounds turn out to belong to the nightmare after all, they are transmuted, either through manipulation (say, by making them louder or by distorting them), or through the addition of other sounds, such as music, that signal a surreal state. In The Dream Warriors, for instance, Jennifer watches TV. She burns herself with a cigarette in an attempt to stay awake. The TV program soon takes an odd turn and starts to address Jennifer directly. Finally, Freddy's voice emerges; he welcomes her to prime time, the TV sprouts arms and it kills her. Something similar occurs in The Dream Child, where Dan, driving to see Alice, turns on the radio only to hear his mother on a call-in show berating him and Alice. Freddy soon materializes in the passenger seat, takes control of the truck, and ultimately kills Dan. The principle of surreal sound synthesis once again operates here, where the dream simulates the sounds of reality only to transmute them into elements of the nightmare. Occasionally, the imitation can be pitch perfect, even when we know it to be a simulacrum, as when Nancy's dad appears near the end of Dream Warriors. Here, her inability to detect the simulation becomes lethal, as this vision of her father quickly turns into Freddy.[25]

However surreal the world of the nightmare may be, it is not radically other; and Freddy is not radically other, either. Both nightmare and Freddy remain bound to the reality they transform. When the score opts for a more characteristic synthesizer sound, it turns not for the most part to the weird, eerie sounds of earlier horror or science fiction, but rather to those synthesizer patches common to popular music. Following the general trend in filmmaking during the 1980s, the amount of popular music increased substantially over the course of the series. The first film features little popular music—a snippet on the radio in Tina's house, Glen listening on his headphones, and most prominently "Nightmare" on the end credits.

Freddy's Dead, by contrast, included more than eleven popular songs, including three by the Goo Goo Dolls. Moreover, songs moved from being used exclusively in a diegetic capacity in the first film to occasionally being incorporated non-diegetically in *Freddy's Dead*—though the score remained dominated by orchestral and synthesized underscore. Yet this distinction is somewhat misleading inasmuch as many of the most distinctive gestures of the underscore—synthesizer pads, drum sequencer patterns, guitar riffs—are themselves drawn from popular music. Already in the first film, these gestures tended to be associated with Freddy, especially when Freddy was pursuing his victims. Insofar as the nightmare removes its cloak of the surreal, then, its substance is revealed to be the driving beat of adolescence, linked directly, via music, to the obscene father of psychosis.

This relationship to the surreal is why the score's resemblance to acoustic instruments cannot be discounted merely as a product of cost cutting on the part of filmmakers. The score to the second film, *Freddy's Revenge*, which has a score that deviates from the others in that it mostly eschews the principle of surreal sound synthesis and expresses instead a fundamentally acoustic imagination with respect to instrumentation, is a case in point. This score sounds much more like a traditional horror film than do the others of the series because it mostly avoids synthesized timbres—especially those common to popular music. The third film, by contrast, returned to surreal synthesized palette of the first film, and the subsequent films continued using it.[26] The particular synthesized sound palette of the series was in fact an aesthetic choice that transcended any constraint placed on the score by the budget. Or rather, if cost entered the equation of scoring choices, we should interrogate the social terms of such cost cutting critically: how, if at all, does it conform to the basic thematic concerns of the series? At this level, the soundtrack presents the allegory that the dream of society has literally grown too costly. The social nightmare, in other words, substitutes for the dream of society because the cost of that dream has become too dear. If the figure of the final girl establishes the impotence of external authority, her figure also recognizes the lack of adult ideal and concomitant need for self-realization. Likewise, the incoherence of the narrative, especially with respect to unreliable narration, renders any image of the adult ideal perverse, while placing barriers before all avenues of self-realization that do not proceed through paranoia. That the synthesizer persists to the end, that the end credits use popular music, that we do not, in the end, hear orchestral music in the underscore—all of this suggests that the final girl may have survived, but that she is not yet an adult.[27] To return to the adult ideal of Pomp and Circumstance in the negative: there is no glorious war, only terror and (apparent) survival. If the adults, too, seem in a state of permanent adolescence, this suggests that society can no longer afford to make its adult ideal with pomp and circumstance. Freddy in that respect returns to remind us of that the path to adult society must pass through the terrors of disillusion.

Notes

1   The subgenre was first described in detail by Vera Dika and Carol J. Clover in separate articles, both published in 1987. Vera Dika, "The Stalker Film, 1978–1981," in *American Horrors: Essays on the Modern American Horror Film*, edited by Gregory A. Waller (Urbana, IL: University of Illinois Press, 1987), 86–101; she elaborates on her argument in Vera Dika, *Games of Terror: Halloween, Friday the 13th, and the Films of the Stalker Cycle* (Rutherford, NJ: Fairleigh Dickinson University Press, 1990). See Carol J. Clover, "Her Body, Himself: Gender in the Slasher Film," *Representations* 20 (1987), 187–228; Clover's account is reprinted in revised form in Carol J. Clover, *Men, Women, and Chain Saws: Gender in the Modern Horror Film* (Princeton, NJ: Princeton University Press, 1992). "Final girl" is Clover's term.
2   Clover, *Men, Women, and Chain Saws*, 17.
3   Remnants of the older horror syntax can be seen in *Halloween* (1978), for instance, when at the end Dr. Loomis ultimately takes the role of hero and shoots the killer just as he is bearing down on Laurie.
4   Clover, *Men, Women, and Chain Saws*, 38.
5   Ibid., 17. It is in this sense of saving herself that the final girl fuses the roles of victim and hero, allying her, as Clover notes, with the protagonist of the action film.
6   Robin Wood, "American Nightmare: Horror in the 70s," in *Horror: The Film Reader*, edited by Mark Jancovich (London: Routledge, 2001), 31.
7   Stephen King argues that horror is a conservative genre because it is principally concerned with social order and norms: the abnormal exists in horror only so that it can expose and so also extend the power of the norm:

> Monstrosity fascinates us because it appeals to the conservative Republican in a three-piece suit who resides within all of us. We love and need the concept of monstrosity because it is a reaffirmation of the order we all crave as human beings ... and let me further suggest that it is not the physical or mental aberration in itself which horrifies us, but rather the lack of order which these situations seem to imply (Stephen King, *Danse Macabre*, 3rd edition [New York: Berkeley Books, 1983], 30).

8   Mark Jancovich (ed.), *Horror: The Film Reader* (London: Routledge, 2001), 9.
9   Gary Heba, "Everyday Nightmares: The Rhetoric of Social Horror in the Nightmare of Elm Street Series," *Journal of Popular Film and Television* 23 (1995), 108.
10 Many horror films outside the slasher subgenre also adopt such incoherent structure—the hand reaching out of the grave at the end of *Carrie* (1976), for instance, or somewhat differently the unresolved situation at the end of *The Birds* (1963).
11 Dika, *Games of Terror*, 59–60.
12 Ibid., 86. More specifically, she adds: "By representing adolescents in situations depicting their imminent social passage from a world of childhood into adulthood (*Prom Night, Graduation Day, Hell Night*), they then also dramatize

a young person's coming to knowledge of a world that threatens violence and evil" (129).

13 The original script takes Dan's speech in a somewhat different, unused direction, suggesting that college rather than high school now serves as the principal means of initiating subjects into adulthood. It opens this way: "we stand naked and defenseless before an ever more unimaginable horror—college. High school was only the beginning for some of us. Don't forget: S.A.T. stands for Sadistic, Anti-human, Torture." His call for regression is also more pointed: "Most of us have just this one summer to live . . . and by live I mean . . . paaarty!" The script can be found on A *Nightmare on Elm Street* Companion website at http://nightmareonelmstreetfilms.com/Files/nightmare_on_elm_street_5_script.pdf (accessed 28 March 2009).

14 Slavoj Zizek, *Looking Awry: An Introduction to Jacques Lacan Through Popular Culture* (Cambridge, MA: MIT Press, 1992), 23.

15 Wood, "American Nightmare," 30.

16 Reynold Humphries, *The American Horror Film: An Introduction* (Edinburgh: Edinburgh University Press, 2002), 159–60.

17 Ibid., 160.

18 Heba, "Everyday Nightmares," 114.

19 Ibid.

20 Ibid., 109.

21 Based on the principle of simulation, copying, and counterfeiting, the scores also fit with the other "postmodern" aspect of the slasher, namely its penchant for quotation and allusion. As Dika notes, the slasher genre is grounded in this practice where earlier cinematic devices are isolated, evaluated, and utilized for predictive effect (*Games of Terror*, 36–7). Something similar happens with the synthesizer, which allows for a similar isolation and redeployment of timbre according to the effect that will be produced.

22 Tony Magistrale, *Abject Terrors: Surveying the Modern and Postmodern Horror Film* (New York: Peter Lang, 2005), 165.

23 Jancovich, *Horror: The Film Reader*, 106.

24 Charles Bernstein, composer of the score to the original film, admits that the filmmakers instrumentalized this ambiguity:

> [In the music] I sometimes had to let the audience know they were watching a dream, and sometimes I had to fool them into thinking they were not . . . [S]ometimes just the presence of music will indicate that there's something about that reality that's questionable. In the choice of spotting, if you bring in the music at the beginning of the scene, you're letting them know there's something about the scene that's different from the one that preceded it. Whereas holding off and waiting for another moment was one way of fooling the audience into not realizing that there was a major transition when that scene began.

Quoted in Fred Karlin and Rayburn Wright, *On the Track: A Guide to Contemporary Film Scoring* (New York: Schirmer Books, 1989), 465.

25 If we wonder why the characters are not more suspicious of the appearance of reality in the nightmare, we need to recall that reality also offers a measure of defense against the nightmare. But reality only resists the nightmare when it intrudes upon it and so bypasses or closes down the nightmare's surreal synthesizer. This most commonly happens when a character sets an alarm or someone wakes him or her up, for instance, in the scene from the original film where Nancy is in the bath. As Freddy's hand emerges ominously between

Nancy's legs, her mom's voice warning her to be careful chases his hand away. The sound of reality here intrudes on the dream world very much like the sound of the nightmare, music in particular, will intrude on reality.

26 The different approach to scoring taken in the second film thus alerts us to the fact that it does not fit neatly into the mythology of the rest of the series.

27 Dika formulates the plot structure of the slasher thus: "16. The heroine survives. 17. But the heroine is not free" (*Games of Terror*, 60).

Chapter 11

The Beauty of Horror
Kilar, Coppola, and Dracula[1]

James Deaville

The vampire movie ranks among the most popular of the various subgenres of horror film.[2] Among other endearing features, the myth of the vampire distinguishes itself as inherently possessing the potential for the expression of the "beautiful," of beauty in horror.[3] After all, as Christopher Frayling argues, vampires have been portrayed on film as "fashionably pallid and clean-shaven, with seductive voices and pouting lips, and . . . always sexually attractive."[4] This has not always been the case, as Murnau's *Nosferatu* (1922) attests. Still, the quintessential vampire Dracula has traditionally embodied the duality of "men's [sic] hidden fears *and* desires,"[5] of repulsion and attraction,"[6] or—as Richard Dyer has observed—"the despicable as well as the defiant, the shameful as well as the unashamed . . ."[7] Most film directors from classical Hollywood[8] tended to portray Dracula as a character drawing upon the binary as presented by Bela Lugosi's Count in Tod Browning's *Dracula* of 1931: elegant, suave in appearance and demeanor, while on the inside, as Nina Auerbach describes, he is "so musty and foul-smelling, so encrusted with the corruption of ages, that . . . he is an eruption from an evil antiquity."[9] This Dracula imago persisted into the 1970s, with the character as portrayed by Jack Palance (*Dracula*, 1973) and Frank Langella (*Dracula*, 1979).

Other Hollywood characters of horror have also embodied this duality between urbanely human and savagely animal personae, such as the Wolfman and Dr. Jekyll and Mr. Hyde. Theirs, however, was a diachronic juxtaposition of these attributes, while Dracula's synchronous performance of humanity and bestiality, of Victorian propriety and modern licentiousness, creates an immeasurably more complex character. The potential for breaching or bridging the binarism authorizes directors to explore different subject positions for the vampire, whereby sympathetic readings have enjoyed a history of their own, including Francis Ford Coppola's 1992 film *Bram Stoker's Dracula*.[10]

Historical Context for *Bram Stoker's Dracula*

Tod Browning's 1931 *Dracula* may have initiated formulas that influenced other gothic horror films of the 1930s, including *Frankenstein* (1931), *The Mummy* (1932), and *The Invisible Man* (1933), but it spawned a rather weak field of vampire sequels: *Dracula's Daughter* (1936), *Son of Dracula* (1943) and *House of Dracula* (1945).[11] Musically speaking, not only did Browning eschew all musical accompaniment, but only one film among the three successors credited a composer on-screen (Hans J. Salter for his score to *Son of Dracula*). There were no musical innovators like Max Steiner (*King Kong*) or Franz Waxman (*Bride of Frankenstein*) in early sound films based on the Dracula myth. Indeed, the story did not attract significant cinematic attention—despite the Hammer Studio efforts—until the 1970s, when filmmakers foregrounded its potential for re-interpretation in light of contemporary social issues within the United States. Thus *Blacula* (1972) adopts the myth to decry racial inequity, *Velvet Vampire* (1971) features a lesbian vampire, and *Deathdream* (1974) situates vampirism within the war in Vietnam. At the same time, rising directors such as David Cronenberg and George Romero took interest in vampires, respectively with *Rabid* (1976) and *Martin* (1977). Clearly the times were right for the rise of the vampire: Anne Rice and Stephen King published their first vampire novels *Interview with the Vampire* (1976) and *Salem's Lot* (1975), respectively, while the television series *Dark Shadows* (1966–71) was already garnering significant attention.[12] Unlike the Hammer Studios Dracula films, which featured predictable horror-genre music, the vampire movies from the 1970s displayed a variety of musical approaches, ranging from Ivan Reitman's atmospheric assemblage of stock music for *Rabid* to Donald Rubinstein's "Baroque-jazz" contemporary score to *Martin*.[13]

Tony Scott's *The Hunger* (1983) anticipates Coppola's film, to the extent that it likewise represents a departure from the gore and violence that dominated the cult vampire cinema of the 1970s. Indeed, its often striking visual elements and poetic imagery, coupled with a score that at times draws on slow movements of Bach and Schubert, sets *The Hunger* in stark contrast to the great majority of its predecessors.[14] Music plays such a role that Royal S. Brown has characterized the film as possessing "dazzling cine-musical virtuosity,"[15] even though he fails to observe music's centrality within this stylish, melancholy film. The emphasis on ravishing music, especially to accompany scenes of heightened passion, points ahead to Kilar's score, even though the differences in musical settings are patently evident.[16]

Bram Stoker's Dracula: The Film

The film's ostensibly authenticizing title has drawn significant popular and scholarly attention to the relationship between the 1897 novel and

Coppola's film, the commentary essentially agreeing that *Bram Stoker's Dracula* is not Bram Stoker's *Dracula*. Screenwriter James V. Hart justified the modifications, which included linking Dracula with Prince Vlad Tepes and rendering Lucy the reincarnation of his human love Elisabeta, with the reassurance, "I feel very strongly that I've tried to support his [i.e. Stoker's] narrative rather than mess with it."[17]

Screenwriter rhetoric notwithstanding, Coppola did significantly depart from Stoker's novel, but so has every other film adaptation of *Dracula*. More disturbing for critics were Coppola's deviations from cinematic traditions—David Ehrenstein sardonically summarized the critiques:

> Here he is [at it] again! Ignoring plot and character for décor, costumes, and lighting effects! All he seems to want to do is manufacture one image after another image, incessantly merging and dissolving, turning the screen into a heaving, pulsating mass of God-knows-what![18]

Film theorist Thomas Elsaesser regards the critics as "complaining that the plot was confusing, the allusions gratuitous, or arguing that at a deeper level the film had destroyed the potency of the myth."[19] This last point refers to what Sheehan identifies as the rewriting of Stoker's horror novel into "the tale of a brave prince transformed into a monster by romantic despair, and how a love which survives the ages starts calling him back to humanity."[20] If this re-interpretation and transformation displeased adherents of classical cinema, it also did not sit well with critics of hetero-normativity such as Richard Dyer and Judith Halberstam, who rejected Coppola's inscription of heterosexuality onto the poly-sexual vampire.[21]

Neither friend nor foe denies that *Bram Stoker's Dracula* represents a significant departure from tradition both as a film in general and as a retelling of the Dracula story. Where the commentators differ is in the valorization of those deviating features. Indeed, the very devices that caused Michael Wilmington to proclaim the film as "the best overall movie realization of Stoker's characters and world,"[22] led Iain Sinclair, among other critics, to declare Coppola's film inauthentic to its (ostensible) source and plagiaristic in its references to other films.[23]

The aforementioned article by Thomas Elsaesser uses *Bram Stoker's Dracula* to explore post-classical cinema in the "New Hollywood," situating the film as an example of how Coppola positioned himself and his film "at the crossroads of major changes in the art and industry of Hollywood."[24] By examining Coppola's historical position and this film's approach to such issues as technology past and present, intertextual reference, narrative progression, and audience engagement, Elsaesser develops the argument that *Bram Stoker's Dracula* embodies the shifting sensibilities of Hollywood. He posits that in the film, "the classical, the post-classical and the postmodern find distinct articulations."[25]

While recognizing the role of the aural realm in this example of post-classical cinema—he identifies "a new treatment of sound and the image"—Elsaesser curiously does not address music, as if it were extraneous to the film's "engulfment" through sight and sound:[26]

> Instead of the bounded image, the mode of engulfment works with the ambient image, in which it is sound that now "locates," "cues," and even "narrates" the image, producing a more corporeal set of perceptions.[27]

Still, he leaves the door open to the consideration of the film's musical elements, for example when he draws our attention to "the possibility of different forms of audience engagement, different ways of being inside and outside when it comes to identification and participation."[28] Moreover, the cinematographic devices he identifies—for example, the lack of frame to an image or the unknowability of "where and how a shot ends and another begins"[29]—have musical analogues, and Kilar's score significantly contributed to the overarching project of humanizing Dracula.

"Specularity and Engulfment" does not stand alone among critical assessments of *Bram Stoker's Dracula* in affording (at least the possibility of) agency to its score. Indeed, at least four other film scholars attend to the film's musical content, albeit only on the peripheries of their investigations. Vera Dika writes about the Annie Lennox song from the end credits ("Love Song for a Vampire"), but does not deal with the orchestral score.[30] That music does figure in Carol Corbin's assessment of "postmodern" elements in *Bram Stoker's Dracula*, whereby the author affirms the efficacy of music as support to the images in given scenes: the "arousing music" that helps amplify the erotic encounter between the vampire brides and Harker and the music in the scene with the quick cross-cuts between Lucy's ravishing by Dracula and the wedding of Mina and Jonathan:

> The powerful music, at once both liturgical chant and orgiastic gasping, combines the seemingly distinct imagery into one surreal moment of beauty and death, good and evil, indelibly melded and inseparable as life is from death, and coated with a patina of blood.[31]

Margaret Montalbano deepens the musical discussion further by trying to identify selected musical themes and their instrumentation in the opening and the wedding scenes, even though her attempts are unsuccessful.[32] Finally, one film scholar—Rick Worland—actually mentions Kilar in his discussion of *Bram Stoker's Dracula*, yet his identification of a quotation from the "Liebestod" of Wagner's *Tristan und Isolde* is in error.[33]

These authors recognize the "added value" *Bram Stoker's Dracula* acquires through the soundtrack, while yet failing to interrogate the film's music in any consistent and meaningful manner. To that extent, Elsaesser's positing of "a new treatment of sound and the image," of the merging of sight and sound at key moments in the film, offers a more fruitful, systematic avenue for the study of music's role here. The centrality that Elsaesser assigns to the sonic realm in the regime of the "New Hollywood" certainly justifies a detailed exploration of music's contribution to audio-viewer engulfment through *Bram Stoker's Dracula*.

The Music: The Background

Coppola's choice of composer, the Pole Wojciech Kilar, did not correspond either to traditional selections for horror films (e.g. Jerry Goldsmith and Ennio Morricone) or to the new breed of high-concept composers (James Horner and Danny Elfman, for example). Coppola explained the search for a composer with the following commentary from the 2007 "Collector's Edition" DVD release:

> I very much wanted a classical score, and my knowledge told me that some of the greatest classical composers were in the Eastern European world, particularly in Poland, partly due to the state sponsorship of classical music . . . For a long time, the composer I really wanted to do it was a great Polish composer named Łutoslawski, . . . [but] he wouldn't be able to devote the time to write 30 minutes, 40 minutes of new music . . . But I continued researching Polish composers and I was very interested in Ligeti, Gorecki, many wonderful composers, some of which I heard in Stanley Kubrick's last film . . . Ultimately I was led to consider the notion of Kilar, another Polish composer, to write the score and I approached him, and he was willing.[34]

In an interview for *Film Score Monthly*, Kilar talked about the initial meeting with the director:

> When I met with Coppola in Paris, we sat there for a few days, and in the end he said, "listen, I'm a director, I made the film; you're a composer, you've seen the film, do what you want." . . . Coppola told me, "do what you want, and don't worry about whether it's going to be good or bad."[35]

Kilar was not new to film scoring when the American director approached him: he had already, between 1958 and 1992, composed music for over 120 films and television programs for Polish, German, and French productions. Moreover, he had worked for such noted Polish directors as Krzysztof Kieslowski, Kazimierz Kutz, Andrzej Wajda, and Krzysztof Zanussi, so that Kilar approached Coppola's film with a practiced eye and ear and an established style. *Bram Stoker's Dracula* nevertheless was Kilar's first

US film, which opened the way for scores to Jane Campion's *Portrait of a Lady* and three Roman Polanski films (*Death and the Maiden, The Ninth Gate,* and *The Pianist*). The *Dracula* music not only drew the attention of directors but also won several awards: the 1992 American Society of Composers, Authors, and Publishers (ASCAP) Award for Top Box Office Film and the prize for the best horror-film score at a 1992 festival in San Francisco.

Coppola made several intriguing remarks about the score in the DVD commentary, attributing "three or at the most four cues" to Kilar: "a love theme, a kind of initial very dramatic theme, and then a third theme, and he gave me these three themes and we recorded them." The director asserts that, after completing the film, he and music editor Katherine Quittner adjusted those recordings—"we could play the cue and not play the string section, or not play the brass section"—to make them "work for the whole movie."[36]

This statement about the film's music requires unpacking, since it implies that Kilar was not involved in the actual synchronization of music to film. To what extent should the reader credit Coppola's remarks about the scoring process, since Jean Cocteau famously misrepresented his collaborations with composer Georges Auric through the phrase "synchronization by the grace of God"?[37] Kilar's own comments about his work for *Bram Stoker's Dracula* do not specify the amount of music he provided, even though it is clear that the director let him devise the music without interference.

The following discussion will engage in thematic and stylistic analysis to determine the veracity of Coppola's assertion that Kilar wrote only "three or at the most four cues." A study of music in the film and on the soundtrack CD actually identifies five discrete themes that recur and are associated with people or situations, as well as one motive (the minor third) that permeates the score.[38] Since these themes migrate between cues, it would be more accurate to observe that Kilar provided Coppola and Quittner with themes rather than cues, and that they then edited the music. Moreover, the film incorporates several individual cues of unknown origin that neither return on screen nor appear on the recording.[39] Thus the present study will necessarily sidestep the question of authorship, at least in the traditional sense of one composer as the generator of all musical material.

There may exist uncertainty over the use of his score in the film, but Kilar admitted in the 2001 interview for *Film Score Monthly* (cited previously) that he liked the music he had composed for *Bram Stoker's Dracula*:

> I have to say that I'm happy with my music for *Dracula*. I would say that it is one of my better scores. I like the three scores which I've

written for American films; I don't hide the fact that I feel they're among my best scores ... Overall, I write well for those films in which the image plays a role, where there's something going on in the image, and not for those philosophical films where you just have men talking.

This last comment is interesting in light of Coppola's lavish *mise-en-scène* for the film, which led critics to complain that he was privileging the visual opulence over plot and character.[40] Kilar implies here that his score was inspired by the visual opulence of the film, which justifies not only his rich, varied and colorful orchestrations, but also the use of a 100-piece orchestra and 50-person choir in recording the soundtrack.[41] The "beauty of horror" cannot reside in music alone, but it is hard to imagine that effect being achieved without the significant contribution of the score.

Reading the Orchestral Score

Kilar's themes tend to function leitmotivically—reference to the soundtrack recording is helpful, then, for attributing meanings to them. Reliance upon the track titles as designations for themes is risky, however, since on the one hand certain tracks—"Dracula: The Beginning," "The Storm," "The Hunt Builds," "End Credits"—feature multiple themes, while on the other, one musical idea may recur in variously titled tracks (for example, the same theme comprises the substance of "Mina's Photo," "Love Remembered," "Mina/Dracula," and "Love Eternal"). That Kilar's ideas return in ever-changing timbral guises forms a fitting musical counterpart to Coppola's constant re-shaping of character identity, above all through costume changes and—in the case of the Count—the morphing of his body in a continuum from a wolf and a bat to a young/aged human, with horrifying admixtures in between.

As themes interact with narrative and visual elements, refinements in meaning result—a case in point is the track entitled "Lucy's Party," which first occurs at a party in Lucy's honor. Here Kilar has created a hauntingly beautiful dance (a waltz) that embraces both elegant sensuality and childlike naiveté through its juxtaposing of diatonic theme and chromatic modulation (Figure 11.1, from 21:21) and its highly colorful scoring for strings without vibrato, harp, glockenspiel, piano, and toy cymbals.[42]

That the full cue (as heard at its first occurrence) fades into a prolonged arpeggiation of a diminished triad conveys how this brilliant world is a facade—at that point, a shadow of the Count appears against the wall, threatening Mina with his disembodied spoken words and finally with his full visage. The theme recurs three more times, twice for scenes with

Figure 11.1 Kilar, "Lucy's Party"

Lucy (at 37:46 and 41:00, before her ravishing by Dracula) and then in the key scene when Mina and Dracula first become intimate (1:03:48), with silhouettes of dancers behind them. While, after its first three occurrences, we might still associate the theme with Lucy, the fourth and final use of this music causes audio-viewers to re-think that interpretation: now we hear it evoking the superficiality of Victorian mores, especially considering that the music does not return with Lucy after her nearly fatal encounter with the Count. As if to confirm her transformation into one of Dracula's conquests, a fragment of the theme last occurs in connection with Lucy as accompanied by the music for "The Brides," and there only in the guise of the diminished triad—with one musical gesture, Coppola/Kilar put an end to Lucy's independent existence and signal Dracula's triumph over Victorian morals.

In contrast, the meaning of the pervasive "Love Eternal" theme (Figure 11.2) never seems to change, functioning like one of Wagner's leitmotifs that may appear in tens of different guises yet retains its fundamental signification.[43] Here the tagline "Love Never Dies" seems to come into play, to the extent that the theme's repeated occurrences take Dracula from the loss of his bride at the beginning to ultimate redemption through his love for her in the music track entitled "Love Eternal."[44] We hear this musical idea in ever different orchestrations at such junctures in the film as Dracula's reading of Elisabeta's suicide note (3:50), Harker's revelation of Mina's photo to the Count (16:56), Dracula's encounter with Mina in the streets of London (45:07), and the remaining scenes between those two characters (53:06, 1:38:05, 1:58:15). Needless to say, such thematic occurrences accompany the moments of most heightened passion in *Bram Stoker's Dracula*, wherein Dracula himself becomes more

Figure 11.2 Kilar, "Love Eternal"

real, more "flesh and blood" than Lucy's and Mina's other love interests. Although "Love Eternal" bears resemblance in melodic contour to what might be called the "Dracula" theme (Figure 11.3), it is always characterized by a sensuous sonority, created by the muted dynamic level, warm timbre (low strings and winds), flowing rhythm—it lacks the rhythmic angularity of the other themes—and accompanying non-functional seventh chords. In its fullest statements, like the tracks/cues "Love Eternal" and "Mina/ Dracula," Kilar builds in a rising triplet idea that further intensifies the passion up to the dynamic and emotional climax of the passage—such moments in the score most obviously manifest the principle of "beauty in horror."

Although the "Love Eternal" theme regularly recurs throughout *Bram Stoker's Dracula*, providing one level of structure in the film, Kilar exploits one motive to bring a deeper unity to the entire edifice: the rising and falling minor third. It undergirds Dracula's theme, as well as "Vampire Hunters" and "The Brides" (Figures 11.4 and 11.5), and Kilar/Quittner often exploit the minor-third motive ostinato-like in strongly rhythmic contexts and rising dynamics to build climax, whether leading to battle with the Turks or reflecting the intensifying hunt for Dracula.

It also provides an appropriately menacing counterpoint to the "Love" theme as Dracula gazes at Mina's photo and as van Helsing and company hunt for Dracula but find Mina. Perhaps the most interesting use of the

Figure 11.3 "Dracula: The Beginning"

Figure 11.4 "Vampire Hunters"

Figure 11.5 "The Brides"

motive occurs at the beginning: Dracula enters the chapel to a choral chant that consists of the rising and falling minor third—after he discovers his bride's suicide and while he takes his accursed vow, the motive is taken up by orchestra, but now it is threatening and sinister. In one gesture Kilar has musically captured the transformation of Dracula from an agent of God to His enemy,[45] a process reversed only at the end of *Bram Stoker's Dracula*, through the same motive.

Indeed, a number of film critics and scholars have commented on the framing device of the chapel scenes at the beginning and end of *Bram Stoker's Dracula*.[46] Elsaesser likewise recognizes their functioning as a "baroque spatio-temporal-specular bracket,"[47] yet he fails to observe how the music not only reinforces that frame but also brings the narrative (and the film) to a close, at a point where words seem inadequate. The same quasi-liturgical minor third becomes the bearer of peace and hope at the very end: the opening ecclesiastical motive in a cappella choir accompanies the final panning shot of the chapel's dome with its fresco of a united Dracula and Elisabeta, only this time the musical idea is neither left hanging on the dominant pitch nor extended by instrumental music. This musical ending is nevertheless not conclusive—the melody stops at the subdominant pitch on its downward trajectory—yet through this implication of a quasi-liturgical plagal cadence, the music suggests not only peace, but also the lovers' (Dracula and Elisabeta's) unification and salvation in the unending world-to-come, as Mina's words have already indicated. The Count's invocation of Jesus's final words on the cross adds to the liturgical significance of his "sacrifice,"[48] whereby the minor third atones for his sins even as it brought his sin into the world. Indeed, the framing scenes enable us to understand the function of the pervasive minor third motive, which either belongs to or underlies those themes and cues associated with evil: it represents his fallen nature.

Here we witness how music not only supports narrative, but actually helps to create it as well.[49] Moreover, the use of a recurring motive, a leitmotif, in the manner of the minor third reinforces music's unique ability to create unity over the broad arch of a film.[50] And music gives life (and death) to the characters in *Bram Stoker's Dracula*: the Count himself is arguably the only one who seems to receive his own theme, an angular yet richly scored idea stated at the beginning (Figure 11.3), which supports the contention that Dracula is the most "real" character in the film.[51] This musicality of Dracula contrasts with Coppola's unsympathetic treatment of Harker, who does not have a theme. In fact, the music that accompanies Harker's dramatic escape from the castle does not take his perilous situation into account at all, but rather serves as a continuation of the "Love Eternal" theme, as if he were a mere shadow of the Count. Even the wedding scene, which should have been the high point for Harker, is overshadowed—despite the authenticizing Orthodox chants—by the minor-third motive as Dracula simultaneously exacts on Lucy revenge for the loss of Mina.[52]

In some ways the most effective theme of the score is the simplest: the opening of the CD track labeled "Vampire Hunters" presents a rhythmic idea on one pitch in the strings: it is a triplet followed by three quarter notes in 4/4 time. The theme's second phrase features the minor third, but the initial idea tends to be repeated over longer stretches for the same additive climactic effect observed above with the ostensibly evil minor third. This electrifying motive by Kilar seems to have captured the imagination of filmgoers and filmmakers alike, to the extent that it has found unusually widespread circulation in numerous trailers to other films of the horror genre.[53]

Kilar draws upon a variety of musical parameters to render terrifying the themes for Dracula and for his brides: these are angular themes that feature unusual melodic leaps (including the augmented second and tritone), chromatic motion, irregular rhythms (juxtaposing excessively long and short values) and a minor key. Moreover, they often appear in and are supported by the lowest registers of the orchestra, which darkens the tone as well. As such, these themes of horror provide fitting counterparts to the lyrical, impassioned "Love Eternal" theme. Or do they? In keeping with Coppola's opulent *mise-en-scène*, in particular the exquisite, award-winning costumes by Eiko Ishioka, the Dracula theme in scenes such as Harker's initial encounter with the resplendent Count and Dracula's courting of Mina in the cinema takes on a ravishing quality through timbral sensuality, at a place where violence and sexuality meet. Kilar and Coppola even draw on this theme to humanize the vampire, to render him sympathetic, especially when it occurs in conjunction with the "Love Eternal" theme (such as at the cinema, where "Dracula" gives way to "Love" as Mina falls under his spell).

The "beauty of horror" is most obvious in the inherently savage and sensual musical theme for Dracula's brides (Figure 11.5), which resembles the Count's own musical idea. In the first scene involving the brides and Harker ("Many Strange Things"), their arousing music sensuously and languorously snakes upward in the ever-rising passion of their sinuously intertwining bodies, until Dracula cuts it off with his own theme. Kilar again exploits the musical principle of varied repetition to enhance intensity in a scene. The "beauty" of the voluptuous bodies finds a fitting musical analog, which in its timbral darkness and rhythmic irregularity nevertheless enables the audience to remain cognizant of the brides' threat to Harker.

In comparison, the fierce music assigned to van Helsing and Lucy's suitors—the theme known as "Vampire Hunters"—seems ironically brutal and divested of any human warmth:[54] its two-dimensionality and ostinato reflect at once the shallowness of those characters and their own fixation on revenge. Van Helsing musically contrasts with Dracula on another front, for the Doctor's repeated incantations of Christian truths are blunt and devoid of music, whereas music frames and fills the Count's spiritual path from his fall into blasphemy to his ultimate salvation. It is as if Coppola regards the "flesh and blood" Dracula as the true keeper of faith and spirituality, with his human opponent van Helsing merely superficially invoking the sacred.

The music that accompanies the diabolical storm over the ocean and London is arguably the most horrific of the underscore, but not through harmonic dissonance or timbral distortion. Rather, the music achieves its effect through discontinuous sound editing, consisting of fragmented, distorted themes in quick succession and in varying combinations, punctuated by brass outbursts and militant drumbeats. This style well suits the similarly fragmented visual style of the scene, which values rapid cross-cutting between locations over continuity editing: there is precious little beauty to be found in this horror.

In comparison, the "Whores of Satan" scene towards the end of the film, in which van Helsing and Mina are attacked by Dracula's brides, attempts to create a sense of horror largely through electronic effects.[55] Since this is the only scene that exploits synthesized sounds, they stand out, and not favorably: the electronic sonorities intrude into Kilar's score in general, calling to mind the soundscapes of such vampire films as *Rabid* and *Martin*. The scene begins with the acoustic ululations of "Exeloume" by Diamanda Galás,[56] the most effective aspect of the film cue: with its orientalizing keening, her singing perfectly captures the *mise-en-scène* of the brides' gypsy costumes and their attempts to influence Mina.

The final scene requiring musical explication is the chase in the Borgo pass, where Lucy's three suitors pursue the gypsy wagon bearing Dracula to his castle, just after the "Whores of Satan"/"Ring of Fire" episode. Although the cliché chase music is not by Kilar (it does not share any of the thematic material from the rest of the film), its character in the tradition of the Western supports Coppola's intentions.[57] Mina initially watches the chase unfold through binoculars, which in its washed-out color and in combination with the exciting music does indeed give the scene the appearance of a Western from the 1950s. Here again, the Count appears to be the only character ironically filled with life, the other men more appropriate for a Saturday afternoon matinee.

Elsewhere within *Bram Stoker's Dracula*, short passages of diegetic music help to establish believability and foreground the technologies of modernity, whether the music to accompany the films in the cinemato-graph theatre or the music Mina puts on the gramophone when she is visiting the ailing Lucy. Coppola does not credit the music playing on the gramophone, which clearly dates from the period.[58] As we might expect, the music emanating from the seen and unseen sources of the gramophone and the film projector sounds as if it is being produced through those apparati. In such cases, mechanized musical reproduction seems to underscore Coppola's subtext that seeing and hearing are essential to the audience's experience of engulfment.

Beyond the melodic features of themes, specific timbres find association with characters, places, situations, and moods: the combination of strings without vibrato, harp, glockenspiel, piano, and toy cymbals for Lucy's superficial social circle; the juxtaposition of wildly differing sonorities in "The Storm" to signify the clash of "good" and "evil" with Dracula's arrival in London; and the dark coloration of the Dracula theme that consistently appears in the cellos. One timbral usage that merits special consideration is the piano's hammering upon single notes in its lowest register, whereby Kilar transforms the piano into a percussive instrument and allies it with the darker side of the vampires. Nowhere is this more effectively illustrated than at the beginning of the film, where we hear the sharply struck note A2 in piano repeatedly alternating with the same note in the basses, in crescendo. That a similar sonorous exchange occurs in the first scene between Harker and the brides stands to reason, given the similarities between their music and that of Dracula; however, the percussive piano part is most evident when the Count calls an end to the ladies' orgy, thus ceasing the sensuous crescendo of musico-sexual activity and taking terrifying command (also musically). This timbral gesture in the piano may subvert the traditional role of the instrument as the bearer of melody, yet the rich sonority matches the dark opulence of Coppola's *mise-en-scène*.

Conclusions

Throughout *Bram Stoker's Dracula*, we have observed how music reinforces and even creates narrative. On a structural level the score accomplishes its work through a series of recurring themes/motives that are associated with characters and situations—to this extent Kilar's music does not depart from traditions of classical Hollywood scoring. Still, the composer's uncanny ability to capture the essence of a character in melody, rhythm, and timbre stands out and contributes to the score's success. We witnessed above all the strong musical portrayals of the sympathetic Dracula and his world, which Kilar contrasts with the virtual unmusicality of van Helsing, Harker, and Lucy's suitors. The recurrence of themes helps the audio-viewer to identify deeper levels of unity, relationship, symbolism, and development within *Bram Stoker's Dracula*. Thus while Kilar alters the meanings of certain musical ideas to accommodate the unfolding story, such as the resignification of the minor third between the film's beginning and ending, he forgoes major alterations of others such as the "Love" theme, in order to highlight its unchanging significance for the narrative. Cues that fall outside the thematic network of the whole often serve the purpose of establishing believability, especially for specific technologies of modernity.

At the same time, Kilar has created musical cues that serve as aural analogues to the director's lavish, striking, and often beautiful *mise-en-scène*, and it is here that the composer departs from conventional approaches to scoring horror. Extending Elsaesser's argument about sound, music in *Bram Stoker's Dracula* serves as a primary agent in "unbounding" the opulent image, whereby it extends the engagement of audience participation beyond the "mind and eye," beyond specularity, to incorporate the "ear."[59] This use of music results in a type of celluloid *Gesamtkunstwerk*,[60] in which the diverse aspects of the film conspire to deliver a cinematic experience of beauty that renders the world of the Undead a site of visual and aural pleasure and Dracula himself an appealing, all-too-human character. *Bram Stoker's Dracula* provides a compelling example for how specularity—even augmented by non-musical sound— at best partially accounts for narrative and character in cinema, whether classical or post-classical: only by drawing music also into consideration can the analyst lay claim to understanding how a film engages (and in Kilar's case, engulfs) the listening and viewing subject.

Notes

1 The author is indebted to Sarah Stephens (Carleton University), André Loiselle (Carleton University), and Neil Lerner (Davison College) for valuable contributions made to this essay, both in thought and deed.

2 This popularity is reflected not only in the number of cinematic and televisual settings of the myth, from F. W. Murnau's iconic *Nosferatu* (1922) to the cult television hit *Buffy the Vampire Slayer* (1997–2003), but also in the quantity of scholarly work about vampires, including such monographs as John Flynn's *Cinematic Vampires: The Living Dead on Film and Television* (Jefferson, NC: McFarland, 1992) and Stacey Abbott's *Celluloid Vampires: Life after Death in the Modern World* (Austin, TX: University of Texas Press, 2007).

3 Regarding the "beauty of horror," see for example the interview between Scott MacDonald and Ellen Spiro in *Public Culture* 14, no. 3 (2002): 468–75, especially 470–1, and the 1992 filmed lecture "The Beauty of Horror" by screenwriter Robert McKee.

4 Christopher Frayling, *Vampyres: Lord Byron to Count Dracula* (London: Faber & Faber, 1992), 6.

5 Alain Silver and James Ursini, *The Vampire Film: From Nosferatu to Bram Stoker's Dracula*, revised edition (New York: Limelight, 1993), 55.

6 Milly Williamson, *The Lure of the Vampire: Gender, Fiction and Fandom from Bram Stoker to Buffy* (London: Wallflower Press, 2005), 2.

7 Richard Dyer, "Dracula and Desire," *Sight and Sound* n.s. 3, no. 1 (1993), 11.

8 "Classical Hollywood" is a term from film studies that refers to the predominant cinematic style in Hollywood between the 1910s and 1960s that above all privileged continuity editing.

9 Nina Auerbach, *Our Vampires, Ourselves* (Chicago, IL: University of Chicago Press, 1995), 63. Christopher Lee would carry on this representation in the Hammer Studio Dracula films of the 1950s and 1960s.

10 Williamson's book (Williamson, *The Lure of the Vampire*) explores what she terms "the sympathetic vampire" from Byron to the present, in literature, film, and television.

11 Abbott, *Celluloid Vampires*, 63.

12 Billed as a gothic soap opera, the show introduced the vampire Barnabas Collins in its second season. For a discussion of the efflorescence of horror

film and its music at that point in American culture, see James Deaville, "The Topos of 'Evil Medieval' in American Horror Film Music," in *Music, Meaning & Media*, edited by Erkki Pekkilä, David Neumeyer, Richard Littlefield, Acta Semiotica Fennica XXV, Approaches to Musical Semiotics 11, Studia Musicologica Universitatis Helsingiensis 15 (Helsinki: Semiotic Society of Finland, University of Helsinki and International Semiotics Institute at Imatra, 2006), 26–37.

13 They extended into the 1970s with *Dracula A.D. 1972* (1972) and *The Satanic Rites of Dracula* (1973).

14 Johann Sebastian Bach, Prelude from the Suite for Unaccompanied Cello No. 1 (BWV 1007) and Franz Schubert, Andante con moto from the Piano Trio in E-flat Major, Op. 100 (D. 929).

15 Royal S. Brown, *Overtones and Undertones: Reading Film Music* (Berkeley, CA: University of California Press, 1994), 257.

16 Whereas *The Hunger* pulls together music from divergent sources and styles, *Bram Stoker's Dracula* relies upon a musical score by one composer, which reflects the shaping and unifying hand of one creator. Furthermore, the principle of diegetic music that performs such a key function in *The Hunger* is all but absent from *Bram Stoker's Dracula*.

17 Henry Sheehan, "Trust the Teller," *Sight and Sound* n.s. 3, no. 1 (1993), 14.

18 David Ehrenstein, "One from the Art," *Film Comment* 19, no. 1 (1993), 27.

19 Thomas Elsaesser, "Specularity and Engulfment: Francis Ford Coppola and *Bram Stoker's Dracula*," in *Contemporary Hollywood Cinema*, edited by Steve Neale and Murray Smith (London: Routledge, 1998), 200.

20 Sheehan, "Trust the Teller," 15. Hart explains, "it's about a seductive, powerful warrior-prince who fell from grace and is seeking to come back." (Ibid.) Jacqueline LeBlanc describes Coppola's Dracula as a "hero-villain tragically doomed by his own rebellious righteousness, a sort of Byronic hero" (Jacqueline LeBlanc, "It Is Not Good to Note This Down: *Dracula* and the Erotic Technologies of Censorship," in *Bram Stoker's Dracula: Sucking Through the Century 1897–1997*, edited by Carol Davison [Toronto: Dundurn, 1997], 264.)

21 Dyer, "Dracula and Desire"; Judith Halberstam, "On Vampires, Lesbians, and Coppola's 'Dracula'," *Bright Lights* 11 (1993), 7–9.

22 Michael Wilmington, "A Shtick Through the Heart," *Los Angeles Times* (November 15, 1992): 22.

23 Iain Sinclair, "Invasion of the Blood," *Sight and Sound* n.s. 3, no. 1 (1993): 15.

24 Elsaesser, "Specularity and Engulfment," 191.

25 Ibid., 197. However, Elsaesser does not clearly differentiate what he terms "post-classical" and "postmodern." See especially pp. 199–203, the section entitled "*Fin-de-siècle* cinema: classical, post-classical, or postmodern."

26 In his analysis of the sonic realm in post-classical film, Elsaesser works from the misleading differentiation of sound effects and music. As the dividing line between music and sound blurs in the New Hollywood—certainly the case for most scenes of *Bram Stoker's Dracula*—music has acquired some of same functions traditionally assigned to sound effects.

27 Ibid., 204.

28 Ibid., 197.

29 Ibid., 202.

30 Vera Dika, "From Dracula—With Love," in *The Dread of Difference: Gender and the Horror Film*, edited by Barry Keith Grant (Austin, TX: University of Texas Press, 1996), 388–400.

31 Carol Corbin, "Postmodern Iconography and Perspective in Coppola's *Bram Stoker's Dracula*," *Journal of Popular Film and Television* 27, 2 (1999), 46.

32 Margaret Montalbano, "From Bram Stoker's *Dracula* to Bram Stoker's '*Dracula*'," in *A Companion to Literature and Film*, edited by Robert Stam and Alessandra Raengo (Malden, MA: Blackwell, 2004), 385–98, especially 388–90. However laudable they may be in principle, Montalbano's musical observations nevertheless are not helpful both due to their misattributions of details of scoring and their selectiveness. For example, she is incorrect in identifying in the prologue "Diamanda Galás's vocal effects as Dracula discovers Elizabeta's body" (389): Galas is only heard in the "Ring of Fire" towards the end of the film, while the opening scene features an unidentified soprano.

33 Rick Worland, *The Horror Film: An Introduction* (Malden, MA: Blackwell, 2007), 262. Worland mistakes the "lush chords and melodic lines" of Kilar's "love" theme for the Wagner passage, a "citation" that he attributes to the influence of Bernard Herrmann's score to *Vertigo*, which does allude to Wagner.

34 Commentary from "Watch *Bram Stoker's Dracula* with Francis Coppola," on *Bram Stoker's Dracula*: Collector's Edition, Columbia Pictures, 2007. Coppola refers to Kubrick's last film, *Eyes Wide Shut* (1999), which uses Ligeti's *Musica ricercata* in its soundtrack.

35 Mark G. So, "Lost Issue: Wojciech Kilar Interview Part 3 (Conclusion)," at www.filmscoremonthly.com/articles/2001/19_Jul—-Lost_Issue_Wojciech_Kilar_Interview_Conclusion.asp (accessed May 4, 2009). In another interview, Kilar indicates that he may have also met Coppola in Los Angeles: "Even when I came to Los Angeles to meet up with Coppola . . ., he said 'I did my part, you are the composer. Do what you want'." Agnieszka Flakus, "Speaking Your Own Language," *Plus: Journal of Polish American Affairs* (May, 2006), at www.pljournal.com/music/wojciech-kilar-interview.html (accessed May 4, 2009).

36 Commentary from "Watch *Bram Stoker's Dracula* with Francis Coppola."

37 See James Deaville and Simon Wood, "Synchronization by the Grace of God? The Film/Music Collaboration of Jean Cocteau and Georges Auric," *Canadian University Music Review* 22, no. 1 (2001), 110–31.

38 The end credits present each of these themes in turn: "Dracula: The Beginning"—"Vampire Hunters"—Love Theme—"The Brides"—"Mina's Photo"—"Dracula: The Beginning." The credits may assist audio-viewers in identifying themes from the film they have just experienced, but that music is so discontinuous, with virtually no bridges between themes, that one suspects an amateur at work in the editing room.

39 The soundtrack recording for *Bram Stoker's Dracula* (1992) adds further complexity to the question of the music, since certain tracks (e.g. "Dracula: the Beginning" and "The Brides") do not fully correspond to the versions in the cues from which the tracks have been excerpted.

40 See, for example, the reviews by Terrence Rafferty in *New Yorker* 68, no. 41 (November 30, 1992): 162–3 and Geoffrey O'Brien in *The New York Review of Books* 40, no. 8 (April 22, 1993): 63–9.

41 This observation presupposes the timbral element as the musical analogue to the visual realm of a film. Francis Ford Coppola's uncle, Anton Coppola, conducted the unidentified orchestra—according to Kilar, an assemblage of Los Angeles studio musicians—for the film. The vocal ensemble is the Los Angeles Master Chorale, under the baton of Paul Salamunovich.

42 A review of the CD by Jonas Uchtmann in FilmmusikWelt.de identifies this track as an "attractive contrast to the tragedy and heaviness that pervades

great stretches of the music." This comment overlooks a deeper interpretation of the passage: this waltz exudes an air of sadness, of loss that ultimately reflects not only the decadence of the lifestyle, but also the fleeting nature of love in this artificial world. With the tagline "Love Never Dies," *Bram Stoker's Dracula* ironically portrays Dracula's/Mina's/Elisabeta's love as eternal, in contrast with that of the Victorian (and our) era. See www.filmmusikwelt.de/index.php?D=5de4e35a5a4bc63bc513f83a2ab925ac&V=order&order=name (accessed May 4, 2009).

43 The theme is clearly associated with Mina, but it only occurs whenever she is brought into some form of connection with Dracula, through a photograph, thoughts, or physical contact. It is interesting to observe that at the point of this theme's fullest statement—when Dracula and Mina discover their mutual histories and affirm their love for each other in the scene "Rules Café"—Coppola chooses to comment (in the Collector's Edition) on his choice of composer, as if inspired by the theme to speak about the strengths of Kilar's music.

44 On the DVD, this track is entitled "Resurrection."

45 For a more detailed study of the music in this scene, see Deaville, "The Topos of 'Evil Medieval.'"

46 Among others, Elsaesser, "Specularity and Engulfment," 201–2; Montalbano, "From Bram Stoker's *Dracula*," 388–9; and Corbin, "Postmodern Iconography," 42.

47 Elsaesser, "Specularity and Engulfment," 202.

48 The phrases uttered by the dying Dracula are "Where is my God? He has forsaken me" and "It is finished." An extended discussion of the film's theological implications is presented by Stephenson Humphries-Brooks in "The Body and the Blood of Eternal UnDeath," *Journal of Religion and Popular Culture* 6 (2004) at www.usask.ca/relst/jrpc/art6-dracula.html (accessed May 4, 2009).

49 Claudia Gorbman, *Unheard Melodies: Narrative Film Music* (Bloomington, IN: Indiana University Press, 1987), *passim*.

50 Among others, Justin London supports this traditional interpretation of leitmotifs in film music, in "Leitmotifs and Musical References in the Classical Film Score," in *Music and Cinema*, edited by James Buhler, Carol Flynn, and David Neumeyer (Hanover, NH: Wesleyan University Press, 2000), 85–96.

51 I thank André Loiselle for this insight.

52 Dracula's presence throughout the wedding scene, through visual and sonic cross-cuts, weakens the validity of the ceremony (Harker again as a shadow presence), which then morally sanctions the film's final scene of Dracula's redemption through the love of Mina.

53 The list includes *Demolition Man* (1993), *The Mummy* (1999), *The Mummy Returns* (2001), and *Pirates of the Caribbean: The Curse of the Black Pearl* (2004). It is interesting to observe how "Vampire Hunters" does not figure in any of the high-concept marketing for *Bram Stoker's Dracula* itself, probably because this music had not yet been composed at the time of the creation of the trailer.

54 For an assessment of this theme's affect, see the review of *Bram Stoker's Dracula* by Anthony Quinn in *The Independent* (UK) of January 31, 1992,

55 The track on the soundtrack CD calls this cue "Ring of Fire." Kilar did not compose or orchestrate the passage: the recording indicates that it was "mixed and edited" by Quittner. Moreover, Kilar has traditionally eschewed relying upon "non-acoustic" sounds in his film scores, where rich orchestral sonorities have prevailed.

56 "Exeloume" ("Deliver Me") originally appeared on Diamanda Galás's 1986 album *Saint of the Pit*.

57 This cue does not appear on the soundtrack recording. Worland, *The Horror Film*, calls the scene "strangely out of place" (264), with Coppola justifying it as an homage to John Ford and his 1939 film *Stagecoach*. (Francis Ford Coppola and James V. Hart, *"Bram Stoker's Dracula": The Film and the Legend* [New York: Newmarket Press, 1992], 3.)

58 In his commentary to the film, Coppola unfortunately talks through this scene, so he does not discuss the gramophone music.

59 See, for example, Holly Rogers, "Audio-Visual Biography: The Collaboration of Music and Image in Derek Jarman's *Caravaggio*," *Journal of Musicological Research* 27, no. 2 (2008), 134–68, where the author discusses at length the aesthetic history of the relationship between music, image, and dialogue (143–8).

60 "Total Art Work," a term introduced by Richard Wagner to designate his music dramas (operas) that at least in theory embraced all of the arts on an equal basis. See Scott Paulin, "Richard Wagner and the Fantasy of Cinematic Unity: The Idea of the *Gesamtkunstwerk* in the History and Theory of Film Music," in *Music and Cinema*, 58–84, for a detailed history of that term in its application to film music.

Chapter 12

Quieting the Ghosts in *The Sixth Sense* and *The Others*

Lloyd Whitesell

The Sixth Sense (M. Night Shyamalan, 1999; score by James Newton Howard) and *The Others* (2001, directed and scored by Alejandro Amenábar) display notable similarities of genre, structure, and theme. Both are ghost stories featuring haunted houses and clairvoyant children. Both make use of surprise endings that arrive in a blinding flash of enlightenment and demand drastic reinterpretation of the preceding narratives. Both films ultimately reveal that their protagonists—Dr. Malcolm Crowe (Bruce Willis) in *The Sixth Sense*, Grace Stewart (Nicole Kidman) and her children in *The Others*—who have provided the main viewpoint on unfolding events and with whom the audience has identified, have been dead from the start.[1] It turns out we have been experiencing the ghost story from the wrong side of the barrier between this life and the next. Seth Friedman classifies films such as these, built around a climactic perceptual twist while disguising narrative unreliability under cover of established generic conventions, as "misdirection films."[2] He believes this category constitutes a genre in itself, claiming that the films I have chosen, for instance, would be better described as misdirection films than as horror films. I remain unconvinced on this point. I prefer to see them as ghost-stories-with-a-twist, so as not to lose sight of the initial genre orientation, while understanding the twist (Friedman calls it the "changeover") as a technique rather than a genre-defining frame.[3]

Nevertheless, Friedman's point about "generic duplicity" is a good one. Filmmakers can use the changeover technique to invoke a familiar set of genre expectations in the beginning and middle of a narrative only to substitute an entirely different set at the end, thereby superseding or transforming the initial genre orientation. The present films begin as conventional ghost stories, with the principal characters defending against supernatural intruders; they end as something else. The changeover renders initial narrative goals meaningless, since ghosts are no longer objects of terror. The new goals are therapeutic: resolution is reached when characters come to terms with their own traumatic deaths. To do this, they must give up their insistence upon moral authority and narrative agency, sources of such intense dissonance in the early stages, and accept that they have already passed away. Music is central to this message. Both scores make skillful use of spine-chilling effects (amorphous textures and pitch continua, percussive shocks, disturbing timbres and registers, increasing tension, distorted allusions to religious music) in line with horror conventions. But such passages of fear and menace are nested within musical expressions of grief and consolation. My focus will be on music's role in maintaining generic duplicity, and in particular how the second musical perspective overtakes the first. I will discuss each film in turn, and conclude by interpreting the telltale reversal of genre and perspective in terms of a response to cultural anxieties.

The Sixth Sense

[*Synopsis:* Prologue.] *The Sixth Sense* opens in the home of Malcolm Crowe, distinguished child psychologist, and his wife Anna (Olivia Williams). They discover a break-in. The highly distraught intruder, Vincent (Donnie Wahlberg), is one of Malcolm's patients from years before. After blaming Malcolm for failing to help him, Vincent shoots Malcolm and himself. [Act 1.] As a new chapter opens, we see Malcolm observing a little boy, Cole Sear (Haley Joel Osment), who exhibits odd antisocial behavior. He begins to counsel Cole, visiting his home, school, and hospital bed. Apart from their conversations, we see Malcolm struggling to regain a close relationship with Anna. We see Cole at home with his protective working-class mother (Toni Collette), and with other children from school who treat him as a freak. Cole has suspicious injuries and is troubled by unexplained phenomena. After a particularly traumatic incident, Malcolm persuades Cole to reveal his secret—he can see the walking dead. [Act 2.] After this pivotal moment in the film, we begin to share Cole's visual sensitivity to ghosts who have died violent deaths. Malcolm resists a paranormal diagnosis until, after desperate pleading from Cole, he is driven to retrieve Vincent's taped sessions, where he hears evidence of supernatural visitation. Intuiting that the ghosts are not malign, Malcolm suggests they merely seek help in communicating with the living. Cole successfully passes a video-recorded message from a poisoned girl, Kyra, to her father, revealing her mother as the killer. Having learned to live peacefully with his gift, Cole finally shares his secret with his mother, healing their bonds of trust. In return, Cole tells Malcolm how to communicate with Anna. [Epilogue.] At the sight of his wedding ring dropping from Anna's hand, the realization of Malcolm's own death comes flooding in. Dread gives way to acceptance, allowing him to say goodbye.

After the prologue, the narrative is foggy in its attention to causal sequence. Malcolm himself complains that he cannot seem to keep track of time. Scenes are not clearly linked by transitions; we hardly ever track

Malcolm as he moves from place to place. Mostly this vagueness is a background perception causing a subtle sense of unreality, but it occasionally comes to the fore, as in the recurring motif of the cellar door. We see Malcolm struggling with the locked door, then we see him in the cellar, without learning how he got there. One can gloss over such an ellipsis as inconsequential, though similar tiny oddities accumulate over time, creeping symptoms of a more glaring narrative omission (the outcome of the shooting). As a fitting reflection of the imprecise storyline, the musical score lacks melodic focus. Textures are mostly homophonic, with isolated melodic gestures stirring momentarily to life. One of the main themes, associated with Cole, consists of piano figuration in an accompanimental pattern. In its first appearance, a woodwind duet enters over the piano in languid contours that never quite form a tune. In later appearances, the piano pattern tends to break into fragments. The only musical figure achieving any kind of strong melodic identity is a compact theme rising to prominence at special moments. Because of its singularity and prominence in the score I will call this theme the motto.

But first let me offer a more comprehensive description of the musical materials making up the score. There are four principal strains, respectively keyed to the expression of fright, mystery, innocence and sadness, and consolation:

1   For conventional horror sequences, there is a rich palette of orchestral and electro-acoustic sounds dedicated to fright effects ranging from inchoate menace to sudden shock and violent terror. These musical passages are typically subservient to atmosphere and action.

2   Another musical strain captures the sense of the uncanny associated with the themes of supernatural phenomena and extrasensory perception. The most important expression of this mysterious aura is the motto (Figure 12.1; first stated in the opening titles, as the composer's credit appears on-screen). The motto is expansive and calm, but harmonically ambivalent, slipping chromatically back and forth between a minor chord and a major chord. Its tune sounds unresolved at the end, and includes pitches foreign to the harmony.[4]

Figure 12.1 The Sixth Sense, motto

3   A third strain is associated primarily with Cole. The piano music
    introducing his character (11:40), although tuneless, has a distinct
    rhythmic/harmonic profile and thus projects a strong thematic identity.
    (Malcolm, on the other hand, has no theme of his own.) Cole's
    theme is emotionally ambivalent, evoking innocence in its simple
    rocking figures and sadness in its minor modal color, haunting
    reverberant quality and poignant unresolved harmonies at the end
    of the cue. There is also a subtle intimation of a sinister side to this
    music. The odd metric grouping adds up to 13-beat bars, while the
    woodwind duet sounds like an embryonic reference to the *Dies Irae*,
    the ancient Christian burial chant frequently quoted in concert and
    film music for its macabre connotations. (In a similar way, the dialogue
    Cole supplies for one of his action figures in the subsequent scene
    alludes to an ancient Latin text, "De profundis clamavi ad te"—a cry
    for help taken from Psalm 130.) The initial statement of Cole's
    theme—ordinary and meek in some ways, but at the same time
    abnormal and unsettling—captures the dual aspects of his character.[5]
4   Finally, there is music expressive of consolation. This type of music
    first appears in passing during Cole's entrance, when, scurrying through
    the streets of Philadelphia, he arrives at the door of the church (12:20).
    For a moment the rocking pattern gives way to a calm hymn-like
    texture; orchestral colors are warmer with the addition of harp and
    horn. The tone is still sad, but the passage suggests rest and comfort
    indicative of the church as a place of refuge. More extensive cues of
    consolation occur the first time Malcolm watches the wedding video
    (40:00) and at the end of the film.

These musical strains, while distinct in symbolism, often mingle in
individual cues. Thus in the scene closing Act 1 where Cole reveals his
secret (50:00), menacing music builds to a statement of the motto, menace
returns with greater force, then Cole's theme leads to a melancholy
orchestral coda. Taking a longer view, the score in Act 1 is dominated
by Cole's music, as we are getting acquainted with him and his troubles;
after we have gained greater access to Cole's point of view, horror music
saturates Act 2, until the double resolution at the end.

Of all the elements in the score, Cole's music undergoes the most
variation and transformation. It first appears as an extended musical theme
with continuous repeated patterns in the piano. Later these patterns
break up into brief halting fragments, e.g. at the end of the breakfast
table scene (18:50), or when Cole's mother ponders his photographs
(29:45). When Malcolm attempts to gain the boy's trust with a mind
reading game (23:30), broken pieces of his theme (drenched in reverb)
draw out into woodwind laments; then, hesitantly at first, a new rocking

pattern takes over, recalling the piano and wind duet texture of the original theme while more restricted in movement, as if commenting on his isolation and hopelessness. Near the close of Act 2, on the other hand, Malcolm and Cole's last session together is punctuated by a sweet tranquil cadence in the piano (1:30:50), signaling the resolution of the boy's inner conflicts. The remarkable malleability of his music suits Cole's youth and relatively unformed stage of growth; it also contributes to the complex treatment of his character as the story unfolds.

A brief snatch of piano is enough to evoke Cole as a musical presence, even if this presence is not always readily explained. In one such passage, a consoling piano accompanies the image of the newlywed couple as they kiss on the video (40:15), then underscores Malcolm watching Anna in the shower. After the shot of her antidepressant medicine on the shelf, the piano initiates a more extended and unsettling pattern, as Malcolm struggles with the cellar door. The introduction of Cole's signature timbre into the music of consolation in this scene is puzzling and somewhat unnerving in the context of the adults' intimate relationship (though this musical riddle will be resolved at the close of the film). It suggests the increasing subliminal influence of Cole over Malcolm's thoughts and actions. At certain moments, Cole's music merges with the music of mystery as well. This occurs for instance at the sight of the hanging ghosts in the school. As Cole explains what it feels like when the ghosts are angry, an eerie bell-like keyboard pattern blends with a statement of the motto (58:25). In this musical passage we get an inkling of how Cole has learned to accustom himself to the constant presence of the uncanny.

The motto itself is the most salient element of the score in its melodic/harmonic profile, but the most elusive in terms of its narrative associations. In this regard, it is an instance of an indeterminate musical theme—a prominent idea suggesting semantic content without being clearly anchored in a specific meaning. The use of such a theme can introduce an added layer of intrigue to the unfolding narrative, leading the listener to deduce and weigh possible meanings in the hopes of eventual clarification.[6] Outside of the title cues, one hears the motto eight times in *The Sixth Sense*. During its first appearance in the frantic moments before Vincent shoots Malcolm (9:00), it becomes overloaded with dramatic associations. Given the motto's overt evocation of mystery, it enters appropriately just as Malcolm struggles to solve the urgent question of the intruder's identity—which one of his former patients is he? But it also gestures toward the more cosmic question of human suffering (Vincent has just asked, "Do you know why you're afraid when you're alone?"). As Malcolm searches for the correct name, Vincent surrenders in abject despair ("I am a freak"). Though we only discover this later, his ostracism has resulted from being "cursed" with an uncanny gift. The musical cue concludes as Malcolm solves the small riddle of Vincent's identity. This points the viewer toward Malcolm's talent for communicating with troubled children (Anna had earlier referred to it as his "gift"). Yet he fails to calm Vincent or prevent violence. In sum, the scene links the motto symbolically with narrative riddles or gaps in knowledge, Malcolm's talent but also failure as a therapist, urgent attempts to establish communication, and obscure hints of paranormal sense perception. Furthermore, the intrusion of the adult Vincent, nearly nude and dangerously unbalanced, dramatically personifies the return of repressed trauma. Thus the motto, in its harmonic ambivalence and semantic indeterminacy, marks the end of the prologue with a densely enigmatic musical sign.

The motto next appears subtly during a transition between scenes as Malcolm makes his way home (15:15). A cluster of associations is still in play: his preoccupation with the new problem represented by Cole, whose case resembles Vincent's, as well as the uncanny Latin message passed between worlds, not to mention the other, deceptively trivial narrative riddles (the single table setting, the locked door). Its third appearance underscores the pivotal moment when Cole reveals his secret (50:50). In his hospital bed, Cole is recovering from severe, unexplained trauma. His willingness to talk marks a new stage in therapy and a new level of communication. Though the scene clarifies the paranormal nature of his gift, it leaves many questions unanswered. On a more hidden level, it provides a secret clue to Malcolm's own situation. (To the eerie strains of the motto, Cole tells Malcolm, "They only see what they want to see. They don't know they're dead.") The motto still means too many things: trauma, healing, riddles, hidden messages, the uncanny. A similar indeterminacy continues with its subsequent appearances: prompted by the hanging ghosts (58:25), as Malcolm replays Vincent's tape (1:09:15), and at Kyra's funeral, where we hear two statements back to back (1:19:05, 1:19:35). (I will return later to the significance of the motto's final appearance in the epilogue.) In contrast with Cole's music, the motto undergoes very little alteration. This constancy is in keeping with the motto's transcendent aura and serves to prolong its enigmatic symbolic force. Only once before the epilogue does the score suggest a loosening of the motto's impassive grip, when Malcolm, turning up the volume on Vincent's tape, reveals a ghostly voice crying for help in Spanish (1:11:30). The music at this point (expansive chordal texture, repetitive piano figuration, high string melody) recalls earlier statements of the motto, including a precise reference to its chord structure (Figure 12.2; piano omitted in the example). But the flexible harmonic movement overall breaks through the motto's chordal impasse, while the melody is completely new, climbing steadily upward to a strong arrival. These qualities, together with the dramatic drum rolls, capture Malcolm's epiphany as he begins to believe Cole's story.[7]

Figure 12.2 The Sixth Sense, first epiphany

As for the music of consolation, we can note that for much of the film it lacks a strong enough presence to call attention to itself as a separate strain. Consoling music first appears as a brief interpolation of calm as Cole enters the church, where listeners may not even register it as distinct from the surrounding context of Cole's theme. Its second, more prolonged appearance in the wedding video scene creates a welcome period of tranquility. As Malcolm watches Anna in the shower, an embryonic lulling tune emerges briefly in the piano (Figure 12.3).

But in general the music here seems to support the mood of nostalgia, not yet projecting a thematic presence. The third appearance is hidden like the first. Here Cole wakes to disturbing sounds: his mother is having a nightmare. Fright music accompanies the scene, except for a brief passage of the lulling tune when Cole attempts to comfort her (1:15:06), after which the fright music returns. Though low key, this musical passage contributes toward the thematic profile of the tune, whose character now better matches the dramatic context of offering comfort.

Not until its fourth appearance (nearly at the end of Act 2) does the consolation music come into its own. Events in the preceding funeral

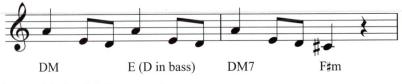

Figure 12.3 The Sixth Sense, comfort

scene have prepared us for the achievement of resolution. In that scene the special weight conveyed by the double statement of the motto signifies several things: the intensified presence of the uncanny, the sense of a crucial step in Cole's passage toward healing, and his acceptance of his role as messenger. As Kyra's father watches her videotaped message, a musical treatment unique within the score heightens the moment (1:25:00). This music clearly belongs to the realm of fear, yet the expression of fear has been transformed. No longer tense, violent, unpredictable, and out of control as before, the music is hushed, composed, and meditative as the tape reveals the secret horror of poisoned motherhood. An eerie, wordless choir groveling in a deep register sets up a repetitive texture suggesting a distortion of religious awe, specifically through disturbing, sinister harmonic dislocations. Fright has turned to a kind of cosmic dread—but dread at a sin that has been exposed in the waking world and can now be rooted out.[8] In passing this test, Cole has gained the wisdom to use his gift (symbolized by claiming the sword as Arthur in the school play). The scene of his final conversation with Malcolm (1:29:10) brings back the tranquil music from the wedding video scene. Earlier, that music had been overcome by fright. Here it expands in duration, the comfort theme recurs, and the harmonies introduce a lulling gesture of their own in alternating between D and E major triads, leading to an untroubled cadence in the piano.

Thus by the end of Act 2 a major shift in musical perspective has already taken place. A consoling voice, at first vulnerable and so meek as to escape notice, finally breaks free to carry the day. Almost all narrative elements appear to be resolved: Cole has been healed, cosmic benevolence restored, and Malcolm's authority as a doctor redeemed. The epilogue, we are led to expect, merely needs to address the marital rift; instead we are stunned by a global narrative reorientation. As the changeover begins (1:37:45), we hear music of the uncanny in its unpredictable, forward-directed guise, heard earlier in the epiphany passage. However, this is an entirely new musical expression of epiphany. Along the way we hear dissonant piano figures, then a span of fright music, leading to an agitated, altered version of the motto (1:38:40), which creates a rush toward the climactic sound of the gunshot (in a flashback to the prologue). The dense jumble of musical information up to this point belies the preceding structural resolution and captures Malcolm's confusion as events reorder themselves in his mind. The musical evocation of epiphany prepares us for a new understanding of the motto, now stated for the last time (1:39:20), accompanying the sight of Malcolm's own blood, both in a recovered memory of the shooting and soaking his body in the present. In relation to its previous associations, the motto now symbolizes: the uncovering of repressed trauma—not in the patient but in the mind of the medical authority himself, that is, the subject of the filmic discourse;

the passing of an unearthly message from Cole *to Malcolm*—more precisely, the unblocking of Malcolm's receptivity to that message; and the revelation of the true secret at the heart of the story, the answer to all the nagging riddles—namely, that Malcolm is dead. The pivotal experience of dramatic reinterpretation points up an intriguing analogy between the microstructure of the motto and the overall narrative structure of the film: the motto embodies a chord shift that reinterprets the melody, moving it from a minor to a major context, echoing the perspectival shift in the situation of the lead characters from suffering to consolation. As the music loses forward drive, there follows an extended passage of consolation (the longest yet), though it takes a while to settle into tranquility. At first the slow harmonies are stressed with dissonance (as Malcolm realizes, "It doesn't hurt anymore"). But after this moment of acceptance, Malcolm is able to say goodbye while the music recounts the entire consoling passage from the end of Act 1, now in a lusher form with a more effusive sense of release. When we arrive at the sweet cadence in the piano, the video image of the embracing newlyweds fades up on-screen. The piano evokes the ghostly presence of Cole at this poignant moment, as if conveying his blessing, but also in recognition of the boy's role in Malcolm's own path to healing.[9]

The Others

[*Synopsis*: Act 1.] *The Others* is set on the island of Jersey just after the Second World War (when it had been occupied by the Nazis). Grace Stewart (Nicole Kidman) and her children, Anne and Nicholas (Alakina Mann/James Bentley), live in a large isolated house from which the servants have disappeared without warning. Three former servants of the house, headed by Mrs. Mills (Fionnula Flanagan), show up to offer their services. Grace is high-handed, pious, and highly strung, suffering from migraines. Her husband Charles (Christopher Eccleston) has never returned from fighting in the war, while the children are dangerously photosensitive and must be kept guarded from sunlight. Anne, chafing at parental authority, teases her brother and hints darkly at an incident not long ago where their mother "went mad." The girl speaks of visitors in the house no one else can see—a young boy Victor, his parents, and an old woman; she is punished for telling lies. Grace herself begins to hear noises coming from empty rooms. After a terrifying encounter in the music room she leaves the grounds to find help, only to be deterred by a dense fog. Mrs. Mills and the gardener are shown conspiring to cover up gravestones. The missing Charles materializes amidst the fog. [Act 2.] Grace retreats into denial about "the intruders," while the servants make ever more suspicious asides. Charles is listless and deathly; one day he is simply gone. The unexplained phenomena grow more threatening. In the climactic sequence, Grace loads her rifle, evicts the servants and rampages through the house in search of an answer. The children climb from their window and discover the graveyard, where the servants' bodies are buried. Stalked by the servants, the children run back upstairs where they come upon the intruders, gathered in a séance. Anne and Nicholas converse with the blind old woman; the changeover is triggered by her question about the manner of their death. Huddling with the children, Grace finally remembers the day she smothered them and shot herself. Mrs. Mills offers comfort by explaining the nature of the afterlife. No longer plagued by illness, the family vows never to leave the house.

The script cleverly uses the general trauma of wartime to disguise the domestic calamity at the heart of the story. Audience members might never suspect any double meanings when servants desert the household, or when characters speak wistfully of the way things were "before." The children's unusual condition also provides an alibi for the family's twilight existence, cut off from society. Though periodically teased with the mystery of "what happened that day" when Mummy went mad, viewers are distracted by more immediate mysteries in line with the conventional horror plot: Who are the intruders? What are the servants up to? Mrs. Mills's many leading statements maintain a thorough ambiguity of intention ("Don't worry—sooner or later, she'll see them. Then everything will be different. There are going to be some big surprises"). In the dénouement, narrative revelations appear to march toward the familiar showdown with evil outsiders, but the reversal tears this error away like a false front, bringing us face to face with the trauma inside the family. Even so, the film persists in making intimate connections between the domestic and national scenes of tragedy (e.g. the parallel between the Nazi invasion of the island and the intruders in the house, or the fierce argument in the bedroom over Charles's duty).

The musical score is remarkably multifaceted, with a variety of expressive tones, themes, and stylistic references, and supple intersections between them. As for expressive tone, the evocation of mystery and foreboding pervades throughout Act 1: e.g. when the children read in separate darkened rooms, or when Grace discovers the posed photos of the dead. The music of fear stands out in the conventional horror sequences, such as when Grace investigates the room draped with dust sheets, or when she faces down the poltergeist in the piano room. The expression of grief is also very important, e.g. when Charles goes away, or when Grace recovers her memory. Some other expressive moods have a significant though limited presence. For example, we almost never see the children at play. When Anne does sing a playful tune by herself (as in the communion dress scene), no orchestra joins in, and she sounds tiny and muted in the empty room. A single expression of untroubled consolation closes the film.

In contrast to *The Sixth Sense*, the score for *The Others* employs a number of recognizable themes and motives. The main theme of the opening titles (which I will call the A theme) is associated with Grace. It begins after we hear her disembodied voice introduce the story of Creation ("Now children, are you sitting comfortably? Then I'll begin").[10] Here, outside the narrative body of the film, the theme has a formal appearance, with parallel phrases, regular meter, and delicate instrumentation, like a courtly dance (Figure 12.4).

Its imaginative, fable-like quality fits well with the stylized graphic tableaux from the story to come (featuring the children), presented in the manner of magic lantern panels. Within the body of the film, A is usually rhapsodic (metrically free), emphasizing the initial plaintive octave and omitting connective tissue. Used sparingly, it seems to accentuate Grace's loneliness, sadness, and pain, while its musical manifestation tends to adapt to the dramatic situation. In the vigil scene, where Grace speaks with Mrs. Mills about the past, the music features the C theme (discussed below); but as she inquires about Lydia's muteness, a solo cello stating A sneaks into the background, as if at a subconscious level (44:00). Grace's lines at this point ("There must have been a reason. These things are always the result of some sort of . . . trauma") hint at her own damaged state. As Grace wades through the fog (53:35), a solitary low flute version of A evokes mystery and isolation. When she reunites with Charles (56:50), A springs up in full-bodied romantic form (cello, strings, and horn). And in her final rampage, we hear a shrieking, chaotic version—Grace gone mad (1:20:45).

Contained within the A theme is an important three-note motive (x; see Figure 12.4) that takes on a life of its own. While maintaining a distinct contour, it varies in interval content. Motive x is actually the first music we hear in the film; its open, tonal shape and dense thicket of woodwinds evoke a pastoral soundscape as if recalling an innocent time outside the story. As Grace and the servants darken the house in preparation for waking the children, the motive enters in distorted, mysterious form in flute and bass clarinet (7:15). At times like these, it projects a general creeping sense of unease at the somber house and the

Figure 12.4 The Others, A theme, titles

family's strange way of life. But the musical connection to Grace (through A) hints that the present malaise may trace back to her. Motive x appears when Grace leafs through the post-mortem photographs (40:30), among which is a portrait of mother and child. The motive marks the transition between the communion dress scene where she tries to strangle Anne, and the bedroom scene where Charles questions her about "that day" (1:09:25). Both of these moments allude to a poisoned motherhood.

A few words about this last idea connecting the two films: both stories reserve a special horror for the image of the lethal mother, as if male violence is less remarkable on the whole, and the failure of maternal instinct an unspeakable aberration. Compounding this taboo is the fear of something going wrong in the private spaces of the home, where mothers exert an unsupervised power over life and death. Furthermore, the idea of stealth villainy plays on the type of paranoia familiar from stories about alien body snatchers or cults of devil worship, where one cannot reliably tell the difference between friends and monsters. To all outward appearances, these characters are good mothers; their crimes do not show. However, the films diverge in the dramatic weight they give to this particular crime. In *The Sixth Sense,* the poisoning scene is one episode amid a parade of human suffering. Kyra's mother acts as a minor foil for the emotional and moral heroism of Mrs. Sear, and a scapegoat destined for removal from society. By contrast, *The Others* treats infanticide as an internal evil that must be owned up to. Blocked knowledge about "that day" proves to be the key obstacle to narrative resolution. The discovery of the truth will incriminate the protagonist herself and snare the viewer in complicity with her guilty self-knowledge.

Returning to the music for *The Others,* the second (B) theme of the title cue is a nursery song, belonging to the children. (Figure 12.5.) Anne sings this tune when playing by herself. In the titles B is accompanied by a motoric pattern in the celesta in imitation of a music box. Aside from diegetic appearances and title cues, the theme never appears intact, always disjointed or traumatized. Just before Grace presents Anne and Nicholas for the first time (7:50), we hear pieces of B harmonically askew in flute and harp, then another fragment on celesta. A mournful, hesitant version in strings and celesta occurs when the children reunite with their

Figure 12.5 The Others, B theme, titles

father (57:50). In the bedroom scene with Charles, as Grace attempts to recall the fateful day, the harp plays a barely perceptible version of B, slow and sad like a dirge (1:10:35).

The film's third theme (C) is introduced in the vigil scene. First appearing as isolated phrases in piano and harpsichord over vibraphone tremolos (43:15), it presently solidifies into a chorale texture in the strings as Grace moves into the children's bedroom to apologize to the sleeping Anne (Figure 12.6). This chorale, with its warm sonority, melancholy harmonies, and religious connotations, serves as the primary vehicle of grief in the score. Yet in this early appearance its precise meaning has not come into focus. The disjointed statement of C corresponds with the memory of better times (but also of plague, death, and trauma); the chorale statement occurs in the context of Grace's futile attempts to comfort the children. The disjointed version returns when Grace and Charles make love (1:12:55). Afterwards, when Charles disappears, one understands the chorale more clearly as expressing Grace's loss—to be precise, her acceptance of the fact that he will never return. (The entire sequence with Charles hints strongly that he is a ghost.) Two other musical passages relate closely to the chorale in sonority and expressive tone. One accompanies an early scene where Grace appeases Nicholas's fears with instructions to say the rosary (18:45); the identical passage concludes the vigil scene as she answers the boy's questions about his father. The other passage creates an elegiac underscore to Grace's reunion with Charles (55:30). All of these passages begin with the same five-note descending scale figure (motive y); all share the same C minor key as the chorale. The final element in the music of grief is a cadential figure (z) in stark parallel fifths, strongly recalling medieval organum (the most primitive form of Christian polyphonic chant; Figure 12.7). First heard at the end of the rosary scene, this figure opens and closes the vigil scene; it becomes prominent after the reversal.

As mentioned, the score evokes reminiscences of church music, nursery songs, and courtly dances, as well as pastoral and elegiac styles. We also

Figure 12.6 *The Others*, C theme, chorale

Figure 12.7 *The Others*, organum cadence z

hear a Chopin waltz (played by unseen hands) and the 1930s popular tune "I Only Have Eyes for You" (sung by Grace to a despondent Charles). This stylistic mélange creates a polyphony of associations—in particular, a tangled web of historical references. Organum is the most distant in time, harking back to the Middle Ages. The A theme in the titles, with its ground bass, harpsichord and harp sonorities, and dotted rhythms, evokes a stylized dance from the Renaissance or Baroque period. The C chorale infuses quasi-Baroque homophonic textures with a Romanticized sentiment; in this regard it echoes Samuel Barber's *Adagio for Strings*.[11] The elegiac passage at the end of Act 1 suggests Romanticism in its intense string sonorities and emotive solo cello. Musical evocations of the past may have a specific narrative point: e.g. the organum formula in connection with the rosary, or the Baroque flavor of C with Mrs. Mills's recollection of the house in its glory days in the vigil scene. The juxtaposition of archaic sounds (harpsichord, chant) with modern ones is also an effective horror convention. But the score's characteristic confusion of temporal coordinates has a more precise thematic significance, hinting at the family's dislocation from earthly existence. The blanketing fog; the strange inversion of darkness in daytime; the references to limbo; the elusive grasp of surrounding circumstances, as in the conflicting statements about whether the war is over—all these elements reinforce the sense of suspension in time and space.

The climactic sequence begins by following familiar horror conventions: fright music prevails (beginning 1:19:55) and contributes to the onrush of action. But the reversal clears the way for a prolonged musical cue (1:34:25) in which a number of thematic elements achieve a new semantic clarification. First we hear a passage expressive of grief, as Grace recounts the murders and her mistaken belief at the time that all of them were still alive, that God had given her a second chance. At the lines, "But now—what does all this mean? Where are we?" the celesta states the C theme (1:36:15). The unique fusing of the theme of loss with the music box sonority encapsulates the newly revealed secret about the children. This realization flows directly into the chorale, whose full meaning is affirmed as the acceptance of death. To reinforce the shift in perspective, the commencement of the chorale coincides with Mrs. Mills's offer to make a "nice cup of tea." Her previous equivocal gestures (supplying pills, making light of Grace's fears) now fall into a pattern of benevolence. The homely tea ritual reorients the family's relation to the horrifying events. (The housekeeper says just before the reversal: "I've been trying to get you to understand . . . about the new situation. We must all learn to live together, the living and the dead.") Mrs. Mills is now free to explain the conditions of their continued life in the house. At the words, "That's the way it's always been," the organum cadence sounds in the horns. Given its antiquity, cadential significance, and stable form throughout the score, this figure now has the positive ring of finality and eternity. To a question from Anne about limbo, Grace replies: "I don't know. I'm no wiser than you are." She then urges the children to repeat, "This house is ours." The music at this point stirs from its lethargy, led by the cello in a repeated version of x that echoes the rhythm of their words (1:38:10). If this appearance of x signals the resurgence of maternal will, the next phrase also pertains to Grace. We see Anne twirling in the sunlight, crying: "It doesn't hurt anymore" (Malcolm's exact words in *The Sixth Sense*). At this moment we hear the sad cello version of A, before the family moves united toward the light. The glimpse of A recalls Grace's pain in one last twinge before the music dissolves into a surge of sentiment leading to an untroubled major cadence; the entire passage is akin to the chorale in its romanticized Baroque rhetoric. Thus this lengthy cue has displayed full emotional progress from grief through acceptance to consolation.

The end title music reiterates important passages related to the C theme (in this order: disjointed C, C chorale, z cadence, cello elegy) before taking up the pristine versions of A and B as heard in the opening titles. Through its symbolic argument, this sequence acknowledges the experience of grief as the key to restoring (musical) wholeness for the main characters. It is worth noting that the only whole statements of A and B exist outside the story, in stylized form, in the overture and coda. This separation creates a kind of ideal, pastoral, or fable time for the title cues, while the narrative unfolds in fallen time. Grace's scream (and the disorienting camera angle) at the outset of the film marks her rupture from pastoral time; the end title cue signals its cyclical return. Both the overture and coda end with the same phrase: a plaintive melody in the pastoral English horn (following the rhythms of A), left hanging in midair, harmonic progression suspended.

Conclusion

According to broad conventions of the horror genre, we expect the protagonist to defend his or her territory and the threatening intruders to be overcome (or appeased, in certain cases of the unquiet dead). These expectations hold in the initial portions of the films under discussion. More than just their physical homes, the protagonists must defend their positions of authority. A disastrous misdiagnosis undermines Malcolm's medical authority; he struggles to save Cole and thereby redeem himself. Subtextually, his patriarchal authority is also under threat from marital alienation and the encroachment of his wife's new suitor. Grace holds class-based authority over land and servants, moral and religious authority within the family. On a more subconscious level, she asserts racial privilege by way of the children, whose skin color represents a marked, heightened whiteness that must be protected from the incursion of light.[12] Grace initially supposes that her tasks consist in maintaining control over the house and servants (as symbolized by the ring of keys), establishing parental rule in the absence of her husband, identifying the nature of the external threat and defending against the intruders (symbolized by the rifle), while maintaining a precarious mental balance. Her insistence on this manifold authority results in intense dissonance throughout the film.

In the case of *The Sixth Sense*, conventions have been modified in a number of interesting ways. First, the leading role has been split into two: Cole (who has little authority) must defend himself against physical and emotional assault, while Malcolm's struggles take place on a more intellectual and spiritual level. Second, Malcolm represents patriarchal authority in a remarkably gentle, compassionate form. (The flavor of Bruce Willis's performance registers the contrast between this vulnerable character and his previous roles as hypermasculine action hero.) Third, Cole's character takes on added complexity through the "queerness" or social deviance of his perceptions and behavior. The film takes time to explore and validate this queer perspective, moving it from an abject, stigmatized position ("freak") to a position of special power and knowledge (condensed in the Arthur story: "Once there was a boy, very different from all the other boys"). Fourth, from the beginning the horror plot shares equal footing with a therapy plot (which will seize global significance after the changeover). Fifth, even before the changeover it is clear that the therapist/patient relationship flows in both directions, and that plot resolution depends on Malcolm giving up a measure of authority. Malcolm's own breakthroughs in opening up about himself, recognizing the paranormal, and communicating with his wife are all due to Cole. Nevertheless, despite these qualifications, Malcolm's attempts to hold onto the dominant role as medical expert and loving husband cause him confusion and frustration throughout the narrative.

At the moment of reversal, the principals learn that their fights were lost long before. They have no authority anymore, nor any agency to affect the narrative. The familiar paradigm that has been driving their actions turns out to be obsolete and counterproductive. The threat against them was never external, but internal all along (Malcolm's shortsightedness, disbelief, and denial; Grace's violence, instability, dogmatism, and denial). Yet the outcome of internal critique in this instance is different from those films in the 1970s that located the monster squarely within the family, as theorized by Robin Wood. In those films the unstoppable evil within the family/society unleashes extreme, even apocalyptic anxiety. According to Wood's analysis, such nihilism acknowledges the "disintegration and untenability" of the dominant social ideology, "as all it has repressed explodes and blows it apart." In most cases, the films stop short of imagining "constructive radical alternatives" to patriarchal capitalism.[13] However, these two films from the turn of the millennium have as their ultimate goal the alleviation of anxiety—not in defense of a conservative power structure but in order that "a kind of transformative recognition can take place."[14] The protagonists must learn to let go of their illusory beliefs and surrender their power. Acceptance and humility provide the keys to psychic healing. The experience of global narrative reversal depends upon a confrontation with an alternative vision. Music conveys this double vision through a shift in perspective from fear to consolation, and from action to a pacific temporal suspension. Musical finales have a particularly important role in acknowledging the passing of an era. In the millennial context in which these films appeared, such a moral easily translates as the fading of dominant cultural status for the subject of racial, class, patriarchal, or scientific privilege. Fittingly, music in the later stages urges peace. It does not dominate, but dies away.

Notes

1 *The Sixth Sense* begins with a prologue in which we witness Malcolm being shot without learning the outcome of his injury. For another recent example of a ghost story with a twist ending, see *El Orfanato/The Orphanage* (J. A. Bayona, 2007; score by Fernando Velázquez).
2 Seth A. Friedman, "Cloaked Classification: The Misdirection Film and Generic Duplicity," *Journal of Film and Video* 58 (2006), 16–28.
3 For a detailed analysis of the twist as a narrative strategy, distinct from considerations of genre, see Erlend Lavik, "Narrative Structure in *The Sixth Sense*: A New Twist in 'Twist Movies'?" *Velvet Light Trap* 58 (Fall 2006), 55–64.
4 The format of an unresolved melody clashing with triadic harmonies strongly recalls Charles Ives's piece *The Unanswered Question*, also meant to evoke mysterious cosmic forces or ideas.
5 It is also tonally deceptive, beginning in D minor and suddenly slipping into C-sharp minor.
6 A famous example is the "Rosebud" motif in Bernard Herrmann's score for *Citizen Kane* (1941). Royal S. Brown discusses another classic example (the "romantic theme") in Erich Wolfgang Korngold's score for *The Sea Hawk* (1940), in his book *Overtones and Undertones: Reading Film Music* (Berkeley and Los Angeles, CA: University of California Press, 1994), 97–117.
7 Note that the epiphany music is important enough to appear in the "overture," i.e. the opening titles.
8 Cynthia Freeland discusses the distinction between dread and other kinds of horror in relation to a recent cycle of films including *The Sixth Sense* and *The Others* ("Horror and Art-Dread," in *The Horror Film*, edited by Stephen Prince [New Brunswick, NJ: Rutgers University Press, 2004], 189–205).
9 This resolves the puzzle of the piano's presence in the earlier video/shower scene.
10 Susan Bruce identifies this voice-over as "the introduction to *Listen with Mother*, a daily BBC radio broadcast during the 1950s and 60s" ("Sympathy for the Dead: (G)hosts, Hostilities and Mediums in Alejandro Amenábar's *The Others* and Postmortem Photography," *Discourse* 27 [Spring and Fall 2005],

21–40; see 33, 38 note 12). For those familiar with this reference, Grace's opening words neatly intertwine domestic and national spheres.

11   For a survey of the use of Barber's *Adagio* in film and broadcast media, and an account of the piece's connotations of loss, sacrifice, tragedy, and the horrors of war, see Luke Howard, "The Popular Reception of Samuel Barber's *Adagio for Strings*," *American Music* 25 (2007), 50–80.

12   Richard Dyer has called attention to a strain of horror film linking whiteness with morbidity and death, thus thematizing the notion that white identity has played itself out as a cultural dominant ("White Death," in *White* [New York: Routledge, 1997], 207–23.

13   Robin Wood, *Hollywood from Vietnam to Reagan* (New York: Columbia University Press, 1986), 192, 88.

14   Susan Bruce, "Sympathy for the Dead," 33. For a contrasting example of a film score whose shift in perspective from anxiety to reassurance upholds ideological conservatism and discourages a critical stance, see Neil Lerner's discussion of *Close Encounters of the Third Kind:* "Nostalgia, Masculinist Discourse and Authoritarianism in John Williams' Scores for *Star Wars* and *Close Encounters of the Third Kind*," in *Off the Planet: Music, Sound and Science Fiction Cinema*, edited by Philip Hayward (London: John Libbey, 2004), 96–108.

Contributors

Julie Brown is Senior Lecturer at Royal Holloway University of London. She has published on Schönberg, Webern, and Bartók as well as on television soundtracks and uses of music in film. Among her publications are *Bartók and the Grotesque* (2007) and the edited collection *Western Music and Race* (2007), which was awarded the Ruth A. Solie Award by the American Musicological Society. She also serves on the advisory board of the journals *Music, Sound, and the Moving Image* and *Music Analysis*.

James Buhler is Associate Professor of Music Theory at The University of Texas at Austin. He is co-editor of *Music and Cinema* (2000) and co-author of *Hearing the Movies: Music, Sound and Film History* (2009). He is currently working on a project concerning the auditory culture of early American cinema.

David J. Code is Lecturer in Music at the University of Glasgow. Previously, he taught at Stanford University on a Mellon Postdoctoral Fellowship, and at Bishop's University in Quebec. His articles on Debussy, Mallarmé, and Stravinsky have appeared in various journals including *JAMS*, *19th-Century Music* and *Representations*; his critical biography of Debussy is forthcoming from Reaktion Press. Current projects include a monograph on Debussyan musical allegory and a study of music in the films of Stanley Kubrick.

James Deaville is Associate Professor in the School for Studies in Art and Culture: Music at Carleton University, Ottawa. His areas of research expertise include music for film and television. He published "The Topos of 'Evil Medieval' in American Horror Film Music" in the collection *Music, Meaning & Media*, co-authored a study about music in the films of Jean Cocteau (*Canadian University Music Review*), and has published contributions about television news music in *Echo: A Music-Centered Journal*, *Music in the Post-9/11 World*, and *Sound and Music in Film and Media: A Critical Overview*. He is currently editing a collection of essays about television music for Routledge.

K. J. Donnelly is Reader in Film at the University of Southampton. He is a historian and theorist of film music and film sound, while also having significant interests in British and Irish cinema, film theory, and popular and experimental music. He is the author of *British Film Music and Film Musicals* (2007), *The Spectre of Sound* (2005), and *Pop Music in British Cinema* (2001); and he is the editor of *Film Music: Critical Approaches* (2001). Having catholic interests, he has also published on subjects as diverse as urban wildlife and "troubles tourism" in Northern Ireland. From time to time he plays music, and he owns exotic instruments including a drum made from the skull of a Tibetan monk.

Ross J. Fenimore, a PhD candidate in Musicology at the University of California, Los Angeles, is writing a dissertation on the songs of Madonna. His other research interests include the divas of the Hollywood studio system (c.1930–60) and popular song in film.

Janet K. Halfyard is Director of Undergraduate Studies at Birmingham Conservatoire where she teaches courses on film music and twentieth century and contemporary music. Her publications include papers on extended vocal technique (which she both performs and researches) as well as on film and television music. She is the author of *Danny Elfman's* Batman: *A Film Score Guide* (2004), several essays on music and performance in *Buffy the Vampire Slayer* and *Angel*, and essays in Miguel Mera and David Burnand's *European Film Music* (2006) and Philip Hayward's volume, *Terror Tracks* (2009).

Claire Sisco King is Assistant Professor in the Department of Communication Studies at Vanderbilt University, where she also teaches in the Film Studies Program. Her research interests include gender, sexuality, and trauma. Her work has been published in such journals as *Text and Performance Quarterly*, *Quarterly Journal of Speech*, *Communication and Critical Cultural Studies*, and *Critical Studies in Media Communication*. She is currently completing a book manuscript on the overlapping discourses of trauma and sacrifice in contemporary American cinema.

Neil Lerner is Associate Professor of Music at Davidson College where he teaches courses in music as well as film and media studies. Attending college at Transylvania University whetted his appetite for work on horror films. His work on film music has been published in journals such as *Musical Quarterly* and *South Atlantic Quarterly* and essay collections including *The Sounds of Early Cinema*, *Off the Planet: Music, Sound, and Science Fiction Cinema*, *Aaron Copland and His World*, and *Wagner and Cinema*. He is co-editor of *Sounding Off: Theorizing Disability in Music* and serves on the editorial boards of *American Music* and *Music, Sound, and the Moving Image*.

Stan Link is Associate Professor of the Composition, Philosophy and Analysis of Music at Vanderbilt University. His papers and publications on the film soundtrack include topics such as the auditory coding of vision, psycho-killers, science fiction, leitmotivic expression, silence, nerds, and the musical visibility of whiteness. Apart from his research in film music and sound, he is an active composer of acoustic and computer music, with pieces available on several compact disks, including a solo disc of electro-acoustic music, *In Amber Shadows*. He currently resides in Nashville with wife, musicologist Melanie Lowe, and their daughter, Wednesday.

Joe Tompkins is a PhD student in Comparative Studies in Discourse and Society in the Department of Cultural Studies and Comparative Literature at the University of Minnesota. His research interests include horror cinema and popular music for film and television.

Lloyd Whitesell is Associate Professor of Music at McGill University, Montreal. He is the author of *The Music of Joni Mitchell* (2008) and co-editor of *Queer Episodes in Music and Modern Identity* (2002). An article of his on Bernard Herrmann's score for the horror film *Hangover Square* appears in *Musical Quarterly* (2005). His current research examines the discourse of glamour in the Hollywood musical.

Index

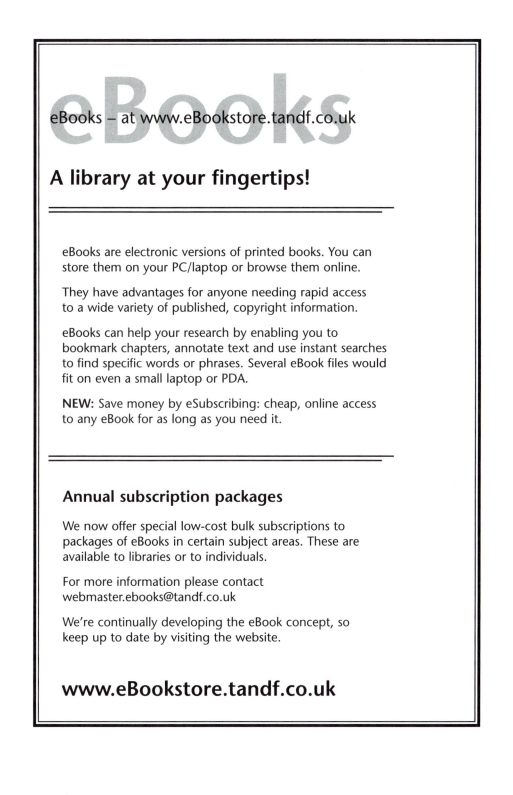